"Shizhou Yang has taken an innovative Global South perspective on literacy autobiographies with stories by himself as an EFL writing teacher as well as those by his students from China in diverse transnational contexts. The result is a fascinating and thought-provoking account that not only contributes to theoretical discussions of concepts such as critical pedagogy, translanguaging, and writing ecology, but also to pedagogical practices that will truly enable and empower the learners, and the teachers, to develop their own voices. As such, it is a major contribution to translingual and decolonising turn in language education research."

Professor Li Wei, *Director & Dean, UCL Institute of Education, University College London, UK*

Like his cicada after its long formation,
Shizhou emerges with translingual poetry
Breaking free from the global and colonizing
Pressures against his voice in literacy.
Not alone, he emerges with his whole musical army—
His students—with their own translingual story.
But these cicadas won't die too quickly;
Their voices will transform the dominant pedagogy.

Suresh Canagarajah, *Edwin Erle Sparks Professor, Pennsylvania State University, USA*

"This is a captivating book about the liberating intellectual journey of Shizhou Yang, who has found his voice and identity as a multilingual scholar through writing his own literacy autobiography. Also featuring the autobiographical writing of the author's students situated in a marginalized context, the book celebrates the power of literacy autobiography as an undervalued genre in EFL contexts, demonstrating how it is intertwined with identity work, voice development, and knowledge creation. I highly recommend the book to everyone."

Icy Lee, *Professor, Faculty of Education, The Chinese University of Hong Kong, Hong Kong Special Administrative Region, China*

"Featuring literacy autobiography and poetic inquiry as methodology, this book has provided EFL teachers and students with a proven way to gain liberation from the shackles of modernism and neoliberalism. It is a must-read for anyone who is keen in search for Southern epistemologies in English language teaching."

Xiaoye You, *Liberal Arts Professor of English and Asian Studies, Pennsylvania State University, USA*

LITERACY AUTOBIOGRAPHIES FROM THE GLOBAL SOUTH

Drawing on autoethnographic research on literacy autobiographies from a Chinese EFL writing context, this book provides unique insights into literacy, voice, translingualism, and critical pedagogy from a Global South perspective.

The book presents literacy autobiographies as a cultural tool for analyzing and refashioning learners' and teachers' sense of self in ever-expanding dialogical spaces. In addition to highlighting teachers' own stories around autoethnographies and translanguaging, it showcases literacy autobiographies from Chinese students themselves. The book theorizes the Global South as an ontological positioning that challenges colonial mindsets and practices concerning literacy, language learning, and narratives. It argues that literacy autobiographies from a Global South perspective can be reimagined as critical pedagogy for EFL writing teaching and learning, as well as teacher development.

Validating and expanding student voices by presenting these literacy autobiographies, this book will be of great interest to researchers and students in the fields of TESOL, applied linguistics, English language teaching, second language writing, and literacy studies.

Shizhou Yang is a second language writer, writing teacher, and researcher in the English Communication Department at Payap University, Thailand.

Global South Perspectives on TESOL
Series editor: Osman Z. Barnawi

Global South Perspectives on TESOL is an international, multidisciplinary series focusing on studies that examine issues of TESOL through recovering the rich histories, theories, and practices of multilingual education developed in traditionally non-English-dominant contexts and communities. Purposefully situated beyond monolingual ideologies, legacies and research theories and practices, this series solicits new studies that critically engage with epistemologies, theories and practices of TESOL, and offer a transformative change that allows the scholarship of TESOL to advance.

The series envisions decolonizing research theories and practices in TESOL and thinking outside the dominance of Western/Northern models as departure points to advancing the field of TESOL. This series will also be a venue for scholars in the Global South to collaborate with Global North scholars in order to promote global harmony in TESOL. It features scholarly works that examine issues surrounding TESOL from new angles, including local theories, pedagogies and practices, and works of novice and under-represented authors.

The series welcomes single-authored or multi-authored monographs and edited volumes on areas including epistemological racism in TESOL; social justice in TESOL; issues of race, gender, and class in TESOL; theories of change in TESOL; translanguaging in TESOL classrooms; Southern theories of TESOL; post-human thoughts in TESOL and decolonizing research theories and practices in TESOL.

Books in the series include:

Transnational English Language Assessment Practices in the Age of Metrics
Edited by Osman Z. Barnawi, Mohammed S. Alharbi and Ayman A. Alzahrani

Literacy Autobiographies from the Global South
Shizhou Yang

Social Justice, Decoloniality, and Southern Epistemologies within Language Education
Theories, Knowledges, and Practices on TESOL from Brazil
Edited by Vander Tavares

For more information about the series, please visit https://www.routledge.com/our-products/book-series/GSTESOL.

LITERACY AUTOBIOGRAPHIES FROM THE GLOBAL SOUTH

An Autoethnographic Study of English Literacy in China

Shizhou Yang

LONDON AND NEW YORK

First published 2023
by Routledge
4 Park Square, Milton Park, Abingdon, Oxon, OX14 4RN

and by Routledge
605 Third Avenue, New York, NY 10158

Routledge is an imprint of the Taylor & Francis Group, an informa business

© 2023 Shizhou Yang

The right of Shizhou Yang to be identified as author of this work has been asserted in accordance with sections 77 and 78 of the Copyright, Designs and Patents Act 1988.

All rights reserved. No part of this book may be reprinted or reproduced or utilised in any form or by any electronic, mechanical, or other means, now known or hereafter invented, including photocopying and recording, or in any information storage or retrieval system, without permission in writing from the publishers.

Trademark notice: Product or corporate names may be trademarks or registered trademarks, and are used only for identification and explanation without intent to infringe.

British Library Cataloguing-in-Publication Data
A catalogue record for this book is available from the British Library

Library of Congress Cataloging-in-Publication Data
Names: Yang, Shizhou, author.
Title: Literacy autobiographies from the global south : an autoethnographic study of English literacy in China / Shizhou Yang.
Description: 1st edition. | Abingdon, Oxon ; New York, NY : Routledge, 2023. | Series: Global south perspectives on TESOL | Includes bibliographical references and index. | Identifiers: LCCN 2022036606 (print) | LCCN 2022036607 (ebook) | ISBN 9781032251981 (hardback) | ISBN 9781032265391 (paperback) | ISBN 9781003288756 (ebook)
Subjects: LCSH: Autobiography--Authorship. | Biography as a literary form. | Literacy--China. | Translanguaging (Linguistics) | English language--Rhetoric--Study and teaching--China.
Classification: LCC PE1479.A88 Y37 2023 (print) | LCC PE1479.A88 (ebook) | DDC 306.442/21051--dc23/eng/20221018
LC record available at https://lccn.loc.gov/2022036606
LC ebook record available at https://lccn.loc.gov/2022036607

ISBN: 978-1-032-25198-1 (hbk)
ISBN: 978-1-032-26539-1 (pbk)
ISBN: 978-1-003-28875-6 (ebk)

DOI: 10.4324/9781003288756

Typeset in Bembo
by SPi Technologies India Pvt Ltd (Straive)

In memory of Michael and Kitty Wilson who loved, laughed, and served faithfully throughout their lives beyond national, racial, and linguistic boundaries

CONTENTS

Editor's Preface   *xi*
Acknowledgements   *xii*

PART I
A Teacher's Stories   1

1 An EFL Writing Teacher's Poetic Autoethnography of Literacy Autobiography   3

2 My Own Literacy Autobiography   18

PART II
Theory and Empirical Studies   35

3 Literacy Autobiographical Writing as Critical Pedagogy   37

4 Pedagogical Translanguaging Behind Literacy Autobiographical Writing   58

5 The Emergence of Translingualism in an EFL Writer's LA   80

6 Voice Construction Beyond Translingualism   97

PART III
Student's Literacy Autobiographies   119

7   My Literacy Rooted in Chinese Culture   123

8   A Learning Cycle of Reading and Writing in English and Chinese   128

9   My Bilingual Journey   133

10   A Literacy History of My Early Twenty Years   136

11   A Journey of Reading and Writing in Chinese and English   140

12   My Footprints of Language Learning   146

13   A Way to Memorize: Reading and Writing   150

14   My Road on Acquisition of Reading and Writing   158

15   My Conquest of Language   161

16   My Journey to Literacy   166

17   Afterword   169

Index   *183*

EDITOR'S PREFACE

Is decolonizing English as a foreign language (EFL) writing education possible? *Literacy autobiographies from the Global South: An autoethnographic study of English literacy in China* grapples with this critical question. Through a poetic autoethnography of his experience and intellectual journey as well as his students with literacy autobiographies (LA) as a foreign genre, **Shizhou Yang**, an L2 learner and writer, addresses the following questions: (1) Why was it so difficult for me to have a voice in Chinese? What does it mean to have a voice, anyway? (2) Why was I drawn to poetry composition in my English L2 writing? What is poetic inquiry in a Chinese sense? (3) Why was literacy autobiography a foreign genre in China?

Through empirical evidence, this timely book demonstrates that literacy autobiographies function as a cultural tool for externalizing, analyzing, performing, and refashioning learners' and teacher's sense of self in ever expanding dialogical spaces. It emphasizes that poetic inquiry may serve as a Global South way of making space for new approaches and new voices in EFL writing teaching and learning as well as teacher development in bi-and multilingual contexts and settings.

For whom has the *Literacy autobiographies from the Global South: An autoethnographic study of English literacy in China* been written? Because of its breadth, depth, and accessibility, this book, a first in its kind, serves a diverse audience, including L2 writing teachers, policymakers, graduate students, researchers, language teacher educators, writing across curriculum specialists, and writing program directors.

Series Editor
Osman Z. Barnawi
Royal Commission for Yanbu Colleges and Institutes, Saudi Arabia

ACKNOWLEDGEMENTS

I thank Xiaoye You, who first told me about the Global South Perspectives on TESOL series and encouraged me to give it a try. I thank Icy Lee, June Yichun Liu, and Barry Lee Reynolds for giving constructive feedback on my proposal and the anonymous reviewers for having faith in my proposed project. I thank the series editor Osman Barnawi, who has shown much enthusiasm about and support for this project. I thank Suresh Canagarajah and Debby Kramlich for commenting on part of my book. I thank the four scholars—Li Wei, Icy Lee, Suresh, and Xiaoye—for endorsing my book so generously, to which I will always be indebted. I also thank He Ting and He Liming for helping me take some photos. I especially thank Bruce Batton for always providing the most encouraging and helpful comments on my writing.

I thank the Routledge editorial team, Anna-Mary Goodall, Ashley Johnstone, Emilie Coin, Josh Swapnil, Kanishka Jangir, for guiding me along with passion, compassion, and dedication. I also thank Suba Ramya Durairaj and Claire Bell for their timely help through the final stage of preparing the manuscript.

I thank Payap University for hiring me and giving me both a reason and much needed time to work on this book.

I thank Wiley for giving me permission to reprint my recent *TESOL Journal* article in this book.

I thank my MTI students for responding to my invitation to tell, research, and compose their literacy experiences. Without their active participation, this book would not have been possible.

I thank my three dear elder siblings in China who are always tender and loving toward me. I thank my wife's family in the United States: Jerry and Julie Fine, Robin Fine and her family, and Sarah Fine and her family, for their embracing arms. I thank my friends in Thailand. Whether I name you or not, I thank you for your words of encouragement, care, and faith along this journey.

I thank my beloved wife Cathryn for her unwavering love, support, and trust. I thank our children Micah, Finn, and Pearl, for their understanding, joy, and perseverance as we go through life's challenges and transitions together.

Last, I thank Christ. The past two years of writing this book was filled with major changes in my life and career: resigning from a university job in China, seeking a new job outside China, making several transnational journeys, and making home in a new country. In all this, my family and I have been kept safe, healthy, and peaceful. We have all experienced his faithfulness, compassion, and provision. May this book echo in some small ways Christ's life mission, as recorded in Luke 4: 18, to "proclaim good news to the poor ... to proclaim liberty to the captives and recovering of sight to the blind, to set at liberty those who are oppressed." As it is in my life, this project is filled with your grace from its conception to its final word.

PART I
A Teacher's Stories

Introduction

The two chapters included in Part I feature my experience as an L2 writing scholar working in a Global South context. Through poetic inquiry and autoethnography, I wrestle with traditions, norms, and practices associated with my heritage and transnational learning and life backgrounds. They set a stage for the rest of my book.

1
AN EFL WRITING TEACHER'S POETIC AUTOETHNOGRAPHY OF LITERACY AUTOBIOGRAPHY

Shizhou Yang

Searching for My Own Voice

Stanza 1

I could hear, in the brisk winter air, sighs of confusion
As my students from skyscraping cities and mountainous lands of China
Cast glances on each other and me, their writing teacher.
"Literacy?" "Autobiography?"
"Never heard of such a thing!"
"Surely, the teacher is speaking a foreign language, but even more foreign is—
Literacy autobiography."
In their dialects of southern, northern, eastern, and western Chinese,
they murmured,
"这LA是什么东西?" "What is this thing called LA?"

Stanza 2

Did I feel the same way in 2006
When I first read a Japanese scholar's literacy autobiography?
Yes, with a feeling of disbelief that this is considered academic writing
And no—
The concept was liberating,
As if a caged bird
Unexpectedly shook loose the iron latch
And, escaping the prison of a spoon-fed life,
Learned again to flutter its wings
To tell the tale of flying

Not by the grammar book of gravity
But by its inherited instinct
To see the world above traffic rules of the ground.

Stanza 3

The journey began long ago
When poetic voices from generations and from deep within,
The countless souls besieged by exams, structuralism, materialism, and native-speakerism ...
Cried like a North American cicada
Who, emerging from the dark damp dungeon underground, after
17 years of waiting, wiggling, and weeping, shrieked like hell,
"I want my own voice,
And
My own tree
To climb."

The teaching and learning of English writing in China has never been a neutral activity. It is tied to the nation's constant struggle for a place on the world stage through pragmatic approaches to foreign language and literacy education, ever since the Opium Wars in the mid-19th century awakened China to its weakness in contrast to the European, especially the English-speaking British, powers (Hu, 2021; Poon, 2010; Shen, 2020; You, 2010). Yet at the same time it is subjected to profound influence by previously unquestioned norms concerning language, literacy, and epistemology that are endorsed by capitalism, colonialism, patriarchy (de Sousa Santos, 2014), and neoliberalism (Surma, 2018). Furthermore, recent changes in high-stakes English test writing task designs (Yu, 2020), the lowered status of English in national policies (Cheng & Li, 2021), and increasing use of technologies in corrective feedback (Wu et al., 2021) have created a new local environment for EFL writing. Caught in these powerful and wide-ranging currents while striving to fulfill their own aspirations, EFL writing teachers and learners have to negotiate their own places, voices, and identities between languages, cultures, literacy practices, and epistemologies.

In this chapter and the following ones, I share and analyze my own literacy autobiography (henceforth LA) and those of my Chinese graduate students to argue that LA writing from a university in southwest China offers a critical contribution to Global South epistemology. According to the United Nations Finance Center for South-South Cooperation, as of 2015, the Global South refers to a list of 77 nations (mostly in Africa and South America) and China. Regardless of whether China (which today contains some very developed and some very undeveloped regions) is formally considered part of the Global South, the Global South perspective is not just about the geographic south, north, east, or west. It is about decolonization in knowledge making. As Pennycook and Makoni (2020) suggested, embracing a

Global South perspective in applied linguistics is essentially about decolonizing the discipline by asking critical questions such as

> How can we deal with the inequalities in global knowledge production, the lack of inclusion of scholars from outside the dominant regions, [and] the imposition of inappropriate frameworks to address language and education outside the central places and institutions?
>
> *(p. 8)*

I believe the research site for this study, a university located in Yunnan, southwest China, is uniquely positioned to address some of these critical questions. First, Yunnan is a relatively impoverished area of China. Second, its educational level lags far behind coastal areas such as Shanghai. Third, it is China's most culturally and linguistically diverse province, with 26 ethnic groups or *minzu*. These three situations are not positions of power. Rather, they fill my students and me with tension and self-doubts concerning whether we can produce new knowledge that addresses global issues. Nonetheless, I feel it imperative to engage in this project to decolonialize my thinking in view of the global epistemological process.

Starting with my three-stanza poem presented above about LA writing, I describe my journey of poetic inquiry. Throughout the book, I will use a similar method, featuring works composed by me or my students, to depict Global South epistemological approaches.

A Poetic Autoethnography

Stanza 1: Teaching LA Writing

In the first stanza of my poem, I tried to recapture the immediate reactions of my Chinese students to an LA writing assignment, which was to last throughout the 18-week semester. My students would soon discover that the class was research-oriented. They were to read sample LAs from Canagarajah's (2020) book *Transnational Literacy Autobiographies as Translingual Writing* and to study Chang's (2008) *Autoethnography as Method*, and then to discuss these texts in class. Creation of multiple drafts was expected. They were to engage in talking, drawing, drafting, and peer-reviewing activities. In the syllabus, I specified the genre ("a memoir … mixing both narrative and academic writing"), audience ("your classmates, friends, teachers, and international readers who are interested in MTI [Master of Translation and Interpreting] education in China"), and purpose ("to develop MTI students' proficiency in Standard Written English while cultivating their sensitivity to the complex nature of academic writing in a second language"), as advised by L2 writing scholars (Matsuda, 2002). By the end of the semester, the students were each to submit a "polished" article for a "self-published book … with the working title of *Languages, Literacies and Identity Work: Narratives of Chinese Multilingual Users*." I anticipated that my students, through this assignment, would create new knowledge rather than just consuming knowledge provided by others.

But why did I say that my students seemed confused about the writing task? One reason is that at the end of the semester, after they had received the self-published document containing their chapters, I organized my students into several groups and asked them to perform different aspects of their learning experiences in the writing class. One group shared their journey with LA writing and revealed their initial confusion at the beginning of the semester.

老师 [TEACHER, AS ACTED OUT BY THE NARRATOR]: 同学们，大家好，这个学期我们的主要任务呢就是写 LA(literacy autobiography) 。(Hello everyone, our main task this semester is to write our LA, literacy autobiography.)
学生 A [STUDENT A]: What, 这是什么东西? (What is this?)
学生 B: 我也不知道。(I don't know either.) [Several students murmuring] (Class recording, January 2, 2020)

My fieldnotes on the first day of teaching (September 12, 2019) reflected a similar concern among my students: "This morning, when I assigned writing task to the class, one of my students said, with disbelief, that it was three pieces of writing!" This brief exchange prompted me to provide a further explanation to my students of my rationale for choosing an LA writing task:

> Although LA writing may appear unacademic, it can actually help us to understand the complexity of (academic) writing as a process and situated activity and to develop negotiation strategies. It also provides us with a way to understand academic literacy in relation to the background that shapes us, so that we can become more capable of making informed decisions about our ways of engaging in reading and writing.

Going through my students' journals, however, I was struck to find that my students responded very positively about the first class, me as their writing teacher, and my teaching approach.

Shi, whose LA is featured in Chapter 14, recorded in her journal a realization of the "writing course" as "art":

> A review of the first writing class
> … At the beginning of the class, Mr. Yang asked us to introduce ourselves in poetry. I thought long and wrote down:
> "This is a girl sitting here.
> A girl with great cheer. …"
>
> Obviously I couldn't continue to make it up because poetry creation is out of reach with my current writing ability. Later, the teacher let us use a word to describe ourselves. We spoke one by one and he gave us feedback with serious record from time to time. I suddenly realized that the writing course is just like an art. A layman as I am now, the teacher is leading us step by step

from the selection of words to the polish of the poetry. And I believe I can really enter the palace of the art one day.

With this trust-filled relationship, we embarked on our shared journey of LA writing for publication.

Stanza 2: My First Exposure to LA Writing

The year 2006 was critical in my academic career. By then, I had finished my M.Ed. at Mercer University in the United States (2000–2002), worked at an international trade company and then taught spoken English to ESL students for a year (2003), returned to my Chinese alma mater (Yunnan Minzu University) to teach for three years (2003–2006), married an American linguist in 2006, and was seeking admission to an applied linguistics Ph.D. program in the Faculty of Education at La Trobe University in Australia. For that application, I needed to draft a research proposal and a personal statement. At that point, I encountered LA writing for the first time and found it, as I wrote in stanza 2, "liberating,"

> *As if a caged bird*
> *Accidentally shook loose the iron latch*
> *And, escaping the prison of a spoon-fed life,*
> *Learned again to flutter its wings.*

In these lines, I featured the LA writing by Paul Kei Matsuda (2001, 2003), whose stories immediately engaged me because they exemplified how a multilingual scholar can write from a marginalized position. His article on voice contained a reflection on his confusion about the "be yourself" instructions that he had received in an undergraduate composition class in the USA (Matsuda, 2001, p. 38). He concluded that "finding my own voice" is a personal journey that involves social participation, specifically "the process of negotiating my socially and discursively constructed identity with the expectation of the reader as I perceived it" (p. 39). Matsuda's experience as an international student from Japan was thus not a problem but a vantage point from which to reconceptualize voice as a dialogical concept. The LA features stood out more clearly in his later writing (Matsuda, 2003), in which he recounted his aspirations, frustrations, and experience of publishing as a graduate student, as he learned how to mask his status as an ESL student while constructing a professional identity. Matsuda's LA convinced me that one's personal background and professional development can actually be closely linked.

Partially influenced by reading Matsuda's LA, I decided to research the EFL autobiographical writing of ethnic minority learners in China to explore their identity work and voice development. As I wrote in my personal statement for La Trobe:

> My years of experience teaching ESL writing to ethnic minorities have aroused my intense interest in this field. ESL writing is not only about learning to write in English, but also a search for one's personal voice and new

cultural identity. Dr. Audrey Grant's reflective article "Potential Space: Narrative Practices and Transformative (Third-Space) Learning," Robert's writing about biographical research, and Matsuda's research on L2 literacy autobiography inspired me to use a biographical research approach to study how the Bai students in Yunnan develop their ESL writing skills, voices and identities, and how an ESL writing teacher can be most effective in the teaching process.

But why didn't I study LA writing? Thinking back, I must have felt that LA writing was too foreign to me. After all, I had never read an LA, let alone composed one, throughout my education in China (1983–1995) or in the USA (2000–2002). In contrast, I was much more familiar with autobiographical writing, in both Chinese and English. Through autobiographical writing, in connection with my evolving life experiences, I discovered multiple meanings of my life experiences and new ways of relating to significant others such as my parents (Yang, 2013). Through autobiographical writing, I wrestled with a constant pain concerning my mother. Mother never went to school. As far as I knew back then, she was illiterate. She belonged to the Naxi ethnic minority group from a neighboring county. Because of a tractor accident, she was paralyzed for 13 years before her death in 2000. In my mind, up until college, I unfortunately associated Mother with poverty, ignorance, backwardness, and illness. She did not have a voice in my world. Yet, to my amazement, while she was alive, Mother repeatedly asked me to write down her stories. I regret that I never did, but I began to think seriously after her death about the significance of stories to those who have been marginalized because they carry various labels such as their education level, ethnicity, and economic status. These labels become their identities in others' eyes, but not their desired identities, which can be constructed only through stories. As I found out later through my uncle, even though Mother never went to school—as the oldest child of the family, she had to help her parents—she taught herself to read newspapers and write simple letters. During the famine years (1959–1961) in China, when Mother was still a teenager, she went to different government offices to beg for food for the whole family. These stories, told after her death, helped me to see Mother as intelligent and courageous. For people living in the margins, whether they are socioeconomically deprived or ethnically positioned outside the mainstream, stories are their livelihood of meanings. They need to tell and retell, write and rewrite their stories until those stories are received with appreciation by others. As I will share more explicitly in Chapter 2, my story was my voice and my identity, or at least how I preferred to be known by my readers.

Stanza 3: Poetic Inquiry and Autoethnographic Research

In stanza 3, I move toward a Global South epistemology, which promotes the legitimacy of non-Western ways of knowing and knowledge making and their contribution to the global knowledge system (de Sousa Santos, 2014). Note that the Global South here is a metaphor, not a geographic reference. As de Sousa Santos (2014) explains, "the [Global] South [is] a metaphor for the human suffering caused by capitalism and colonialism on the global level, as well as for the resistance to overcoming or minimizing such suffering" (p. 18). By evoking the Global South metaphor, I choose to expose my wounds as a researcher (Romanyshyn, 2021), and strive to reveal injustices committed by prevalent ways of knowledge making in EFL literacy education. More specifically, I focus on two ways of making knowledge that feature the self. One is poetic inquiry, which I define as the use of poetic composition to richly explore, concisely capture, and aesthetically represent the inner and outer experiences of the writer in the world. Grbich (2013) provides a more research-oriented definition, treating poetic inquiry as "a qualitative form of research that incorporates poetic forms as data display" (p. 129). The other is autoethnography, which includes artistic texts such as poetry but tends to use narrative prose to document, analyze, and reveal cultural influences (Chang, 2008). In this chapter, I mainly discuss poetic inquiry, saving the discussion and use of prose autoethnographic writing for later chapters.

Something similar to poetic inquiry was part of my family literacy practice. My paternal grandfather, who was killed by the government for being in the wrong social class and for having served in China's Nationalist government, had written several poems and couplets. One of his poems, which I read 50 years after his death, expressed his low regard for money and high hopes for his descendants to be virtuous. A set of 对联 (*dui lian*) or couplets that he wrote once adorned the Temple of Guan Yu in my hometown, a testimony to his reputation as a "县内名士" (a well-known scholar in China's Weixi County). Similarly, I observed my father copying ancient Chinese poems in his calligraphic work and composing his own. During each Chinese New Year, I would assist him in cutting the red paper into sets of three, witness the lines taking shape—stroke by stroke, character by character—and paste the couplets on our doorposts. Sometimes, he would invite me to compose the couplets together with him. Gradually, poetic inquiry has become an integral part of my literacy experience, first in Chinese and then in English, and it has extended to my academic publishing (Yang, 2013).

Recalling how often I composed poetic lines to express my intense emotions and ponderings over the meanings of my life and relating to my family's literacy practice, I wrote:

> *The journey has long begun*
> *When poetic voices from generations and from deep within*
> *The countless souls besieged*
> *by exams, structuralism, materialism, and native-speakerism …*
> *Cried like a North American cicada*
> *Who, emerging from the dark damp dungeon underground, after*
> *17 years of waiting, wiggling, and weeping, shrieked like hell*
> *"I want my own voice,*
> *And*
> *My own tree*
> *To climb."*

I never really liked cicadas when I was living at the foot of the Himalayas in Weixi. Hearing the ear-piercing and unceasing shriek of thousands of cicadas during hot summer days and nights in Macon, Georgia in August 2000 made it worse. I wanted them dead. However, perhaps because I made a Christian commitment a few months later, I began to appreciate these insects more, as part of the creation. Or perhaps the difference was that I had learned an amazing fact (McKeever, 2021): North American cicadas typically live underground for 17 years before they (at least, the successful ones) emerge; once out in the light, they live for only about a month. *What an amazing creature!* I thought to myself. *If I were a cicada, I would make as much noise as well. Because now, I finally see light.* In fact, I began to identify myself as a cicada who had been one of the "countless souls besieged by exams, structuralism, materialism, and native-speakerism" and was trapped in the "dark damp dungeon underground." I was in a culture and an educational system that did not encourage me to speak my own mind. I existed, but I did not have my voice, nor did I dare to express it. Nonetheless, I desired more for myself. This desire lay behind all my efforts as a learner, a teacher, and a professional. Hence these lines of a poem that I discovered in 2000 (I have not been able to identify the original author):

I want my own voice
And
My own tree
To climb.

These poetic lines not only resonated with me; they expressed a shared desire of multilingual professionals trying to find their own voices in a discourse community dominated by self-distancing academic prose (Iida, 2017). Furthermore, they foreground the intense struggles involved in academic writing, particularly in demarcating the ownership of words, which, according to Bakhtin (1981), are "half-ours and half-someone else's" (p. 345).

Poetic inquiry is also a disciplinary critique on science-oriented research and writing practices that have dominated in social studies. Influenced by postmodern suspicion of any claims of universal truth in social studies and motivated by a vision of producing engaging ethnographic writing, the sociologist Richardson (1997) argues that qualitative researchers should write both creatively and critically. She then demonstrates with her own examples how this can be done. She names her approach Creative Analytical Process (CAP) writing, invoking three images she associates with CAP: the head as both body and mind, instead of just the body or just the mind; the headwear, or the discourse of a profession; and the Capitalist. Using a CAP approach thus acknowledges one's multiple positionings, related privileges, and ideological underpinnings.

Richardson further suggests that poetic writing is one productive form of CAP writing. With regard to her first attempts to use poems for ethnographic writing, she argues that poetic representations of ethnographic knowledge are, in spirit, devising storylines, which is consistent with the poststructualist assumption that "knowledge systems are narratively constructed" (Richardson, 1997, p. 197). The rise of postmodern and feminist scholarship has provided such possibilities for alternative knowing and voicing. As Richardson (1997) reflects:

> Postmodernist culture permits us—indeed, encourages us—to doubt that any method of knowing or telling can claim authoritative truth. We have a historical opportunity to create a space for different kinds of social practice. As one possible practice, I have modeled here [through *Nine Poems*] a feminist-postmodernist practice [in which] dualism—"mind-body," "intellect-emotion," "self-other," "researcher-research," "literary writing—science writing"—[is] collapsed.
>
> (p. 186)

Poetic inquiry is, therefore, a postmodernist approach to challenging the positivist conventions of doing social studies and reporting research findings, which tend to adopt a detached stance. It constitutes an alternative way of knowing that features narrative, connections, and contextualization, all of which will be explored further in this book.

A Critical Reflection on the "Foreign" from a Global South Perspective

So is LA as foreign a genre as I initially positioned it in my poem? Are poetic inquiry and autoethnographic research foreign methods? Upon reflection, I am more inclined to say that they felt foreign to me and my students because they have been first named in English by scholars in the English-speaking world. However, the spirit of all three has been present in the lives of those in the margins of formal education, under the sway of global market forces.

First, LA was a marginalized genre in universities, especially those outside the English-speaking world. In such contexts as the United States and Australia, the rise of a process approach to writing education since the 1980s set the stage for learner-writers to explore their own experiences, emotions, and imaginations, and not least, the mysterious "voice" (Elbow, 1998; Graves, 1983; Kamler, 2001; Shen, 1989). However, universities offer no safe haven from the permeating power of capitalism and neoliberalism (de Sousa Santos, 2020; Surma, 2018). Consequently, when North American scholars noticed signs of LA writing falling out of favor in college composition—for instance in the 2010s—they observed a dwindling market for literacy narrative according to booksellers or publishers (Bryant, 2013). Nonetheless, writing teachers in English-speaking countries have continued to adapt literacy narrative in their teaching, sometimes turning it into a multi-modal composition (Angu, 2019; Canagarajah, 2020; Carstens, 2013; Corkery, 2005; Pennell, 2014; Sladek, 2019). In contrast, as we will see more closely in Chapter 5, scholarship on LA writing in the EFL context is extremely limited.

To date, I can find only two published examples, one from China (Qian, 2019) and one from Japan (Fujieda & Iida, 2015).

Here, then, is a paradox. Despite the overall absence of LA writing in the EFL context, the spirit of LA writing has actually long been present there. Four shared epistemological gazes in which LA writers, poetic inquirers, and autoethnographic researchers engage have actually been practiced for centuries, if not longer, in countries such as China, Korea, Japan, and several others with a non-Western cultural heritage. Specifically, one gazes back (on one's own and others' past), outward (on nature, society, culture, and related events), inside (on mental, emotional, and philosophical experiences), and forward (on imagined possibilities). I did this in the present chapter when I used a poem to recount my students' reactions to an LA writing assignment and my own experience of encountering LA for the first time (gazing back). I then suggested possible hurdles such as "grammar books" and "a spoon-fed life" (gazing outward). Next, I revealed my thoughts and wonders concerning the LA as "liberating" (gazing inside). Last, I envisioned a new life for "a caged bird" to "see the world above traffic rules of the ground" (gazing forward). The poetic expressions are the natural culmination of these gazing acts.

A similar argument can be made about autoethnographic writing. Long before this term was coined, some early colonial writers already engaged in such gazing acts. I have in my mind Guaman Poma's bilingual (in Spanish and Quechua) letter to the king of Spain from over 400 years ago. Pratt (1991) provided an insightful analysis of the transcultural nature of this letter in *Arts of the Contact Zone*. Pratt explained that in the letter, Poma, a native of Peru, gazed back on history, both that of humanity based on the Bible and that of Andeans based on stories told by Inca elders; gazed outward on colonialization; gazed inside to express "Andeans values and aspirations" (p. 555); and gazed forward with "a revisionist account of the Spanish conquest" (p. 503). Pratt (1991) suggested that the letter be treated as autoethnographic because it is "a text in which people undertake to describe themselves in ways that engage with representations others have made of them" (p. 501) in the written language of the other. Autoethnographic texts do not take knowledge as given; they interrogate, complicate, contextualize, and critique such knowledge. Thus, as Pratt (1991) also suggested, such texts "often constitute a marginalized group's point of entry into the dominant circuits of print culture" (p. 502). The spirit of autoethnographic research has long breathed through texts written by the marginalized. Therefore, although these epistemological gazes were rarely directed toward literacy itself, they have been frequently practiced in history. If that is the case, then we can relate to LA writing in a fundamentally different way. Rather than viewing it as completely foreign, we can treat it as a mobile genre whose spirit is historically and widely present and yet whose specific manifestations, including the use of the language, differ across diverse contexts and times. Because LA—through its first appearance in print, its naming, and related pedagogical and research practices—was first known in the English-speaking countries, its mention tends to evoke a sense of foreignness among those from other countries. The absence of LA writing in these contexts marks its similarities to texts outside the Western cultural centers. That's why both my students and I failed to recognize its native-ness initially.

The same is true of poetic inquiry. Even though this term now appears in postmodern North American research literature (e.g., Faulkner, 2019), the practice has had a long history outside the Western political sphere. In China, for example, the spirit of poetic inquiry was manifested by Qu Yuan 屈原 (340?–278?), "the first man ever to be known in China for his poetry" (Sukhu, 2017, p. 9). Qu Yuan, though competent and loyal in his service to the Chu state as a minister, was slandered by other court officials and subsequently demoted and exiled by the king and his successor. Feeling desperate before his suicide, which the Chinese Dragon Boat Festival was originally introduced to commemorate, the poet wrote, "路漫漫其修远兮，吾将上下而求索" (Long is the road, and I will ever search its ups and downs). The two short lines capture two worlds: that of the road and that of the self, the "I" who takes the position of a humble but determined explorer. They imply that the road of knowledge is an ongoing process of searching for the most truthful answers. Similarly, his poem *Tianwen* 天问 ("Ask the Sky"), originally written on bamboo strips, features a wide range of questions about "the origin of the cosmos, the formation of the heavens, ancient myths, and ancient history" along with his search for understanding (Sukhu, 2017, p. 13).

Although Qu Yuan fell out of favor with two kings in his own lifetime, his voice has been heard ever since through his poetic cries. Wu (2019) distinguished two types of poetic inquiry. The first type, known as poetic inquiry (lowercase), has been in practice for thousands of years in many countries, including China. The second type, which he termed Poetic Inquiry (with capitalization), refers to recent theorizations and experiments by postmodern and feminist scholars seeking to provide a non-positivist epistemology. Both types can serve to challenge positions of marginalization. Scholars adopting the approach spoke from the margin to address imbalances in knowledge production within their fields. Consider the case of Park (2013), a Korean ELT professional who interpreted and reinterpreted the multiple meanings of her poem about two chrysanthemum gardens. They represent the conflicting worlds of a bilingual individual in the English-speaking context: both privilege and marginalization, voice and silence, enrichment and deprivation. Or consider Wu (2019), a Chinese scholar who used a wide array of poetry—poems in classic Chinese, his own freestyle translations of some of these poems into English, and freestyle English poems—to make sense of challenging aspects of his family life history, such as his father's death in a truck accident and mistreatment by his aunt and uncle as a child. By applying Poetic Inquiry, these bilingual scholars managed to understand the complexity of their experiences and to articulate and share their preferred interpretations. Poetic Inquiry enabled them to adopt positions in the world as curious explorers of new possibilities. In Wiebe's (2015) words, "to inquire poetically is to attune our senses to this world" and discover "right distance between the self and other, between the researcher and the participant, and between the poet and the poetry" (p. 153). In other words, LA writing, Poetic Inquiry, and autoethnographic research are not really foreign to individuals with less power in imbalanced cultural dynamics. Sharing the same searching spirit by gazing inwardly, outwardly, to the past, and to the future, these forms of expression are alternative ways of knowing and representing knowledge. They allow the voiceless to find their voices in cultural and disciplinary spaces dominated by voices of the powerful. Embracing such an epistemological stance is a necessary step to disrupt the state of silence and being silenced in the face of the seemingly foreign ways of knowing and representing.

A poem by He Zhizhang (659–744), from the Tang Dynasty, captures this kind of misrecognition and tension well. He wrote:

> 回乡偶书
> 少小离家老大回，乡音无改鬓毛衰。
> 儿童相见不相识，笑问客从何处来。
> *On Returning to My Hometown*
> (my translingual[1] translation)
> Young—far away—from my kind.
> Old—back—the same accent kept.
> My sideburns, now gray, "*Where are—
> you from, sir?*" Kids smiled and asked.

Although this poem originally described a (domestic) diaspora member's struggle with geographical relocation, I reimagine it as an imaginary and humorous ode to personified LA writing, poetic inquiry, and autoethnographic research. All the "I" references in the poem can metaphorically point to these three forms of exploration and expression with the same gazing spirit. During the travel of the same gazing spirit, its accent has persisted, yet its appearance has changed (as indicated by the graying of his sideburns). Confused by this odd mixture of both the same and the different, my students and I were like the kids who smiled at the seeming stranger, as expressed in the final line of the Chinese poem: "笑问客从何处来" (which literally means "smiled and asked, 'Visitor, where are you from?'") It invites us to consider the mobility of things at a global scale in both colonial and postcolonial times (Pennycook, 2012), to recognize the importance of wrestling with writing differences in transnational and translingual terms (You, 2010, 2016, 2018), and, above all, to respond to the pressing call to engage in English writing education from a Global South epistemological perspective (Comaroff & Comaroff, 2013; de Sousa Santos, 2014).

Structure of the Book

This book contains four parts. The two chapters in Part I foreground the teacher's stories. Building on Chapter 1, the next chapter presents my own literacy autobiography, which I wrote with my Chinese students. It highlights my process of constructing identity and voice as shaped by culture, ideology, and social interactions.

Part II has four chapters. Chapter 3 reconceptualizes EFL literacy autobiographical writing as critical pedagogy from a Global South perspective. Chapter 4 describes my own pedagogical and research processes that shaped the students' EFL literacy autobiographical writing and identity construction, featuring especially the relationship between translanguaging/translingual practice and classroom writing ecology. Chapter 5 presents a case study of Chen, who demonstrates strong signs of "translingualism" (Canagarajah, 2020) in her final literacy autobiography. Her evolving subjectivity can be partially attributed to the transnational literacy experiences of her upbringing and was further facilitated by the classroom writing ecology, which featured a dialogical approach, multi-drafting process, and autoethnographic research. Chapter 6 presents an analysis of voicing patterns of multiple EFL student writers still through the lens of "translingualism" but with a critical consideration for internal and external translanguaging conditions.

Part III contains ten chapters, featuring literacy autobiographies of representative EFL learners. In an afterword, I reflect on EFL literacy autobiographical writing and the book project as a whole, and I offer suggestions for future research.

Note

1 By this, I mean that I not only translate the meaning of the poem, but also try to retain some stylistic features of the original Chinese poem, which contains seven characters in each of the four lines. In my translation, I used seven syllables in each line.

References

Angu, P. E. (2019). Understanding voices from the margins: Social injustice and agency in first-year students' literacy narratives. *Journal of Further and Higher Education*, *43*(8), 1152–1162. https://doi.org/10.1080/0309877X.2018.1458977

Bakhtin, M. M. (1981). *The dialogic imagination: Four essays* (M. Holquist, Trans.). University of Texas Press.

Bryant, L. (2013, July 24). Is the literacy narrative dead? https://lists.asu.edu/cgi-bin/wa?A2=WPA-L;3cd259b.1307&S=

Canagarajah, A. S. (2020). *Transnational literacy autobiographies as translingual writing*. Routledge.

Carstens, A. (2013). Using literacy narratives to scaffold academic literacy in the Bachelor of Education: A pedagogical framework. *Journal for Language Teaching*, *46*(2), 9–25. https://doi.org/10.4314/jlt.v46i2.1

Chang, H. (2008). *Autoethnography as method*. Left Coast Press.

Cheng, J., & Li, W. (2021). Individual agency and changing language education policy in China: Reactions to the new "Guidelines on College English Teaching." *Current Issues in Language Planning*, *22*, 117–135. https://doi.org/10.1080/14664208.2019.1700055

Comaroff, J., & Comaroff, J. L. (2013, November 13). Writing theory from the south: The global order from an African perspective. *World Financial Review*. https://worldfinancialreview.com/writing-theory-south-global-order-african-perspective/

Corkery, C. (2005). Literacy narratives and confidence building in the writing classroom. *Journal of Basic Writing*, *24*(1), 48–67. https://doi.org/10.37514/JBW-J.2005.24.1.04

de Sousa Santos, B. (2014). *Epistemologies of the South: Justice against epistemicide*. Routledge.

de Sousa Santos, B. (2020). Decolonizing the university. In B. de Sousa Santos, & M. P. Meneses (Eds.), *Knowledges born in the struggle: Constructing the epistemologies of the Global South* (pp. 219–239). Routledge.

Elbow, P. (1998). *Writing without teachers*. Oxford University Press. (Original work published 1981).

Faulkner, S. L. (2019). *Poetic inquiry: Craft, method and practice*. Routledge.

Finance Center for South-South Cooperation. (2015). *Global South countries: Group of 77 and China*. http://www.fc-ssc.org/en/partnership_program/south_south_countries

Fujieda, Y., & Iida, A. (2015). Literacy autobiography in EFL contexts: Investigating Japanese student language learning experiences. In D. Shaffer, & M. Pinto (Eds.), *Embracing change: Blazing new frontiers through language teaching* (proceedings of the KOTESOL/KAFLE international conference) (pp. 97–104). Korea TESOL Organization.

Graves, D. H. (1983). *Writing: Teachers and children at work*. Heinemann Educational Books.

Grbich, C. (2013). *Qualitative data analysis: An introduction* (2nd ed). SAGE Publications.

Hu, G. (2021). English language policy in Mainland China. In E. L. Low & A. Pakir, *English in East and South Asia* (1st ed., pp. 19–32). Routledge. https://doi.org/10.4324/9780429433467-3

Iida, A. (2017). Expressing voice in a foreign language: Multiwriting Haiku pedagogy in the EFL context. *TEFLIN Journal—A Publication on the Teaching and Learning of English*, *28*(2), 260–276. https://doi.org/10.15639/teflinjournal.v28i2/260-276

Kamler, B. (2001). *Relocating the personal: A critical writing pedagogy*. State University of New York Press.

Matsuda, P. K. (2001). Voice in Japanese written discourse: Implications for second language writing. *Journal of Second Language Writing*, *10*(1–2), 35–53. https://doi.org/10.1016/S1060-3743(00)00036-9

Matsuda, P. K. (2002). Epilogue: Reinventing giants. In L. L. Blanton, & B. Kroll (Eds.), *ESL composition tales: Reflections on teaching* (pp. 163–171). University of Michigan Press.

Matsuda, P. K. (2003). Coming to voice: Publishing as a graduate student. In C. P. Casanave, & S. Vandrick (Eds.), *Writing for scholarly publication: Behind the scenes in language education* (pp. 47–62). Lawrence Erlbaum Associates.

McKeever, A. (2021, March 17). Millions of cicadas will soon emerge in the U.S. Here's why. *National Geographic*. https://www.nationalgeographic.com/animals/article/millions-cicadas-emerging-now-united-states

Park, G. (2013). My autobiographical-poetic rendition: An inquiry into humanizing our teacher scholarship. *L2 Journal*, *5*(1), 6–18. https://doi.org/10.5070/L25115768

Pennell, M. (2014). (Re)placing the literacy narrative: Composing in Google Maps. *Literacy in Composition Studies*, *2*(2), 44–65. https://doi.org/10.21623/1.2.2.4

Pennycook, A. (2012). *Language and mobility: Unexpected places*. Multilingual Matters. https://doi.org/10.21832/9781847697653

Pennycook, A., & Makoni, S. (2020). *Innovations and challenges in applied linguistics from the Global South*. Routledge.

Poon, A. Y. K. (2010). Language use, and language policy and planning in Hong Kong. *Current Issues in Language Planning*, *11*(1), 1–66.

Pratt, M. L. (1991). Arts of the contact zone. *Profession*, *91*, 33–40.

Qian, Y. (2019). Motivation to English academic writing: Chinese students' literacy autobiography. *Theory and Practice in Language Studies*, *9*(5), 530–536. http://doi.org/10.17507/tpls.0905.06

Richardson, L. (1997). *Fields of play: Constructing an academic life*. Rutgers University Press.

Romanyshyn, R. D. (2021). *The wounded researcher: Research with soul in mind*. Routledge.

Shen, F. (1989). The classroom and the wider culture: Identity as a key to learning English composition. *College Composition and Communication, 40*(4), 459–466. https://doi.org/10.2307/358245

Shen, Q. (2020, July 22). *xīn zhōng guó wài yǔ jiào yù guī huá qī shí nián: fàn shì biàn qiān yǔ zhànlüè zhuǎn xíng* [70 years of foreign language education planning of China, Paradigm changes and strategic shifts]. Chinese Academy of Social Sciences. http://www.cssn.cn/yyx/202007/t20200722_5158699.shtml

Sladek, A. (2019). Literacy as threshold concept: Building multiliterate awareness in first-year writing. *Composition Studies, 47*(2), 108–126.

Sukhu, G. (2017). *The songs of Chu: An anthology of ancient Chinese poetry*. Columbia University Press.

Surma, A. (2018). Writing is the question, not the answer: A critical cosmopolitan approach to writing in neoliberal times. In X. You (Ed.), *Transnational writing education: Theory and practice* (pp. 61–76). Routledge.

Wiebe, S. (2015). Poetic inquiry: A fierce, tender, and mischievous relationship with lived experience. *Language and Literacy, 17*(3), 152–163. https://doi.org/10.20360/G2VP4N

Wu, B. (2019). *Poetic inquiry: My journey in language* [Unpublished PhD dissertation]. The University of British Columbia.

Wu, L., Wu, Y., & Zhang, X. (2021). L2 learner cognitive psychological factors about artificial intelligence writing corrective feedback. *English Language Teaching, 14*(10), 70–83.

Yang, S. (2013). *Autobiographical writing and identity in EFL education*. Routledge.

You, X. (2010). *Writing in the devil's tongue: A history of English composition in China*. Southern Illinois University Press.

You, X. (2016). *Cosmopolitan English and transliteracy*. Southern Illinois University Press.

You, X. (Ed.). (2018). *Transnational writing education: Theory, history, and practice*. Routledge.

Yu, C. (2020). The washback of the new writing tasks in China's national matriculation English test. *English Language Teaching, 13*(1), 99–111.

2
MY OWN LITERACY AUTOBIOGRAPHY

Shizhou Yang

In view of my humble rural roots, perhaps no one, especially those who grew up with me, expected me to go so far in my journey with literacy, particularly reading and writing in English. But here I am, teaching at a Chinese university and reflecting—in English—on how my rural life has taken a different turn through learning English. Slowly, English has become *my* language, "my bread and butter, or to be culturally more accurate, my rice, steamed buns, and noodles" (Yang, 2021, para. 1). In this literacy autobiography (henceforth LA), which I first wrote while guiding my graduate students in China to draft their own LAs (2019–2020) and then revised when I was teaching a similar writing course to international students at a university in Thailand (2020–present), I narrate, analyze, and attempt a cultural interpretation of my process of becoming a reader and writer in Chinese and English, and of eventually developing an L2 writing teacher identity. Although this study features my LA, its end goal is to address some outstanding issues in the TESOL profession. Increasingly, the hegemonic status or so-called "epistemological racism" of the Global North or Western-centric TESOL scholarship is being questioned (Pennycook & Makoni, 2020). Meanwhile, there is a pressing need to study L2 writing teachers' multiple identities (Racelis & Matsuda, 2015), personal experiences (Cheung, 2017), and cognition as teachers. As Lee (2018, p. 5) pointed out, "Scant attention has been paid to writing teachers' own beliefs about themselves and experiences as writers." These gaps in scholarship prompted me to engage in LA writing. Using autoethnographic research (Chang, 2008) allows me, like other multilingual TESOL professionals, to speak from my marginalized position (Kim & Saenkhum, 2019; Yazan et al., 2021). Furthermore, by adopting a Global South perspective to foreground contradiction-induced knowledge (Santos, 2014, 2020), I hope to contribute a critical voice to the still-emergent scholarship on L2 writing teachers' dynamic and situated identity work (Canagarajah, 2016; Cheung, 2017;

Lee, 2013, 2018; Lee & Canagarajah, 2019; Racelis & Matsuda, 2015). Teacher identity, after all, has important implications for teaching practice (Goh, 2014).

Early Exposure to Reading

I was born in Weixi Lisu Autonomous County in northwest Yunnan, China in 1977 (This was around the time when the College Entrance Examination was finally restored after the disastrous ten-year Great Cultural Revolution came to an end). Although Weixi, an important station on the Ancient Tea-Horse Road, was inhabited by many ethnic minority groups such as Tibetans, Bai, and Yi, I was not interested in learning any of these languages, including Naxi, my mother's language. I lived at the edge of the county seat, where people spoke a southwest dialect of Chinese. That was my language until when I went to school and discovered another language: Mandarin Chinese. This was a language of the powerful and educated—government officials, teachers, actors, actresses, and announcers on the TV, which had just begun to appear in my hometown. By comparison, to my young and prejudiced mind, all other languages belonged only to the drunkards, tobacco smokers, and rice farmers in the villages and mountains. As for Naxi, it was the secret language my mother would use to communicate with her siblings when they came to visit once or twice a year. But it was for them, not for me. I wanted to learn Mandarin Chinese like my elder siblings.

My first lessons in reading and writing, all in Mandarin Chinese, began when Mother sent me to her friend Madam Wei's class to *pangting* instruction in the one-story schoolhouse about a five-minute walk from home. I was only six years old, too young to be officially enrolled. Both Father and Mother had to work in the cornfields, so school was the only place for me to go. Besides, I had wanted to go to school because I hoped to carry a school bag as the older kids in my neighborhood did.

But soon, I realized that school was tough. As I wrote in 2008 in a story called "My First Picture," to share with my research participants in an extracurricular writing group that I led:

> However, much to my disappointment, the school turned out to be a difficult place: no playing with clay, nor hunting of crickets, but repeatedly reading after the teacher things I could not understand. Worst of all, I was constantly bullied by bigger kids. Now that I think about it, what I did not understand back then must have been Chinese characters and *pinyin*. Having never learned anything about them before elementary school, as there was no preschool or kindergarten in the countryside at that time, I was at a loss about what the teacher was teaching. Of course, being bullied increased my anxiety at school, making it hard for me to focus.
>
> I persevered, however. In part, I was comforted by Mother's visits to school. But I also began to understand that my only way to beat the rough

guys was not through any physical strength, but through study. After all, I was thin and frequently sick as a child, and consequently I also looked weak. Although I toyed with the idea of studying with some kung fu master, I knew I could never do that. So I just continued doing whatever my teachers required of me at school.

Learning to read and write in Chinese was my first potential game changer. By learning what the school was teaching, despite the unfriendly environment, I hoped to compensate for my small physical size with greater cognitive power.

Reading for fun was seldom a part of my childhood experience. In fact, until college, I hardly read anything other than textbooks. My family was not well off. My parents were farmers who also ran a small family business on the side, making and selling tofu and distilled corn whiskey at times. I clearly remember wearing plain blue clothes made by Mother, having eggs only on my birthdays or when I got 100 on my tests, and occasionally Father buying a thin, illustrated book to comfort me when I had to go to the hospital. A bankbook that I inherited from my father around the early 1980s also testifies to how little money we had as a family back then. It usually had a balance of just a few yuan RMB (less than one U.S. dollar), deposited for several weeks or even months and earned from sales of tofu or whiskey. Thus, my parents had to use every penny frugally so that my three older siblings and I could all attend school. This explains why we had so few books at home and why I envied my friend Yong, who had all kinds of books including the "*Four* [Chinese] *Classics*." Both of his parents were government employees, so his family could afford to buy numerous books for him.

Also, I had it drummed into me that it was a crime to read for fun. Students who read *lianhuanhua*, little pocket-sized storybooks with black-and-white illustrations, at school would be criticized by teachers; if you read kung fu, martial arts, or romance novels, you would surely be criticized too. The central message in all these criticisms was that reading anything other than textbooks was a waste of time and would jeopardize your opportunity to go to high school and eventually college.

College, what a glorious thought! I knew I had to study hard for it; it was probably my second game changer, one that could help me (as we Chinese would say) to jump the dragon gate and leave a farming life behind. With this prospect in mind, our teachers and parents would do everything they could to keep us on track, repeating to us the stories of scholars of old times who studied diligently for the imperial exams. There was not a complete absence of leisurely reading, but it was very rare, happening occasionally when one of my primary-school math teachers would end the afternoon class with a ghost story from *Liaozhaizhiyi* (Strange Stories from a Chinese Studio). It was scary and exciting at the same time, a welcoming change from textbooks loaded with facts and formulas. About as infrequently, I would lay my hand on some *Gushihui* (anthology of stories) and read them like a thief, because doing so often evoked in me a sense of guilt that I was not studying as seriously as I should.

Besides this perceived conflict between reading for fun and studying, I was restricted in my reading because I had to help my family with housework. In 1987, when I was age ten and in fourth grade, my mother had a tractor accident and broke her spine. From then until her death in 2001, she could no longer stand up straight, let alone work in the cornfields. To lighten the family burden, my siblings and I began to shoulder various family responsibilities. I soon learned to cook rice over our family fire pit and to make *baozi* (steamed buns) and yak-butter tea, a traditional Tibetan drink. I washed dishes by hand every day and my own clothes every week. I learned to mend my own shoes. "穷人的早当家" (The children of the poor learn to manage the household early), as the Chinese often say. If I had any free time after school, I was busy cooking, cleaning, washing, or doing whatever useful service I could find at home. Reading for fun was out of the question. Living in a poor family, I developed a poverty mindset with regard to reading.

Learning to Write in Chinese

My limited early reading did not prepare me well for Chinese writing. I felt—as one of my later ethnic Bai students, Anne, once did—unable to write good compositions in Chinese due to my limited vocabulary and inability to use 华丽的辞藻 or flowery expressions (Yang, 2013). In modern Chinese writing, especially writing for exams, the use of flowery expressions, which range from four-character set phrases to historical allusions, is an important indicator that the writer is well-read, educated, and a member of the cultured class. However, my family situation and my teachers' words placed me in a tug of war between a low and a high literacy level, a reality and an aspiration. I wanted to read widely, but I was constrained both externally and internally.

As in most traditional Chinese families, my father did not encourage me to speak my mind. "Children are to be seen, not heard" was the unspoken rule at home. It was implicit in my father's raised voice and stern look when I tried to tell jokes. It must have happened so many times that I began to internalize the rule, becoming very quiet and hardly ever talking to others, including my own family, of my own accord. "Nobody wanted me to say anything" was a message I repeated constantly in my mind. I even began to embrace the cultural saying "沉默是金" (silence is golden) as my motto. Yet in my heart, I still wanted to express myself and to communicate with others.

I turned to music. I liked singing, so I started copying some song lyrics—popular patriotic Chinese songs to sing praises to the motherland, as well as songs from Hong Kong and Taiwan such as 我的中国心 (*My Chinese Heart*) and 爸爸的草鞋 (*Baba's Straw Sandals*), which expressed a Chinese sentiment. Music, after all, was my family inheritance. My father played the *erhu*, a string instrument, all his life and was a renowned folk musician in my hometown. So was his father, whom I had never met but who (or so I heard) played the flute very well. But I also invested my creativity in writing letters and diaries. Two experiences especially stand out from this time: doing calligraphy and writing a letter.

When I was in elementary school, I had to practice calligraphy almost every day. It was a regular assignment from my Chinese teacher. I practiced by tracing a model calligraphic work first and then by means of exercise books with measured squares and lines. The repeated practice reinforced in my mind and muscles not only the formation of each Chinese character, but also a notion of traditional Chinese value. The character "人," for instance, was used by both my teacher and my father, who emphasized the importance of writing it properly. "It should be upright and balanced, standing straight on the two feet!" This was no simple teaching of skill. Rather, it entailed a philosophical question of how to be a proper human being, and the answer was by striving for righteousness. "字像人形" was frequently evoked by my teachers, whether they taught Chinese, math, or physics. This word means that how characters are written actually manifests both the writer's appearance and inner qualities. If your handwriting is good, you are praised; if not, you are criticized. In both cases, one's way of writing Chinese characters is equal to one's identity. Years later, in a 2001 letter, my father admonished me for my deteriorating handwriting. "It is too hasty and careless; it does not match the advanced education you are receiving." I was then studying at Mercer University in Georgia (2000–2002), obtaining my M.Ed. in English, and would occasionally write letters to my family. But this indictment of me was still based on how carefully I put the strokes together and how properly I wrote my Chinese characters.

The content of my calligraphic practice as a child was usually "Tang Poems," a collection of works by famous ancient poets such as Li Po from the Tang Dynasty (618–907 AD). They are highly valued in Chinese education. As one saying goes, "熟读唐诗三百首，不会作诗也会吟" (If one is familiar with the 300 Tang poems, one would know how to read a poem, if not to compose one). Thus, Tang poems are a household item in China. For me, copying Tang poems in my calligraphic practice not only exposed me to the themes of traditional poetry and its rhythmic beauty, but also taught me some life philosophy and developed in me some Chinese sentiments. The lines "谁知盘中餐，粒粒皆辛苦" (Don't you know each grain/on the plate comes from farmers' /toil and sweat?), which even my five-year-old daughter knows by heart, would condemn me if I wasted any food. The lines "举头望明月, 低头思故乡" (I lift my head to gaze at the moon; I lower my head, missing my hometown) guided my thoughts when I visited foreign lands. A poem favored by both my father and myself is "登鹳雀楼" (Climbing the Guanque Building). It was contained in my father's gift to my sister, copied in his fine calligraphy. The idea that "one should climb one story higher to see farther," as expressed in this poem, resonated with my search for a home away from my birth home. I quoted this poem to summarize my father's life, which was filled with losses, pain, illness—in short, all kinds of sufferings—and his unyielding desire to bring his family to a higher place. My childhood exposure to the Tang poems thus nurtured a poetic sentiment within me.

The other major event in my Chinese literacy journey was writing a letter. I was probably in fifth grade. One day, my second Chinese teacher, Madam Wu, asked the students to write a letter to a relative. I wrote my letter to my uncle, who was living in Beijing. I remember asking him if he was doing well there. I then thanked him for sending the medicine to help my mother, who had been paralyzed in her tractor accident about a year earlier. To my surprise, Madam Wu selected my letter to read to the whole class, as was customary with model essays in Chinese writing classrooms. She even praised me, saying that my letter "表达了真情实感" (expressed my true emotion), a quality that makes writing good in China. This was the beginning of seeing myself as a writer through my teacher's eyes. It taught me what is valued in Chinese writing. Nonetheless, my negative view of myself as a writer in Chinese remained dominant.

I wonder why I wrote to my uncle in Beijing in the first place. Perhaps my teacher had asked us to write to a relative living in a big city, and I happened to have an uncle in Beijing. Or I might have chosen my uncle because he was the first college student in my extended family. Or I was trying to claim my right to speak, my voice, despite my limitations in Mandarin Chinese. The sociologist Bourdieu (2004) proposed two forms of capital: material and symbolic. Whereas material capital refers to items of tangible value such as money, houses, and cars, symbolic capital refers to things like credentials and backgrounds. Both play an important role in deciding whether one can speak or deserves a hearing. Since I had so little reading to draw upon from my extremely restricted literacy experiences, I needed an extraneous form of capital, the symbolic kind, to speak and write in Chinese.

My English Learning Journey

As an English language learner, I reaped what I sowed into imagined identities. Norton (2000) theorized that individuals' imagined identities shape their investment in language learning to complement the psychological construct of motivation. Darvin and Norton (2015, 2018) proposed further that learners' investment is concurrently shaped by identity, capital, and ideology. Similarly, Dörnyei (2014) theorized that behind each individual's language learning trajectory is a self-system, including an "ought-to L2 self" pointing to social expectations to learn an L2, a "feared L2 self" constructed of situations one tries to avoid, and most powerfully an "ideal L2 self" or what one aspires to become through an L2. In other words, language learning is not just a mechanical process; it is a process of profound identity work (Kramsch, 2009; Pavlenko & Lantolf, 2000).

These theories resonate with my experience. My six years of investment in English learning during middle and high school (1989–1995) were characterized by a burning desire to leave my rural birthplace behind and connect with the outside world. My imagined identity or ideal L2 self was built around the idea of English becoming my own language. It guided my English learning, not just as a school subject, nor perfunctorily or rebelliously as my local male culture dictated. In fact, I dreaded becoming a member of the local gang, whose members often joked that "English knows me, but I do not know English" or "I cannot even pronounce the 26 alphabets." Such were my feared L2 selves to avoid. I wanted instead to learn English so well as to pass the College Entrance Exam, on which the subject of

English used to carry as much weight as Chinese and math. To actually use English was not yet my immediate goal. After all, I had no one in my life, either relatives or teachers, who could show me how they used English to communicate with others. English in my hometown was strictly locked in the classroom, written on the blackboard as grammatical rules, and recited word by word from textbooks by the whole class, some students doing it more fluently than others. It was a "foreign" language and "the devil's tongue" (You, 2010) to my peers but the language of cream in my dreams, my third game changer. Nonetheless, as I wrote in a personal essay about my early English learning experience (Yang, 2021, para. 2):

> I diligently memorized the vocabulary and texts, took copious notes from the blackboard, and tried to commit to my heart the past-tense forms of irregular verbs such as *is*, *go*, and *fly*, and constantly reminded myself that *two* and *too* are different. I did all these for the faint hope that English could help me pass the College Entrance Exam.

My hard work eventually paid off. In 1995, I was admitted, with a scholarship, to Yunnan Minzu University (YMU), majoring in English. I was one of the only three high-school graduates (out of 150) in my county that year to enter college successfully. Studying in Kunming, the capital city of Yunnan, I gained a clearer sense of my "imagined identity," which Norton (2000) defines as some future self that one aspires to become. I wanted to study abroad, in the United States, just as my aunt in Hong Kong had encouraged me. Or, as my father had shockingly told me when I was in high school, "Shizhou, you should think about studying abroad!" I had never thought that my father had such high expectations for me. But my level of English was a galaxy away from my dream. I was tongue-tied, because of both my poor English pronunciation and my shy personality. My grammar was poor. My vocabulary was limited. I was in every way like "癞蛤蟆想吃天鹅肉" (a toad dreaming of eating a swan).

That's when my agency kicked in. Agency, defined by Ahearn (2001, p. 116) as "a socioculturally mediated capacity to act," plays a central role in successful language learning (Pavlenko & Lantolf, 2000). This was the case with me. As I recounted in my personal statement in 2006, while applying for a Ph.D. program in Australia:

> At university, I worked very hard to develop both my English language skills and a more outgoing personality. To improve my spoken English, I listened to English radio programs every day and went to English corners every week. To expand my vocabulary, I read the *Oxford Pocket English Dictionary* from front to back in my sophomore year. In my dorm room, I was the first one to get up and the last one to go to bed. Meanwhile, I worked for the departmental Students' Union and actively participated in English speech contests, singing contests, and other extracurricular activities as a way to help myself break

free from my fear of speaking in public. My persistent hard work contributed greatly to my later success. I was the only undergraduate in my school to pass not only the TOEFL [Test of English as a Foreign Language] and GRE [Graduate Record Examinations], but also Band 8 of the Test of English for English Majors [TEM-8], the highest English-language proficiency test in China. My outstanding achievement as an English major and student leader convinced the Foreign Language Department to employ me as a teacher of English majors immediately after my graduation.

During my four years in college, I went home only twice. As no one in my family had the influence to get me a job in the city, I spent all my holidays, as well as weekends, studying English. My learning surpassed the requirements in my textbooks. I listened to and recited Martin Luther King Jr.'s "I Have a Dream" speech in the back of the university teaching building. I read aloud, with a mirror in my hand, the international phonetic alphabets one by one, to ensure that my tongue was touching the roof of my mouth when pronouncing "L" and that I could indeed put two fingers between my upper and lower teeth when pronouncing "a" as in apple, just as my intensive reading teacher, Mr. Ma, had suggested. I also read the English Bible, acting upon the advice of someone I had met at an English corner (a place where people gather to speak English to each other in China), who said, "If you really want to learn English well, you should also read the English Bible!" Furthermore, I listened to audiotapes of American conversations repeatedly, while waiting in line in the canteen or even when going to sleep, hoping that I would soon enter the superior state of dreaming in English.

I portrayed in my personal statement an identity as a diligent and successful English learner. My efforts were congruent with my desired future identity for myself, as someone studying in an English-speaking country.

Becoming an L2 Writing Teacher

When I graduated from college in 1999, I had three job offers: one from a Dutch company, one from a five-star hotel, and one from my alma mater YMU. I decided to become an English teacher—*just to try it out. At least, teaching at a university would make it easier for me to study abroad*, I reasoned. That began my career as a language teacher. Like most of my English teachers in college, I had never received any training in teaching. However, one big advantage was that I was the one of the few students from my class to have passed the TEM-8, the most advanced English proficiency exam in China. Besides, through my years of diligent study, I had already become a confident and fluent speaker of English, which helped me immensely as I started my own English-medium instruction.

I was assigned to teach intensive reading, which emphasized close reading of selected texts, although it also included a writing component in each unit. Untrained as a teacher, I implemented what I thought effective teaching should consist of (e.g., humorous, relaxing, and all in English) and tried to avoid some of my former teachers' ways of interacting (e.g., speaking sarcastically about students when they made grammar mistakes or mispronounced words). Although I held this position for only one year, by the time I left China in 2000, I knew that I actually enjoyed teaching English.

Studying at Mercer University in Macon, Georgia (2000–2002) was a critical phase of my life both spiritually and professionally. I lived with Michael and Kitty Wilson, two of my former American teachers, who treated me like their son. I went to a Baptist church with them, attended a Sunday school for international students, sang in the church choir every week, and read the Bible every day. Gradually, I experienced a spiritual awakening and became a Christian. In an essay, I wrote that God is the ultimate teacher and the world is the classroom. Thus, God's words began to inform my thinking and writing.

A short teaching experience at the Baptist church intensified my desire to continue as a teacher. One day, Mrs. Stockstill, one of my Sunday-school teachers and an experienced ESL instructor, asked me to teach a few Chinese words without speaking any English. The learners were adults from the church who had volunteered to tutor ESL students. The purpose was to sensitize the volunteers to the immense psychological challenges associated with learning a new language. I taught the class some simple words such as *shu* (book) and *zhuozi* (table) by using the total physical response method. Although the session lasted for only five minutes, it had a profound impact on me. After the class, Mrs. Stockstill said, "Nicholas [my American name], you have a gift for teaching!" Her words both surprised and encouraged me, because up to that point, I had never thought that I had any gift, let alone a gift for teaching! Nonetheless, I trusted her insight and decided that I would pursue teaching as a vocation.

Studying at Mercer University also encouraged me to engage in creative writing in English. During my two years there, besides completing academic writing assignments for education-related courses, I wrote several life narratives for a contemporary essay course and several autobiographical poems for an Introduction to Poetry course. The workshop approach adopted by my American professors opened my eyes. For the first time, I experienced a democratic way of teaching writing. Everyone, including the professor, would sit in a circle to share their drafts with the whole class. After reading a piece of writing, the class would ask questions such as "How did you come to the topic?" or "What do you mean by …" and make comments such as "I really liked …" Once, I read two of my poems, "MT: Music of the Tomb" and "MW: Music of Water," which featured, respectively, my traumatic family history and my later conversion to Christianity (see Yang, 2013). I will forever cherish the feedback I received from my poetry professor and classmates. I experienced initially a long silence of admiration, followed by positive verbal and written comments from both my professor and my American classmates. My poetry professor wrote later on my portfolio how much he had enjoyed my poems. Writing experiences such as this one encouraged me to see myself as a creative writer and to consider the possibility of teaching L2 writing.

My identity formation as an L2 writing teacher can be divided into three phases. The first phase featured my initial exploration and experimentation. Starting in 2003, when I resumed my teaching position at YMU, I decided to make the teaching and researching of L2 English writing my niche. The vacuum was huge. At YMU, English writing was typically assigned to foreign teachers. Concerned about the potential heavy workload of responding to students' essays, none of my Chinese colleagues wanted to teach writing. When they had to do so as part of a language course, they commonly overemphasized matters of form, overlooking the writer, the content, and the process, as was typical when literacy education was test-oriented (Yang & Nong, 2019; Ye & White, 2012; You, 2004). Drawing on sociocultural theory of learning (Vygotsky, 1978) and my positive creative writing experiences in the United States, I introduced autobiographical writing projects to my students, asking each of them to produce an autobiography in English. At the end of the semester, they were to read a selection of their autobiographies to their class. Unbeknownst to myself, I was promoting meaningful literacy (Hanauer, 2012) in an EFL context. It was an innovation in that I did not restrict my students to argumentative writing, nor did I assign writing tasks for them to complete within 30 minutes, as was typical in exam-oriented teaching. However, my teaching practice was not yet informed by L2 writing scholarship, with which I was not familiar.

My second phase involved extensive reading and research as a Ph.D. student at La Trobe University in Australia (2007–2011). My topic was EFL autobiographical writing and identity, partially rooted in my reflection on the autobiographies written by my Chinese students. As I wrote later:

> My students' English "autobiographies" showed me that they were not a homogeneous group, nor did they conform to stereotypes such as deficit [deficient] and backward at worst or "能歌善舞" (good at singing and dancing) at best. Instead, they were people with stories, albeit rarely written about. Three students especially influenced me in choosing EFL autobiographical writing and identity as my research topic. One student, a Han Chinese from northern China, started her autobiography by writing[,] "Thank you for giving me this opportunity to make such a big statement of myself!" Her stories featured travels around China with her parents. Another student, a Yi boy, filled many pages with his struggles as the son of a drinking and gambling father. The third student, a Naxi girl, complained that the stories she wrote with care were commented on only casually. These and others taught me that the opportunity to write their stories in English mattered to them. They prompted me to devote myself to exploring EFL autobiographical writing, hoping to understand both their stories and them.
>
> *(Yang, 2013, p. 5)*

The generous scholarships I received from the Australian government and La Trobe University helped me focus on my studies. I was on a Ph.D. research track, so I spent most of my days reading and writing. Once every other week, I met with my advisors in the Faculty of Education: Dr. Audrey Grant, an adult literacy expert; Dr. Peta Heywood, specializing in transformative learning; and Dr. Howard Nicholas, a leading scholar in applied linguistics. My three advisors encouraged me to engage in my research from an interdisciplinary perspective, merging narrative theories and dialogism with literacy and applied linguistics. Eventually, based on the ethnographic data I collected from an extracurricular writing group that I led at a university in China for nine months in 2008, I wrote my Ph.D. thesis. I also started attending conferences and writing for publication. I was especially encouraged when Brian Street, one of the three external reviewers of my Ph.D. thesis, called it "an outstanding thesis [that] well deserves not simply the award of the Ph.D. but also publication." Two years later, I published my first book through Routledge. My four years of Ph.D. study had not only broadened my vision but also helped me to view myself as an emergent L2 writing scholar.

My third phase (2011–2020) featured a deepened involvement with the teaching and research of L2 writing. During this period, I taught a wide range of writing courses in English: composition, reading and writing, academic writing, and creative writing. My students came from diverse disciplinary backgrounds: Chinese college students majoring in English or translation, Chinese graduate students in translation, and international students majoring in business. Equipped with my Ph.D. program experience, I became more confident in tapping into my students' backgrounds in my teaching as well as in my own academic writing. I continued implementing autobiographical writing projects in some of my writing courses. However, now I was more deliberate in guiding and supporting my students through their projects. I also began to write with my students, as my American poetry professor used to do. Furthermore, I continued my research on L2 writing and attending conferences, including the Symposium of Second Language Writing and a conference on the teaching and research of English writing in China.

In 2014, I received a postdoctoral scholarship from the China Scholarship Council to be a visiting scholar at Purdue University with Professor Tony Silva, the founding father of the L2 writing field. After my return to YMU, I invited several L2 writing scholars including Paul K. Matsuda, Icy Lee, June Liu, and Xiaoye You as guest speakers to present lectures and workshops at my institute. These teaching, researching, and professional development activities gave an additional boost to my growth as an L2 writing scholar.

A Reflection from a Global South Perspective

A Global South perspective emphasizes speaking from one's epistemological margin within the global knowledge system so that those who have been formerly marginalized can use their own experience to contribute new knowledge (Santos, 2014). My LA illustrates how this can be done. First, I recounted a narrative of deficit and lack of resources due to my geographical location (rural China), ethnicity (being a Naxi minority), socioeconomic background (my family having been too poor to buy books), ideology (the view that reading non-textbooks was a waste of time), and consequently a lack of experience in extensive reading. Nonetheless, two successful stories were being constructed at the same time. One story featured my gradual upward social mobility, facilitated by passing high-stakes national exams such as the College Entrance Exam and international English exams such as the TOEFL. The other story progressed from my initial lack of a voice in Chinese to gradual discovery of my voice through creative writing in English.

Second, my multi-phase personal identity work was mediated by the learning of English. It included a constant pursuit of and investment in an imagined identity as an international student in the United States, the gradual formation of an identity as an English language teacher, and the eventual embrace of an L2 writing teacher identity. My narrative shows how my multiple identities were always there in the background, informing my emergent L2 writing teacher identity.

Furthermore, my ongoing teaching, research, and self-initiated professional development activities have contributed to a more confident L2 writing teacher identity. As such, my LA demonstrates the power of narrative knowing about my identity as complex, dynamic, and evolving, that is, entailing a sense of both constancy and change (Menard-Warwick, 2005; Yang, 2013). Even as I wrestled with the challenging aspects of living in the margin, I discovered and performed an alternative storyline of myself being an agent, who pursued and realized what I desired to become professionally.

L2 writing teacher identities are not a given, nor are they formed only through professional development. In my case, my L2 writing teacher identity is closely tied to my marginal ethnic, linguistic, and socioeconomic background as well as my much-cherished opportunities to grow professionally, and the enthusiasm with which I have seized them. By writing my LA, I have found a way to narrate my humble roots, my lofty aspirations, and the winding trajectory that connects my past with my present and future. Given the capacity of LAs to make all these things more apparent, I would suggest that LA writing can play an important role in helping an L2 writing teacher to manage the personal and professional aspects of this role. As Matsuda (2002) concluded in his personal essay:

> No amount of professional preparation or resources will help teachers see farther than the giants can see today unless new teachers themselves are willing to struggle with various issues and develop their own personal knowledge base, situated as it is in the context of their own teaching.
>
> (p. 169)

Like Matsuda, I was marginalized. Like Matsuda, I speak from my marginal place. Through my LA, I turned my struggles into a resource and a developmental stage. As a resource, LA writing allowed me to relate to my student writers genuinely, not from a position of superiority but of humanity—that is, featuring shared struggles and hopes. As a developmental stage, LA writing provided a textual space for me to foreground my dreams, efforts, and accomplishments—in short, my agency for social and professional mobility, as mediated by my investment in related language and literacy practices.

Since my life has taken such a positive turn through learning English, does my example indicate that English is a magic language that can bring justice to all? Of course not. Granted, language is the very tool we use to construct our identities. Without English, I would not have become an English learner, teacher, or eventually an L2 writing teacher. Nonetheless, language in itself does not promise anything, although it has afforded me more than I had imagined possible within a specific historical context. Reading memoirs such as *Wild Swans* (Chang, 1993) and English language teacher narratives such as Matalene (1985), I am reminded of how fortunate I was to be born at a time in Chinese history when the College Entrance Examination had been restored, English was no longer treated as the language of the capitalists, the government had adopted an open-door policy at large, and the teaching and learning of English was encouraged nationwide. My life, both personally and professionally, has been intertwined with and expanded by English language and literacy. But in this regard, I can speak only of its impact on myself, who was formerly marginalized and voiceless due to my ethnic, linguistic, and socioeconomic background. I am reluctant to overgeneralize from my positive experience.

Additionally, my evolving language ideology has had a huge impact on my language learning and teaching practices. Even though I lived in a multilingual society, I have long occupied a monolingual position from elementary school all the way to college. At first, I wanted only to learn Mandarin Chinese; later, I wanted only English. I sided with the dominant discourse about what language is valuable. After all, Mandarin Chinese was the language of the powerful others whose professional status appealed to me. As for English, the school sowed a seed of native-speakerism in me through a text about how Karl Marx learned English. Marx forgot his native German and soon learned to speak English very well. As the first lesson of my high school English textbook taught me:

> In one of his books, Marx gave some advice on how to learn a foreign language. He said when a person is learning a foreign language, he [sic] must not always be translating everything into his own language. If he does this, it shows he has not mastered it. He must be able to use the foreign language, forgetting all about his own. If he can not [sic] do this, he has not really grasped the spirit of the foreign language and can not [sic] use it freely.
>
> (Dong & Liu, 1984, p. 3)

Not having many resources in the countryside, I believed that Marx's approach was the best and decided that if I could not advance myself through Chinese language and literacy, I should try to do so in English. I took this mindset to college and implemented it by spending all my time learning English—listening, speaking, reading, writing—and even in multiple varieties, first British English and then American English. In contrast, I did not read or write anything in Chinese unless I had to. I must admit that my accomplishment as a language learner can be at least partially attributed to my extreme monolingualism. It was so pervasive that in my first year of teaching, I sought to reproduce my way of learning by turning my class into an all-English environment.

Fortunately, and only many years later, my language ideology shifted to become more multilingual and translingual. As I wrote in the following poem (originally drafted in 2008 and revised in 2009):

Find a Friend in English

As a child, I found myself awkward at school—
for I could not speak Mandarin;
at home, I seldom spoke—
for a kid was to be seen, not heard.

So I became dormant as a winter grass
until English,
like a spring breeze,
wakened me, my pen and my fingers.
She minds not my shabby dialect,
nor my timid personality.
In the quiet of wilderness, she whispers to me love
is beyond language
and prayers can be
many: dialect or English.

Containing two lines ("prayers can be many: dialect or English") not found in the version that was published (Yang, 2017), this poem draft captured my emergent understanding from both a Christian and a professional perspective. As a Christian, I have grappled with the vision that one day all nations, tribes, and languages will appear before the heavenly throne (Revelation 7:9); the obvious implication is that people are accepted by God regardless of their linguistic backgrounds. This vision challenged me to distance myself from the practice of assessing the worth of a language solely in terms of its market value and to critically examine dominant language ideologies of my society and scholarship from the Global North. Thus, as I have explained elsewhere (Wang & Yang, 2022), I "elevated" the status of my dialect Chinese to that of the English language. It was a gesture of reclaiming my heritage backgrounds, a past I had previously regarded with shame but that nonetheless has become my own unique place to discover new ways of relating to languages. At least in my own private space, I refuse to marginalize my heritage as I formerly did.

Professionally, as an L2 writing teacher who aspires to contribute to the field of L2 writing at large, I have struggled with several contradictions in my particular context. They include clashes between a pay-to-publish local culture and publishing as a noble scholarly endeavor, between a constitutional right to speak ethnic languages and an educational discourse that favors dominant languages (Wang & Phillion, 2009), between Western-fashioned theories (Canagarajah & Gao, 2019) and Eastern realities, and between L2 writing as a field some experts expect to disappear (cf. Santos et al., 2000) and translingualism as an increasingly trendy yet controversial intellectual movement (Atkinson et al., 2015; Matsuda, 2014). My strategy is to speak from my local context, to voice my own epistemological position, and to reinvent my own pedagogical practice. As I have indicated elsewhere (Yang, 2015, 2020c), I welcome a dynamic view of language and an appreciative attitude toward language difference, as promoted by translingual scholars. At the same time, I believe that effective practice of translingualism is contingent on the user's proficiency in the standard language, room for negotiation, and aspects of non-linguistic capital such as one's professional status, transnational affiliations, and publications. Thus, I believe that "maybe it is individual writers like me who can eventually help reconcile the tension between translingual and L2 writing [scholarship] for the maximal benefits of our students" (Yang, 2020a, p. 3). At least, this is what I have done myself, first in my mind and eventually in my classroom. I wish to be sensitive and intentionally selective about promoting scholarship that seeks to serve the marginalized—of whom I used to be a member—lest efforts to help them turn into unintended hurt. Through this mindful inquiry, I have turned "from a fish to a dragon" (Pawan et al., 2017) or, more accurately, from a farmer to an L2 writing teacher who actively pursues meaningful and critical literacy education in my own and others' EFL classrooms (Yang, 2018, 2020b, 2020a; Yang & Nong, 2019).

Conclusion

My journey with literacy had a humble beginning. In the spirit of a Global South perspective, I composed this LA to facilitate narrative understanding of my marginal status. In particular, I have revisited and analyzed my process of learning to write in Chinese and English, which was shaped by family situations, educational discourses, and my pursuit of imagined identities. My LA demonstrates that literacy in Chinese is inseparable from its cultural underpinnings. It further exhibits my dynamic and evolving language ideology, as informed by my earlier education, later Christian conversion, and ongoing professional development experiences. Finally, it reveals the gradual, contextual, and agentive formation of an L2 writing teacher identity. I hope my story can inspire other TESOL professionals to engage in similar reflective inquiry in their own contexts from a Global South perspective.

References

Ahearn, L. M. (2001). Language and agency. *Annual Review of Anthropology, 30*, 109–137. https://doi.org/10.1146/annurev.anthro.30.1.109

Atkinson, D., Crusan, D., Matsuda, P. K., Ortmeier-Hooper, C., Ruecker, T., Simpson, S., & Tardy, C. (2015). Clarifying the relationship between L2 writing and translingual writing: An open letter to writing studies editors and organization leaders. *College English, 77*(4), 383–386.

Bourdieu, P. (2004). The forms of capital. In S. S. Ball (Ed.), *The Routledge Falmer reader in sociology of education* (pp. 15–29). Routledge.

Canagarajah, A. S. (2016). Translingual writing and teacher development in composition. *College English, 78*(3), 265–273.

Canagarajah, S., & Gao, X. (2019). Taking translingual scholarship farther. *English Teaching & Learning, 43*(1), 1–3. https://doi.org/10.1007/s42321-019-00023-4
Chang, H. (2008). *Autoethnography as method.* Left Coast Press.
Chang, J. (1993). *Wild swan: Three daughters of China.* Anchor Books.
Cheung, Y. L. (2017). Writing teacher identity: Current knowledge and future research. In G. Barkhuizen (Ed.), *Reflections on language teacher identity* (pp. 246–251). Routledge.
Darvin, R., & Norton, B. (2015). Identity and a model of investment in applied linguistics. *Annual Review of Applied Linguistics, 35,* 36–56.
Darvin, R., & Norton, B. (2018). Identity, investment, and TESOL. In J. I. Liontas (Ed.), *The TESOL encyclopedia of English language teaching* (pp. 1–17). John Wiley & Sons.
de Sousa Santos, B. (2014). *Epistemologies of the South: Justice against epistemicide.* Routledge.
de Sousa Santos, B. (2020). Decolonizing the university. In B. de Sousa Santos, & M. P. Meneses (Eds.), *Knowledges born in the struggle: Constructing the epistemologies of the Global South* (pp. 219–239). Routledge.
Dong, W., & Liu, D. (1984). How Marx learned foreign languages. In W. Dong, & D. Liu (Eds.), *Gāo jí zhōng xué kè běn yīng yǔ dì yī cè bì xiū* [Senior high school textbook: English (required)] (Vol. 1). People's Education Press.
Dörnyei, Z. (2014). Future self-guides and vision. In K. Csizér, & M. Magid (Eds.). *The impact of self-concept on language learning* (pp. 7–18). Multilingual Matters.
Goh, C. C. M. (2014). Foreword. In Y. L. Cheung, S. B. Said, & K. Park (Eds.), *Advances and current trends in language teacher identity research* (1st ed., pp. xii–xiv). Routledge.
Hanauer, D. (2012). Meaningful literacy: Writing poetry in the language classroom. *Language Teaching, 45*(1), 105–115.
Kim, S. H., & Saenkhum, T. (2019). Professional identity (re)construction of L2 writing scholars. *L2 Journal, 11*(2), 18–34. https://doi.org/10.5070/L211242088
Kramsch, C. (2009). *The multilingual subject.* Oxford University Press.
Lee, E., & Canagarajah, A. S. (2019). Beyond native and nonnative: Translingual dispositions for more inclusive teacher identity in language and literacy education. *Journal of Language, Identity & Education, 18*(6), 352–363. https://doi.org/10.1080/15348458.2019.1674148
Lee, I. (2013). Becoming a writing teacher: Using "identity" as an analytic lens to understand EFL writing teachers' development. *Journal of Second Language Writing, 22*(3), 330–345.
Lee, I. (2018). Future directions for writing teacher cognition. In J. I. Liontas (Ed.), *The TESOL encyclopedia of English language teaching* (pp. 1–7). https://doi.org/10.1002/9781118784235.eelt0563
Matalene, C. (1985). Contrastive rhetoric: An American writing teacher in China. *College English, 47*(8), 789–808. https://doi.org/10.2307/376613
Matsuda, P. K. (2002). Epilogue: Reinventing giants. In L. L. Blanton, & B. Kroll (Eds.), *ESL composition tales: Reflections on teaching* (pp. 163–171). University of Michigan Press.
Matsuda, P. K. (2014). The lure of translingual writing. *PMLA, 129*(3), 478–483.
Menard-Warwick, J. (2005). Both a fiction and an existential fact: Theorizing identity in second language acquisition and literacy studies. *Linguistics and Education, 16*(3), 253–274. https://doi.org/10.1016/j.linged.2006.02.001
Norton, B. (2000). *Identity and language learning: Gender, ethnicity and educational change.* Pearson Education.
Pavlenko, A., & Lantolf, J. P. (2000). Second language learning as participation and the (re)construction of selves. In J. P. Lantolf (Ed.), *Sociocultural theory and second language learning* (pp. 155–177). Oxford University Press.
Pawan, F., Fan, W., Miao, P., & Wang, G. (Eds.). (2017). *Teacher training and professional development of Chinese English language teachers: Changing from fish to dragon.* Routledge.

Pennycook, A., & Makoni, S. (2020). *Innovations and challenges in applied linguistics from the Global South*. Routledge.

Racelis, J. V., & Matsuda, P. K. (2015). Exploring the multiple identities of L2 writing teachers. In Y. L. Cheung, S. B. Said, & K. Park (Eds.), *Advances and current trends in language teacher identity research* (1st ed., pp. 203–216). Routledge. https://doi.org/10.4324/9781315775135

Santos, T., Atkinson, D., Erickson, M., Matsuda, P. K., & Silva, T. (2000). On the future of second language writing: A colloquium. *Journal of Second Language Writing, 9*(1), 1–20.

Vygotsky, L. (1978). *Mind in society*. Harvard University Press.

Wang, G., & Yang, S. (2022). Socializing strategies, family language policies and practices: An auto-ethnographic study of a transcultural family in southwest China. In J. Gube, F. Gao, & M. Bhowmik (Eds.), *Identities, practices and education of evolving multicultural families in [the] Asia-Pacific* (pp. 15–30). Routledge.

Wang, Y., & Phillion, J. (2009). Minority language policy and practice in China: The need for multicultural education. *International Journal of Multicultural Education, 11*(1), 1–14. https://doi.org/10.18251/ijme.v11i1.138

Yang, S. (2013). *Autobiographical writing and identity in EFL education*. Routledge.

Yang, S. (2015). [Review of the book *Translingual practice: Global Englishes and cosmopolitan relations* by A. S. Canagarajah]. *Iranian Journal of Language Teaching Research, 3*(1), 145–147.

Yang, S. (2017). Find a friend in English. *The Font—A Literary Journal for Language Teachers, 2*. http://thefontjournal.com/on-friendship/

Yang, S. (2018). Left foot on traditional literacy, and right, on transliteracy. *International Journal of Virtual and Personal Learning Environments (IJVPLE), 8*(2), 1–9.

Yang, S. (2020a). Critical pedagogy for foreign-language writing. *L2 Journal, 12*(2), 110–127.

Yang, S. (2020b). Meaningful literacy and agentive writer identity. *MEXTESOL Journal, 44*(4), 1–15.

Yang, S. (2020c). [Review of the book *Transnational literacy autobiographies as translingual writing*, by A. S. Canagarajah]. *Journal of Second Language Writing, 48*, 1–5.

Yang, S. (2021). From hoeing the cornfields to teaching English. *The Font—A Literary Journal for Language Teachers, 1*. https://thefontjournal.com/from-hoeing-the-cornfields-to-teaching-english/

Yang, S., & Nong, M. (2019). Making new books in rural middle schools in China: A preliminary exploration of local realities and community-oriented literacy projects. *Asian EFL Journal, 23*(5), 97–139.

Yazan, B., Canagarajah, A. S., & Jain, R. (2021). *Autoethnographies in ELT: Transnational identities, pedagogies, and practices*. Routledge.

Ye, H., & White, J. (2012). Writing without fear: Creativity and critical pedagogy in Chinese EFL writing programs. *Journal of Asian Critical Education, 1*(1), 8–20.

You, X. (2004). The choice made from no choice: English writing instruction in a Chinese University. *Journal of Second Language Writing, 13*, 97–110.

You, X. (2010). *Writing in the devil's tongue: A history of English composition in China*. Southern Illinois University Press.

PART II
Theory and Empirical Studies

Introduction

Part II has three chapters. Chapter 3 theorizes EFL literacy autobiographical writing as critical pedagogy. Chapter 4 describes my own pedagogical and research processes that shaped the students' EFL literacy autobiographical writing and identity construction, featuring especially the relationship between translanguaging/translingual practice and classroom writing ecology. Chapter 5 presents a case study of Chen, who demonstrates strong signs of translingualism (Canagarajah, 2020) in her final literacy autobiography. Chapter 6 presents a creative autoethnography that features EFL writers' voice construction by drawing on a collection of LAs and other classroom-based data.

3
LITERACY AUTOBIOGRAPHICAL WRITING AS CRITICAL PEDAGOGY

Shizhou Yang

读写自传非自成，内审外视文化情。
方言汉语携英语，融会贯通书人文。

Literacy autobiography (LA), also known as literacy narrative, is defined as "a narrative about how we become literate in community, academic, and professional discourses" (Canagarajah, 2020, p. 4). LA writing, according to Schmertz (2018, p. 280), has been "a rite of passage or initiation of sorts" in composition at North American colleges since the 1980s. The popularity of LA writing in English-speaking countries can be partially attributed to its pedagogical benefits, such as enhancing learner writers' confidence (Corkery, 2005) and revealing their literacy backgrounds (Williams, 2003). As Carstens (2012, p. 15) summarized, after listing several other benefits:

> Literacy narratives are useful tools to assist students, lecturers and course designers to grapple with (multi-) literacy, multilingualism and identity in a diverse society. They are also a unique vehicle for conveying theory and practice about teaching, and they are useful tools to assist lecturers in designing and developing curricula that both draw upon students' capabilities and initiate them into academia and their chosen professions.

These stated pedagogical benefits, however, still need to be empirically proved in the EFL context, where pedagogical use of LAs is rare and conditions for writing are different.

Furthermore, to avoid importing the LA writing task blindly into the EFL context, we need to consider existing critiques. First, we must scrutinize the kind of identity work promoted by encouraging the reading of recommended LAs (Corkery, 2005; Williams, 2003). Second, we also need to contextualize LA writing.

DOI: 10.4324/9781003288756-5

As Canagarajah (2020) commented, existing research tends to overlook how contexts shape LA writing. In this chapter, I extend these and other critiques to reconceptualize LA writing in the EFL context as critical pedagogy. As LA writing begins to make its way into EFL literacy education, I hope to provide a disciplined classroom practice for the use of this genre.

Promises and Pitfalls of LA Writing

Promises

The rise of LA writing in English-speaking countries was motivated by several perceived pedagogical benefits of personal writing. First, LA writing has been frequently used to serve basic writers, "who are also usually minority, immigrant, and working-class students" (Soliday, 1994, p. 512). Working from a multicultural perspective, Corkery (2005) suggested that LAs, which often feature a triumphant story of the writer overcoming challenges to gain a desirable form of literacy, can enhance basic writers' confidence in developing competence in academic literacy. Similarly, Soliday (1994) argued that LA writing can legitimate the home culture of basic writers and allow them to explore their language-mediated identity work as informed by both home and school cultures. Using a classroom example, Soliday illustrated how LAs can promote "a more dialogical, multicultural curriculum that includes—indeed, that both respects and responds to—the voices and stories of individual writers" (p. 523). For instance, she found that her student Alisha had used her LA to foreground her identity as a creative user of different styles of English without committing herself to a standard style. Therefore, LA writing may expand basic writers' identity options in various ways, not solely through assimilation.

Scott (1997) identified three additional benefits of LA writing. He suggested that LA writing (which he called literacy narrative) can validate students' existing identities as writers. Furthermore, LA writing within first-year classes contributes to an emergent community for both language use and narration. Lastly, LA writing can facilitate discussions of implicit writing theories and practices. In short, the practice can be helpful in mediating students' learning about themselves as literate beings.

The rise of LA writing has also been driven by a narrative turn in language and literacy research since the 1990s (Norton, 2000; Pavlenko, 2007). Drawing on LA writing as the primary data, studies of this type featured the literacy experiences of ESL students (Canagarajah, 2015, 2018; Sladek, 2019; Steinman, 2007), multilingual language professionals (Belcher & Connor, 2001), and a combination of both groups (Canagarajah, 2020) to showcase literacy as multiple, complex, and identity-bearing. Canagarajah's (2015, 2018, 2020) studies, in particular, revealed how LA writing was tied to the writer's linguistic and cultural backgrounds and greatly influenced by the pedagogical context. He argued that multilingual writers tend to write their LAs from the perspective of the transnational spaces they inhabit and may develop a translingual orientation that favors their non-English cultural and linguistic traditions. These studies exemplify a narrative turn in writing studies (Journet, 2012) in the Global North, in which composition scholars such as Wallace (2014) advocated the writing of personal stories, in contrast to self-distancing academic writing, to disrupt systematic injustices against the marginalized. These "unwelcome stories" from the margin, wrote Wallace (2014), are important in "exposing our individual and collective complicity in the ongoing systems of oppression and discrimination that marginalize many groups in our culture" (p. 547). Canagarajah's (2015, 2018, 2020) studies illustrate well how classroom-based use of LAs can challenge the deeply entrenched monolingual ideology and rigid ways of conceptualizing academic writing that typify North American higher education and English-medium publications.

Pitfalls

LA writing has its own pitfalls, though, of which Corkery (2005) discussed two. First, LA writing can function as an elite genre. That is, it may be more friendly to students who have already been socialized into school literacy. Second, LA writing may favor students with a strong literacy background over those with an oral tradition. These concerns call for critical consideration of whose interests LA writing actually serves, lest the marginalized remain marginalized.

Furthermore, the political agenda promoted through LA writing can be problematic. Scott (1997), for instance, cautioned against overly politicized use of LA writing, primarily as texts to engage in "resistance and/or assimilation of dominant ideologies" (p. 115). He explained, "Such approaches can misrepresent and patronize students; the writing of a literacy narrative is neither a revolutionary act nor a conversion experience for most students" (p. 115). Scott's point is clear: LA-based studies should not be overtaken by the researcher's own agenda, nor should writing teachers confine their students to only politically savvy tropes of becoming.

Canagarajah (2020) observed another pitfall: treating LAs as autonomous texts or "self-standing products without [giving] consideration to what motivated their shaping" (p. 37). Autobiographical data need to be contextualized. As Pavlenko (2007) suggested, a holistic interpretation of personal narratives should consider not only their multiple realities, but also the means (for instance, L1 or L2, spoken or written) through which these realities are constructed. In other words, LAs must be understood in view of their contexts of production.

Unfortunately, emergent studies on LA writing in the EFL context seem to have fallen victim to one of these pitfalls: the decontextualized use of LAs. Two illustrations come from the studies by Fujieda and Iida (2015) in Japan and Qian (2019) in China. Fujieda and Iida (2015) collected six LAs from Japanese undergraduate students majoring in English. Although the instruction followed a process approach involving multi-drafting, peer review, teacher feedback, and revision, no details were provided as to how the teaching process shaped the students' LAs. Similarly, Qian (2019) treated the students' LAs as primary data to "understand how both L1 and L2 academic writing courses influenced their engagement [with academic writing]" (p. 531). These LAs were written at the beginning of the semester, with little guidance from the instructor and without an opportunity for revision. Furthermore, other contextual factors such as writing only in English were not critically examined. In addition, even though the LA data were rooted in the Global South, both studies relied primarily on scholarship from the Global North, suggesting an epistemological tendency to use the south for only data mining.

Reconceptualizing LA Writing as Critical Pedagogy

Studies of LA writing in the EFL context, as represented by Fujieda and Iida (2015) and Qian (2019), have left some unanswered but critical questions about our knowledge of EFL writers and their LA writing. How was the LA writing influenced by assessment criteria and societal expectations concerning the personal genre? How did the instructors balance their multiple roles as evaluator, teacher, and researcher? Are the EFL students proficient enough to write their LAs *only* in English, as required by the instructors? Are the students' LAs providing a transparent window into their lived experiences, or would other stories be told if they had the opportunity to talk and write about their literacy experiences in their heritage language? Would the students produce the same types of stories if they were to compose LAs in non-pedagogical contexts? Who were the real beneficiaries of these LAs? If the use of LA writing is pedagogically motivated, should its interaction with the pedagogical context be given due attention? What systematic injustices, if any, was the LA writing designed to address?

As noted earlier, these studies adopted a decontextualized approach to LA writing. They did not follow Pavlenko's (2007) suggestion to consider personal narratives in their historical contexts, material conditions, and language(s) in use. Furthermore, these studies did not scrutinize the shaping effects of the pedagogical contexts in which the LAs were produced. As Canagarajah (2020) explained, commenting on LA-based studies as a whole, the final drafts of the learners' LAs are treated as "self-standing products" without considering how "pedagogical activities or classroom conditions" or "social interactions" have shaped the texts (p. 37). Whereas Canagarajah (2020) called for more attention to the research and pedagogical processes underlying LA writing, I argue for a reconceptualization of LA writing as critical pedagogy to disrupt a global epistemological hegemony. The first step is to view LA in its contexts.

Contextualization

To contextualize LA writing is to recognize the multiple contexts that influence its conception, composition process, resulting text, and related realities. Canagarajah (2015, 2018, 2020) offered a useful starting point for such contextualization. According to Canagarajah (2020), LA writing is "shaped" in that "the [LA] text or identity [constructed through it] doesn't originate from the writer or his mind; they are mediated and influenced by diverse historical, social, environmental, and rhetorical factors" (p. 37). These contexts can be further understood from micro, macro, and in-between perspectives.

At a micro level, LA writing is especially shaped by its immediate context of production. Canagarajah (2020) used Pratt's (1991) concept of a "contact zone" to focus on geographic places such as classrooms where LA writing occurs. He suggested further that LA writing should be examined within its classroom writing ecology. This ecology entails four key elements. The *human agents* are the writer, teacher, and peers who influence the LA writing directly or indirectly. The *process* concerns pedagogical and research design and their implementation, which situate LA writing in particular ways. The *structure* concerns the forces, such as curriculum, that are external to the classroom reality but nonetheless exert influence on the pedagogical design and practices. Finally, teaching *artifacts*, such as textbooks, articles, and writing samples, inform the LA writing. To see LA writing in context is therefore to view it as "part of a network of relationships, among social participants, other texts, and ecological resources that constantly shape each other, progressively reframing the terms of communicative interaction" (Canagarajah, 2020, p. 42). Rather than being autonomous, LA as seen from a classroom writing ecology perspective bears diverse traces of pedagogical and research influences.

At a macro level, LA writing is shaped by historical, rhetorical, and transnational contexts (Canagarajah, 2020). The historical context concerns how social realities of a given time period influence ways in which self-narratives are told and selves are constructed. For instance, autobiographies by early immigrants to the USA tended to feature a rags-to-riches storyline without emphasizing language issues, whereas later autobiographies tended to reflect more on issues of language identity (Pavlenko, 2007). As Canagarajah (2020) explained, the *rhetorical context* concerns ways of voicing that become accepted and normalized within particular disciplines. For instance, currently, reflective genres such as LA writing are gaining legitimacy in academia, making it more likely that composition teachers will assign LA writing to their students. The *transnational* context points to the premise that all multilingual writers naturally reside in some liminal space, which features the writers' multiple ties beyond national boundaries due to human migration and the movement of materials and information.

At the meso or in-between level, contexts concern contact, interaction, and hybrid possibilities. In her multi-storied framework to literacy and narrative (see Yang, 2013, pp. 54–56 for a detailed discussion), Grant (1997, 2001) made several points that may be relevant to LA writing in context. First, each of these multiple contexts—described in terms such as personal, social, and global—deserves its due attention, to ensure that an interpretation does not romanticize nor remove individual agency. Second, contexts do not function in isolation but in contact with each other. Third, the mingling of these contexts provides a space for individuals to move to new practices and identity options that feature human agency beyond prescribed trajectories.

As for the personal context, we may consider Ivanič's (1998) notion of the *autobiographical self*, which highlights the rich, diverse, and complex backgrounds informing individuals' writing and LAs. It can be connected to critical approaches to literacy education, which emphasize the importance of linking literacy with learners' lives, emotions, and imaginations (Freire, 1970; Giroux, 2020; Hanauer, 2012), and with their ongoing identity work through language and literacy activities (Kramsch, 2009; Norton, 2000, 2013; Yang, 2020b). Case studies (Canagarajah, 2015; Yang, 2013; Zhao, 2015) have shown that multilingual writers' past life and literacy experiences are critical in shaping their writing dispositions. These studies have also demonstrated that multilingual writers' subjectivity can be expanded to include creativity and criticality within new learning contexts (Canagarajah, 2020; Cox et al., 2010; Yang & Reynolds, 2022). Attending to the writer's personal context is thus pedagogically important. It helps us to treat learners not as a blank slate, but as flesh-and-blood individuals with histories, backgrounds, existing dispositions, and emergent subjectivities.

The other context concerns material conditions. In a recent article, Canagarajah (2021) argued that material realities, which have often been neglected, actually play important roles in shaping LA writing. These realities can be uncovered by asking *how* questions: How much time does the writer have to compose an LA? How are texts used in the teaching process? How are drafting and revision, if relevant, accomplished? How are interactions between the writer and readers mediated? How many drafts are expected? By attending to the material context, we can be more sensitive to the conditions a writing classroom provides for students to complete their LA writing. These issues deserve attention, especially since LA writing from the Global South involves very different material conditions from those typically found in the Global North.

Lastly, studying LA writing in context recognizes the dynamic interactions between the writing experience and the broader context. Canagarajah (2021) borrowed two concepts from Silverstein (2019) to elucidate such dynamics and the important contribution of the *how* questions in LA writing to narrative knowing. The first concept, *recontextualization*, concerns the ways in which a text suggests its shaping context, or how the context is implicated in the text. It is about seeing a text in the shadow of its contexts. The other concept, *entextualization*, concerns the ways in which a text takes form under the influence of the contexts. In other words, recontextualization is about how a text points to its contexts, whereas entextualization is about how a text incorporates elements from its contexts. Here, I use the plural form "contexts" to emphasize the multiple—micro, macro, meso, personal, and material—settings in which LA writing occurs and takes its specific and changing forms.

Repertoire

Existing studies of LA writing have considered writers' repertoire, or what can be used for writing, from three main perspectives. The first perspective emphasizes the use of individuals' linguistic resources other than standard English alone. Canagarajah's (2018, 2020) case studies of international students' LA writing illustrate this perspective well. For instance, both his own LA and that of a Japanese student, Kyoko, included deliberate embedding of heritage-language passages within English prose. Canagarajah (2020) described this feature as a manifestation of translingualism, i.e., "an orientation to communication and competence that treats words as always in contact with diverse semiotic resources and constantly generating new grammars and meanings out of this synergy" (p. 6).

Here, we may need to evoke a similar term: translanguaging. To me, translingualism and translanguaging are synonyms. They both refer to multilingual speakers' synergistic or synergic use of their diverse semiotic resources, including dialects and modalities. However, they come from two different disciplinary homes. Whereas writing and composition scholars often refer to translingualism (Canagarajah, 2013; Horner, 2017; You, 2018), applied linguists and bilingual educators tend to use "translanguaging" instead (García & Kleifgen, 2020; Li, 2011; Li & Zhu, 2013). I use the two terms interchangeably to emphasize that in literacy education, it is important not only to see things from multilingual writers' perspective, but also to imagine new literate identities outside monolingual frameworks.

The second perspective emphasizes the writer's transnational connections. By this, Canagarajah (2020) invited us to consider "the transnational space as the location of our writing, teaching, and analysis [of LAs]" (p. 5). Being transnational is an historical phenomenon, which is accentuated in modern times due to such factors as increased ease of human migration and mobility of information through Internet-based technologies (Canagarajah, 2018). Accordingly, writing education needs to make a transnational turn (Ordeman, 2021; You, 2018) to account for identities and literacy activities that transcend nation-state boundaries (Canagarajah, 2020). Canagarajah went on to argue that being transnationally situated provides ideal conditions for individuals to engage in translingual writing or synergic language use. I agree with this claim, but I would add that although being transnational can often function as a resource with regard to LA writing, it can also involve tension, particularly when translingual writing goes against official language ideologies.

The third perspective emphasizes the writers' prior literacy experiences, which the personal context, as described, has already implicated. Yet more needs to be said. Knowledge of the writers' prior literacy experiences may be the major contribution LA writing offers as a composition assignment and research tool. It reveals the nature of literacy as both personal and social, both experienced and narrated. Literacy as featured in LAs by language professionals (Belcher & Connor, 2001; Canagarajah, 2020) and marginalized writers alike is "a process, not a fixed point or a line of demarcation" (Davidson, 2004, p. 126). A Bakhtinian interpretation of former slave Frederick Douglass's LA, for instance, shows three phases of his literacy journey: his initial view of literacy as a pathway to freedom, as suggested by his master; his discovery of literacy as both freeing and limiting; and his later understanding of literacy in spiritual and African-American terms (Sisco, 1995). Similarly, when people write LAs, their prior literacy experiences are thus turned into a resource for composition, reflection, and critical analysis of literacy. Granted, the extent to which the analysis is critical and yields new interpretations depends in part on contextual factors. Nonetheless, by reconnecting with these prior experiences, LAs provide these writers with textual space to trace their individual trajectories, wrestle with diverse conceptions of literacy, and construct a literate identity of their own.

Thus conceived, LA writing as grounded in the writers' prior literacy experiences can provide an artistic form to interpret their literate identities dialogically as if they were "a polyphonic novel" (Hermans, 2001, p. 248).

However, although I endorse these three perspectives, I have reservations about the translingual aspect of LA writers' repertoire (Gevers, 2018; Yang, 2015, 2020c). My concerns can be summarized by the following questions. What roles does proficiency in a language play in effective synergic use of one's linguistic repertoire? What about metalingual awareness? What about non-linguistic resources such as one's professional identity and social networks? Can negotiation happen effectively without some implied norm, with the difference being embedded only in intelligible prose or speech? Silva (2021, p. 15) raised these questions about norms: "Is a clear understanding of norms a prerequisite for discussing differences; otherwise how can we know whether something is different or not? Should conventions be viewed as merely restrictive and oppressive linguistic norms? Might teaching norms enhance writer agency?" I think the answers to these questions are all positive. Additionally, I am concerned about multilingual writers' experiences of genres that exist, for the time being, only or mainly in their heritage languages. Should they also be regarded as part of their repertoires? Otherwise, meaningful literacy through Korean Sijo (Kim & Park, 2020), Japanese Haiku (Iida, 2017), and Chinese Da You Shi (Zhang, 2019) would not remain meaningful any more.

Accordingly, I believe that we need to expand our views of writers' repertoire in at least three ways. First, we need to be open to any genre experiences that writers have had in both their heritage language and the English language. Second, we need to consider the writers' use of their expansive semiotic resources during the composition process, instead of observing such use only in the final LAs. For instance, are non-English languages used during class discussion? Are dialects of their heritage languages used? What about non-linguistic resources? Third, we need to adopt a dynamic view of the writers' repertoires. That is, even as they read sample LAs and interact with others in the classroom contact zone, the writers are also expanding their repertoire for communication. With this expansive and dynamic view of writers' repertoires, we can understand how and why these writers move from one draft to another and, at times, represent the same experience differently and agentively.

Agency

In LA studies, Canagarajah (2020) defines agency as individuals' "ability to act strategically within the available constraints and affordances" (p. 76). This conception is consistent with the premise that agency cannot be understood only as resistance, nor romantically as free will (Ahearn, 2001). Furthermore, the verb *to act* can be understood in a narrow and broad sense. The narrow sense of acting is similar to performing. It links LA writing to literature on writing as constructing one's discursive identity or performing a certain kind of desired persona (Ivanič, 1998; Matsuda, 2001; Yang, 2013). The broad sense of acting is equally important.

It entails a broad range of possible actions related to language and literacy activities such as investment (Norton, 2000) and alignment (Horner, 2017). Yet individuals do not act at will. Their capacity to act, whether in terms of identity work or other actions, is contingent on contextual affordances and constraints. Ivanič (1998) used the phrase *possibilities of selfhood* to foreground this contextual shaping. Advancing a similar argument, in his recent LA-based studies, Canagarajah (2015, 2020, 2021) emphasized the critical role played by a classroom writing ecology, including material realities, in shaping individual writers' agency through translingual practice. A contextualized notion of agency is important in understanding LA writing.

Nonetheless, two additional considerations about agency may be needed to release the full potential of LA writing for marginalized learners. First, individuals' intentions need to be foregrounded. Although Canagarajah's definition of agency is more specific than "individuals' socioculturally mediated capacity to act," as provided by the linguistic anthropologist Ahearn (2001, p. 112), both definitions have unwittingly neglected intentions as fundamental to agency (Brockmeier, 2009). Narrative theorists have argued that human desires are the ultimate locomotive of their actions, shaping profoundly who they become (White, 2007). Similarly, in her review of agency and language learning theories, Duff (2012) remarked, "A sense of agency enables people to imagine, take up, and perform new roles or identities (including those [as a] proficient L2 speaker or multilingual [speaker]) and to take concrete actions in pursuit of their goals" (p. 417). Thus, as in narrative counseling (White, 2007), to offset narrow and negative conceptions of the self that essentialize oneself, it is important to encourage the telling of stories that feature individuals' intentions such as desires, hopes, and commitment. If we fail to give due attention to individuals' intentions, agency becomes more reactive than proactive.

Second, the notion of material mediation can be broadened. To start with, a wider range of genres should be considered. Commendably, Canagarajah (2020) recognized LA as a hybrid genre that mixes academic with narrative writing. However, this view of hybridity fails to accommodate other non-narrative and non-academic genres, such as poems and music, that multilingual writers may bring into LA writing from their heritage language and literacy experiences. It may also be blind to certain literacy events in multilingual writers' heritage languages simply because these are not yet recognized as literacy by English-centric scholarly literature. In contrast, Canagarajah (2020) was careful to acknowledge the presence and value of heritage-language poems, Internet expressions, and heritage cultural references in his international students' LA writing. It is, therefore, a healthy move to conceptualize material reality as also including the extent to which LA writers are encouraged to integrate any genres and literacy events rooted in their heritage languages.

Furthermore, besides these hidden genres and literacy events, we may need to consider translanguaging in the LA composition process. In Canagarajah's (2015, 2018, 2020) studies, translanguaging or translingual practice has been acknowledged mainly in the final LA drafts. Although this perspective is important, it is equally important to identify ways in which translanguaging, as part of the material reality, occurs during the LA composition process. Translanguaging, after all, started as a bilingual education strategy that recognized the usefulness of two languages, Welsh and English, for teaching and learning purposes (see García & Kleyn, 2016). Translanguaging has also been widely used by diaspora multilingual speakers and writers and in classroom instruction. Moreover, recent studies have emphasized the synergic use of languages and modalities from a translanguaging lens as facilitating subject learning. Acts of translanguaging are transformative in that they create or expand spaces for others to also engage in translanguaging, thus disrupting the dominance of monolingualism in such spaces (Li, 2011). By considering the classroom writing ecology and its material reality, a translanguaging lens thus points to the extent to which the synergic use of communicative resources is modeled, experienced, and encouraged, or the lack of such conditions.

Lastly, we need to consider space for negotiation. This space differs from Canagarajah's (2020) notion of transnational space as a liminal or borderland area for multilingual writers to draw upon in their LA composition. It concerns the asymmetrical power relations between LA writers and critical readers such as the instructor, the researcher, and (if the writing is for potential publication) reviewers and editors. Depending on their priorities, these critical readers may or may not provide opportunities for negotiation. Some obvious considerations include whether multiple drafts are expected, whether the writer is given a fixed amount of time for composition or revision, and whether a critical reader tolerates linguistic deviations. Certain journals, for instance, may reject a paper (LA included) without giving the author a second chance if it contains too many expressions that differ from the accepted norms. Such material realities must be recognized if multilingual writers' agency is to be interpreted in situ, as it should be.

At any rate, agency is a rich concept featuring individuals' hopes for new possibilities and concrete actions toward achieving these possibilities. By attending to individuals' ability to *act*, including performing and other actions in line with their intentions, we come closer to recognizing their personal ways of actualizing their goals. By attending to the often implied or neglected material realities—such as time for composition, translanguaging in the process, and room for negotiation—we are better positioned to see agency as situated in and mediated by diverse conditions. Thus equipped, we can begin to see LA writers exercise their agency proactively and simultaneously as afforded and constrained by specific situations.

Epistemological Disruption

What roles, then, does LA writing play besides building basic writers' confidence—or besides providing data for researchers? I would suggest that LA writing, systematically reimagined, actually may disrupt existing epistemological hegemonies that dominate literacy education and research. I will develop this position by first describing two parallel epistemological hegemonies in practice. I will then consider a dialogical notion of voice and affordances provided by LA writing for multilingual writers to compose polyphonic texts from their marginalized positions so as to challenge, or at least address, the epistemological center. Finally, I will outline key pedagogical and research features of systematically re-imagined LA writing, highlighting especially the cultural answerability from the Global South perspective.

Hegemonic Relations

In the global knowledge system, there seem to be two dominating hegemonies. The first hegemony concerns literacy education in English as a foreign language, which tends to favor values, visions, and practices from English-speaking countries. The EFL context is typically positioned within this hegemony as importers and consumers of norms and pedagogies that were produced in the West (Canagarajah, 2005; Min, 2009; Muchiri et al., 1995). I will offer two recent examples. One is translingual scholarship, the center and leading advocates of which remain based in Anglo-Saxon environments (Canagarajah & Gao, 2019). The other is meaningful literacy, which also began in North America and has recently begun to be exported to places such as Taiwan and Japan. Although it had been long pointed out that the EFL context has very different historical, material, and ideological realities for English literacy education (Leki, 2001; You, 2010), there is still a trend according to which writing teachers from this background often teach in the shadow of writing scholars from or based in the West. Lost in this tendency is any possibility of acknowledging and validating local writing teachers' personal knowledge developed within a particular EFL teaching context. Also lost is the humanity of EFL student writers, who are positioned to receive writing education as conventions, with little to no room for creative and critical engagement.

The other hegemony concerns research practice in literacy education in the EFL context. Similar to the trend of importing pedagogies from the economically more developed West, EFL writing researchers have largely relied on imported methodologies, approaches, and concepts to interpret local realities. This importing is necessary, in part, because of the much longer and more extensive development of research traditions in composition, rhetoric, and English L2 writing in the West than in the rest of the world. It is also driven by non-Western scholars' need to write for international publication. They need to utilize established norms to join the conversation, often at the cost of burying local epistemologies or what Santos (2016) called "epistemicide." A popular approach to academic literacy in China, for instance, is corpus linguistics, which studies how Chinese students differ in their use of lexicons and lexicon bundles, as measured by frequency, from native speakers of English and other published authors. One implication drawn from these studies is that Chinese students typically need to approximate published authors' language use. Relatively little attention, however, is given to the fact that language use is only part of the epistemological game concerning knowledge representation, which should be secondary to viewing oneself as a potential maker and contributor of new knowledge.

Hegemonies have a far-reaching impact through their naturalizing ideologies and infrastructure. It is a commonly accepted view that *of course* the EFL world should look to English-speaking countries for the best teaching practices, and that *of course* one should engage in scientific research as the West has prescribed. This is the power of the *authoritative discourse* (Bakhtin, 1981) wielding its scepter in teaching and research, requiring all its subjects in the global empire to submit to its seemingly divine rule. This rule is further assisted by the existing and expanding infrastructure, which includes education ministries, policies, institutions, curricula, examinations, publications—in short, anything that seeks to normalize language use at personal levels.

Consequently, these hegemonies have produced two typical dehumanizing relations at the global level in the EFL world. The first features an oppressive teacher-student relationship, in which the teacher seeks diligently to help the students produce English writing according to Western-based conventions. In this way, the students are deprived of humanity because in practice they are positioned as containers of writing knowledge, as is typical of the banking model of education critiqued by Freire (1970). The teacher's humanity is also lost or at least compromised in this process, because his or her value does not go much beyond deciphering, transmitting, and evaluating the students by the idealized norms of native English speakers. The second dehumanizing aspect concerns the relationship between the researcher and the subject being researched. By embracing Western-originated research paradigms, theories, methodologies, and approaches, the researcher produces knowledge mainly through replication, which, at its best, will reveal findings contrary to those of similar studies. At its worst, such research will continue to reify the truth claims made by Western epistemologists, thereby locking the research participants forever in the marginal position of anonymous informants who tell their stories only through the researcher's Westernized interpretations and representations.

Cultural Dynamics

How, then, can LA writing disrupt such epistemological hegemonies and their local chieftains? I suggest that we can do so by reimagining LA writing at the ground level. More specifically, LA writing can be reconceptualized from a Global South perspective as critical pedagogy that embraces cultural and dialogical relations, thereby turning the project into a channel of gaining voice through reflective teaching and participatory research.

First, culturally speaking, LA writing can reverse a historical trend of approaching language and literacy education only in a utilitarian manner. In the case of China, You's (2010) study of the history of English writing education from the 1840s to the 1940s revealed a constant English-as-a-tool official discourse. A review of six periods of English education in China by Hu (2021) showed a similar pattern: English is taught and learned primarily for the purposes of achieving national agendas such as modernization. As Kramsch (2006) objected, both second- and foreign-language education tended to overlook "the flesh and blood [sic] individuals who are doing the learning" (p. 98). Such a pragmatic approach to English language and literacy education neglects the profound impact exerted by additional language and literacy on learners' identity (Cox et al., 2010; Kramsch, 2009; Norton, 2000; Yang, 2013). Language and literacy are promoted globally as if they were culture- and value-neutral and therefore universally applicable. In the EFL context, learning writers are often taught to memorize model essays and to rely on templates when producing their own essays (Yang & Nong, 2019; Ye & White, 2012), leaving little room for creative and critical voices. To usurp this tendency, EFL writing teachers can assign LA writing and create a nurturing classroom writing ecology. This ecology should not just encourage students to explore the literacy experiences in their heritage languages that have been habitually neglected in formal education. It should also challenge them to articulate and critique taken-for-granted cultural meanings so as to facilitate the emergence of more culturally inclusive writing subjectivities. This can be considered a revolution at the head and heart levels that will recognize the existence of diverse literacy cultures and their varying impact on one's literate identities.

The impact of LA writing, however, is not just cognitive or emotional. It produces artifacts or, more specifically, emergent literary texts that enrich the cultural ecology of the world. According to Gunn's (1980) review, cultural ecology was proposed by anthropologists in the early 20th century and focuses on the dynamic relations between human activity, culture, and environment. Literature as cultural ecology, according to Zapf (2016), plays three roles in shifting established hegemonies. Drawing on literary works by Emily Dickinson, Poe, and others, Zapf (2016) proposed that literature as cultural ecology should first "deconstruct," that is, expose and denaturalize dominant ideologies and structures. Furthermore, literature as cultural ecology also constructs by providing "imaginative counter discourse" to contest the dominant ideologies and structures. Third, literature as cultural ecology may "reintegrate interdiscourse," yielding new positions and texts that amalgamate perspectives from both dominant and marginal discourses.

The function of literature as a medium to rebalance the relationships between culture and nature, however, is not reserved only for celebrated writers. Even emergent EFL writers can contribute significant prose. Zapf's explanations can help us perceive this possibility:

> Literary culture provides one such form of cultural knowledge, which in the course of cultural evolution has developed unmistakable functional and discursive features that lend imaginative texts a special potential of representing, exploring, and communicating fundamental dimensions of human life within the overarching culture-nature-relationship [sic].
>
> *(Zapf, 2016, p. 89)*

Here, Zapf is essentially saying the act of writing always involves some kind of "literary culture," which consists of the deeply rooted ways of understanding and representing culture and nature dynamics. Applied to LA writing in the EFL context, at least two sets of literary cultures are instantiated: the local and the foreign.

However, we must also note that the literary cultures evoked in EFL LA writing are not simply added, one on top of another, without integration, interaction, or transcending. In fact, because this process simultaneously gazes upon the first language-mediated literacy experiences yet recomposes them in a foreign language, it constitutes an act of expanded vision (Bakhtin, 1981), involving both one's understandings of self (the local culture) and of other (the foreign culture). As Zapf concluded about the importance of literature as cultural ecology:

> As a form of cultural textuality that stages the tension between regimes of discursive civilizational power and prediscursive life processes, literature is therefore both discourse and a "non-place" (Foucault) of discourse. It constitutes itself in a "counter space" or an "in-between-space" of discourses as a paradoxical form of writing which constantly transgresses and shifts the boundaries of what can be known, said, and thought within a culture by opening them toward their excluded other, toward what remains unsayable and unknowable within its rules of discourse.
>
> *(Zapf, 2016, pp. 92–93)*

Put in simpler terms, literature as cultural ecology can facilitate the telling of untold stories from some "in-between-space" or "contact zones" between cultures (Pratt, 1991). LA writing from a Global South perspective as literature invites EFL learners to look back on, explore, and represent literacy experiences that are formerly considered (by cultural discourses joined with educational institutions) irrelevant, trivial, or meaningless. The cultures in contact give shape to the literature created. Creating such emergent literature, as exemplified by narratives of professionals and student writers alike (Canagarajah, 2020; Herawati, 2021; Nunan & Choi, 2010; Riyanti, 2015; Yazan et al., 2021), thus amounts to a gesture of contestation of ruling discourses that habitually discourage such telling.

Dialogical Voice

Before I turn to a dialogical notion of voice, it may be helpful to review this notion's modernist or individualistic predecessors. Emphasizing the authenticity of the self, these earlier conceptions of voice were especially popular in pedagogical discourses in composition and rhetoric in North America before the turn of the century (Coles, 1988; Elbow, 1981; Macrorie, 1985). Voice from this perspective is like a mythical beast; it is much talked about but not clearly explained. Elbow (1981), for instance, defined voice in elusive terms such as "juice," "magic potion," "mother's milk," and "electricity" (p. 286). His book equated writing with voice and writing with power and life. As Matsuda (2015) pointed out, such conceptions of voice presume a "modernist conception of self as singular, coherent, and static" (p. 142). Voice thus conceived is a personal property; one either has a voice or one does not.

We can relocate voice for epistemological disruption by drawing on critiques of individualistic notions of voice (Hashimoto, 1987; Kamler, 2001;

Ramanathan & Atkinson, 1999). One critique, in particular, concerns the teaching of voice to L2 writers. Not sharing the same cultural assumptions about self and identity, L2 writers may find it difficult to respond to the pedagogical discourse of "just be yourself" (Shen, 1989, p. 460) that commonly circulates in U.S. college composition classrooms. As Matsuda (2001) reflected, "As an international undergraduate student at a U.S. university. … I, too, struggled every time I was told to 'be yourself'" (p. 38). Eventually, Matsuda (2001) found his voice through "the process of negotiating my socially and discursively constructed identity with the expectation of the reader as I perceived it" (p. 39). He then redefined voice as "an amalgamative effect of the use of discursive and non-discursive features that language users choose, deliberately or otherwise, from socially available yet ever-changing repertoires" (p. 40). Voice was thus relocated as a result of negotiation in written communication. Whether one writes in an L1 or an L2, one's voice, or one's textual or *discoursal* identity (Ivanič, 1998) is always projected and interpreted based on a text's overall features. It is not an individualistic voice *within* oneself, but a dialogical voice *between* the writer and the reader, as mediated by the text.

Along this dialogical line of thinking, the relationship between voice and identity can be further expanded. First, extratextual identities and identity as a process must be considered. Canagarajah (2015) proposed an interpretive framework for a dialogical notion of voice as the result of negotiation. It entails a dynamic relationship between the writer and the reader featuring their *identity, role, subjectivity*, and *awareness*. According to Canagarajah (2015), identities point to one's linguistic, ethnic, and citizenship ties; roles are different ways in which an individual is positioned in social institutions such as family and school; subjectivity refers to conventionalized ways with words that inform an individual's voice; and awareness features individuals' reflective agency in their identity work. Being aware of the self and its constraints, individuals can seek alternative ways of being via deliberate language use. As Canagarajah (2015) noted, "The fact that language is creative and polysemous provides resources for writers to rise above historical, social, and ideological impositions, register a reflexive awareness of their constraints, and adopt a strategic footing in relation to them" (pp. 124–125). This framework of voice implies that when we are interpreting a writer's voice dialogically, we should consider not only the diversity and dynamics of the writer's identity work, but also the writer's situated agency. From this framework, even "possibilities of selfhood" (Ivanič, 1998) are not fixed but negotiated.

Second, writer identity and identity work need to go through a similar dialogical transformation to serve the marginalized more effectively. That is, writer identity should entail components of imagination, narrativity, and morality. Regarding imagination, Norton (2000, 2013) proposed a poststructuralist theory of identity in which she argued that imagined identity is critical to language and literacy education. In essence, imagined identities point to individuals' investment in line with their aspirations, as mediated by their first and/or additional languages and literacies. From this perspective, we should consider not only who the writers already are, as captured by "identity" and "role" in Canagarajah's (2015) heuristics of voice, but also who the writers want to become. Regarding narrativity, several scholars (Menard-Warwick, 2005; Price, 1996; Yang, 2013) have contended that the poststructuralist theory of identity has overlooked the possibility that identity could stay constant through narration. A dialogical reconceptualization of writer identity thus acknowledges its diverse and dynamic nature on one hand (Cox et al., 2010; Li, 2007) and on the other hand its continuity through holding onto the same identity categories and storylines (Yang, 2013, 2018). Lastly, regarding morality, Zhao (2014) offered a powerful critique that Western conceptions of identity in general are overly individualistic and that identity should include ethical considerations as well. This argument is especially relevant in a society such as China, where literati are endowed with a cultural responsibility to convey ethical truth through their writing. This responsibility was famously captured by Zhou Dunyi (周敦颐 1017–1073), a Neo-Confucianist scholar, who stated, "文所以载道也" (Writings are meant to convey ideas and ethics) (Chinesethought.cn, n.d.). From this perspective, to write is to seek what is morally right and to right the wrongs in other people's writing. Integrating these three strains of literature, a dialogical reconceptualization of writer identity recognizes writers as moving toward their inspirations, embracing their own stories, and pursuing social justice through literacy activities. The voice effect they thus pursue involves the self but is not self-centered.

I have now summarized, as I see them, the epistemological affordances of LA writing from a Global South perspective. For the marginalized, including language learners, LA writing provides a textual space to enter into a dialogic relationship with the world that has already been named, that is, marked by perspectives and intentions of the privileged. Within the particular contexts of composition, drawing on their repertoires and exercising their own situated agency, these writers may disrupt hegemonic relations and unbalanced cultural dynamics by developing their own voice that orchestrates the visions, values, perspectives, and practices of both those in the center and those in the periphery. As Eldred and Mortensen (1992) observed in their reading of Shaw's *Pygmalion* as a literacy autobiography, there is always potential for the taught subject (in this case, Eliza the pupil) to resist the literacy of the powerful (Henry the teacher): "Literacy narratives sometimes include explicit images of schooling and teaching; they include texts that both challenge and affirm culturally scripted ideas about literacy" (p. 513), including a dichotomic view of body and mind. LA writing thus allows writers to wrestle with dominant literacy conceptions, values, and practices, and, concurrently and as a consequence, *to be* (i.e., to discover, embrace, or discard their own I-positions or ideological stances) and *to voice* dialogically (i.e., to express agreement or disagreement or anything in between with regard to the voices of others, including the dominant discourse). Through this systematic reconceptualization, LA writing becomes a critical pedagogy, the ultimate mission of which is to restore humanity to both the teacher and the learners in language and literacy education within a global context, by honoring their human backgrounds, feelings, subjectivities, and imaginations (Freire, 2000; Hanauer, 2012; Yang, 2020a).

Conclusion

This chapter has reconceptualized LA writing as critical pedagogy from a Global South perspective. It first reviewed the rise of LA writing in English-speaking countries and the complications related to this method's migration into the EFL context. It then reconceptualized LA writing in relation to context, repertoire, agency, and epistemological disruption from marginalized positions. This disruption concerns pedagogical and research practices that address hegemonic relations, imbalanced cultural dynamics, and dialogical voice. Although this chapter has focused on theory building, the evidence of its influence should be evident in the rest of the book, attesting to both the need for a reshaping of the global epistemological system and LA writing's potential to serve this purpose.

References

Ahearn, L. M. (2001). Language and agency. *Annual Review of Anthropology, 30*, 109–131.
Bakhtin, M. M. (1981). *The dialogic imagination: Four essays* (M. Holquist, Trans.). University of Texas Press.
Belcher, D., & Connor, U. (2001). *Reflections on multiliterate lives*. Multilingual Matters.
Brockmeier, J. (2009). Reaching for meaning: Human agency and the narrative imagination. *Theory & Psychology, 19*(2), 213–233. https://doi.org/10.1177/0959354309103540
Canagarajah, A. S. (Ed.). (2005). *Reclaiming the local in language policy and practice*. L. Erlbaum Associates.
Canagarajah, A. S. (2013). *Translingual practice: Global Englishes and cosmopolitan relations*. Routledge.
Canagarajah, A. S. (2015). "Blessed in my own way": Pedagogical affordances for dialogical voice construction in multilingual student writing. *Journal of Second Language Writing, 27*, 122–139. https://doi.org/10.1016/j.jslw.2014.09.001
Canagarajah, S., & Gao, X. (2019). Taking translingual scholarship farther. *English Teaching & Learning, 43*(1), 1–3. https://doi.org/10.1007/s42321-019-00023-4
Canagarajah, A. S. (2020). *Transnational literacy autobiographies as translingual writing*. Routledge.
Canagarajah, S. (2018). Transnationalism and translingualism: How they are connected. In X. You (Ed.), *Transnational writing education: Theory, history, and practice* (pp. 41–60). Routledge. https://doi.org/10.4324/9781351205955-3
Canagarajah, S. (2021). Materializing narratives: The story behind the story. *System, 102*. Advance online publication. https://doi.org/10.1016/j.system.2021.102610
Carstens, A. (2012). Using literacy narratives to scaffold academic literacy in the bachelor of education: A pedagogical framework. *Journal for Language Teaching, 46*(2), 9–25. https://doi.org/10.4314/jlt.v46i2.1
Chinesethought.cn. (n.d.). Key concepts in Chinese thought and culture. Retrieved from https://www.chinesethought.cn/shuyu_show.aspx?shuyu_id=2193
Coles, W. E. (1988). *The plural I—And after*. Boynton/Cook Publishers.
Corkery, C. (2005). Literacy narratives and confidence building in the writing classroom. *Journal of Basic Writing, 24*(1), 48–67. https://doi.org/10.37514/JBW-J.2005.24.1.04
Cox, M., Jordan, J., Ortmeier-Hooper, C., & Schwartz, G. G. (Eds.). (2010). *Reinventing identities in second language writing*. National Council of Teachers of English.
Davidson, C. N. (2004). *Revolution and the word: The rise of the novel in America* (Expanded ed.). Oxford University Press.

Duff, P. (2012). Identity, agency, and second language acquisition. In S. M. Gass, & A. Mackey (Eds.), *Handbook of second language acquisition* (pp. 410–426). Routledge.

Elbow, P. (1981). *Writing with power: Techniques for mastering the writing process.* Oxford University Press.

Eldred, J. C., & Mortensen, P. (1992). Reading literacy narratives. *College English, 54*(5), 512–539. https://doi.org/10.2307/378153

Freire, P. (1970). *Pedagogy of the oppressed.* Penguin.

Freire, P. (2000). *Pedagogy of the oppressed* (30th anniversary ed). Continuum.

Fujieda, Y., & Iida, A. (2015). Literacy autobiography in EFL contexts: Investigating Japanese student language learning experiences. In D. Shaffer, & M. Pinto (Eds.), *Embracing change: Blazing new frontiers through language teaching* (pp. 97–104). Korea TESOL Organization.

García, O., & Kleifgen, J. A. (2020). Translanguaging and literacies. *Reading Research Quarterly, 55*(4), 553–571. https://doi.org/10.1002/rrq.286

García, O., & Kleyn, T. (2016). Translanguaging theory in education. In O. García, & T. Kleyn (Eds.), *Translanguaging with multilingual students: Learning from classroom moments* (pp. 9–33). Routledge.

Gevers, G. (2018). Translingualism revisited: Language difference and hybridity in L2 writing. *Journal of Second Language Writing, 40,* 73–83. https://doi.org/10.1016/j.jslw.2018.04.003

Giroux, H. A. (2020). *On critical pedagogy* (2nd ed.). Bloomsbury Academic.

Grant, A. (1997). A multi-storied approach to the analysis: Narrative, literacy and discourse. *Melbourne Studies in Education, 38*(1), 31–71.

Grant, A. (2001). Understanding the contexts of vernacular literacy. *READ Magazine, 36*(1), 11–13.

Gunn, M. C. (1980). Cultural ecology: A brief overview. *Nebraska Anthropologist, 149,* 18–27.

Hanauer, D. (2012). Meaningful literacy: Writing poetry in the language classroom. *Language Teaching, 45*(1), 105–115.

Hashimoto, I. (1987). Voice as juice: Some reservations about evangelic composition. *College Composition and Communication, 38,* 70–80.

Herawati, H. (2021). Learners as story writers: Creative writing practices in English as a Foreign Language learning in Indonesia. In D. Bao, & T. Pham (Eds.), *Transforming pedagogies through engagement with learners, teachers and communities* (pp. 71–87). Multilingual Matters.

Hermans, H. J. M. (2001). The dialogical self: Toward a theory of personal and cultural positioning. *Culture & Psychology, 7*(3), 243–281. https://doi.org/10.1177/1354067X0173001

Horner, B. (2017). Teaching translingual agency in iteration: Rewriting difference. In B. Horner, & L. Tetreault (Eds.), *Crossing divides* (pp. 87–97). University Press of Colorado.

Hu, G. (2021). English language policy in Mainland China. In E. L. Low, & A. Pakir, *English in East and South Asia* (1st ed., pp. 19–32). Routledge. https://doi.org/10.4324/9780429433467-3

Iida, A. (2017). Expressing voice in a foreign language: Multiwriting Haiku pedagogy in the EFL context. *TEFLIN Journal: A Publication on the Teaching and Learning of English, 28*(2), 260. https://doi.org/10.15639/teflinjournal.v28i2/260-276

Ivanič, R. (1998). *Writing and identity: The discoursal construction of identity in academic writing.* John Benjamins.

Journet, D. (2012). Narrative turns in writing studies research. In L. Nickoson, & M.P. Sheridan (Eds.), *Writing studies research in practice: Methods and methodologies* (pp. 13–24). Southern Illinois University Press.

Kamler, B. (2001). *Relocating the personal: A critical writing pedagogy.* State University of New York Press.

Kim, K. M., & Park, G. (2020). "It is more expressive for me": A translingual approach to meaningful literacy instruction through Sijo poetry. *TESOL Quarterly, 54*(2), 281–309. https://doi.org/10.1002/tesq.545

Kramsch, C. (2006). Prview article: The multilingual subject. *International Journal of Applied Linguistics, 16*(1), 97–110. https://doi.org/10.1111/j.1473-4192.2006.00109.x

Kramsch, C. (2009). *The multilingual subject*. Oxford University Press.

Kramsch, C. (2010). Afterword. In D. Nunan, & J. Choi (Eds.), *Language and culture: Reflective narratives and the emergence of identity* (pp. 223–224). Routledge.

Li, X. (2007). Souls in exile: Identities of bilingual writers. *Journal of Language, Identity, and Education, 6*(4), 259–275. https://doi.org/10.1080/15348450701542256

Li, W. (2011). Moment analysis and translanguaging space: Discursive construction of identities by multilingual Chinese youth in Britain. *Journal of Pragmatics, 43*(5), 1222–1235. https://doi.org/10.1016/j.pragma.2010.07.035

Li, W., & Zhu, H. (2013). Translanguaging identities and ideologies: Creating transnational space through flexible multilingual practices amongst Chinese university students in the UK. *Applied Linguistics, 34*(5), 516–535. https://doi.org/10.1093/applin/amt022

Leki, I. (2001). Material, educational, and ideological challenges of teaching EFL writing at the turn of the century. *International Journal of English Studies, 1*(2), 197–209. https://doi.org/10.6018/IJES.1.2.48301

Macrorie, K. (1985). *Telling writing* (4th ed). Boynton/Cook Publishers.

Matsuda, P. K. (2001). Voice in Japanese written discourse: Implications for second language writing. *Journal of Second Language Writing, 10*(1–2), 35–53. https://doi.org/10.1016/S1060-3743(00)00036-9

Matsuda, P. K. (2015). Identity in written discourse. *Annual Review of Applied Linguistics, 35*, 140–159. https://doi.org/10.1017/S0267190514000178

Menard-Warwick, J. (2005). Both a fiction and an existential fact: Theorizing identity in second language acquisition and literacy studies. *Linguistics and Education, 16*(3), 253–274. https://doi.org/10.1016/j.linged.2006.02.001

Min, H.-T. (2009). A principled eclectic approach to teaching EFL writing in Taiwan. *Bulletin of Educational Research, 55*(1), 63–95.

Muchiri, M. N., Mulamba, N. G., Myers, G., & Ndoloi, D. B. (1995). Importing composition: Teaching and researching academic writing beyond North. *College Composition and Communication, 46*(2), 175–198.

Norton, B. (2000). *Identity and language learning: Gender, ethnicity and educational change*. Longman.

Norton, B. (2013). *Identity and language learning: Extending the conversation* (2nd ed.). Multilingual Matters.

Nunan, D., & Choi, J. (Eds.). (2010). *Language and culture: Reflective narratives and the emergence of identity*. Routledge.

Ordeman, W. (Ed.). (2021). *Creating a transnational space in the first year writing classroom*. Vernon Press.

Pavlenko, A. (2007). Autobiographic narratives as data in applied linguistics. *Applied Linguistics, 28*(2), 163–188. https://doi.org/10.1093/applin/amm008

Pratt, M. L. (1991). Arts of the contact zone. *Profession, 91*, 33–40.

Price, S. (1996). Comments on Bonny Norton Peirce's "Social identity, investment, and language learning": A reader reacts. *TESOL Quarterly, 30*(2), 331–337. https://doi.org/10.2307/3588147

Qian, Y. (2019). Motivation to English academic writing: Chinese students' literacy autobiography. *Theory and Practice in Language Studies, 9*(5), 530–536. http://dx.doi.org/10.17507/tpls.0905.06

Ramanathan, V., & Atkinson, D. (1999). Individualism, academic writing, and ESL writers. *Journal of Second Language Writing*, *8*(1), 45–75. https://doi.org/10.1016/S1060-3743(99)80112-X

Riyanti, D. (2015). An exploration of voice in second language writing. *The Nebraska Educator: A Student-Led Journal*, *2*, 28–48.

Schmertz, J. (2018). Writing our academic selves: The literacy autobiography as performance. *Pedagogy*, *18*(2), 279–293.

Scott, J. B. (1997). The literacy narrative as production pedagogy in the composition classroom. *Teaching English in the Two-Year College*, *24*(2), 108–117.

Shen, F. (1989). Identity is key to composition. *College Composition and Communication*, *15*(2), 478–512.

Silva, T. (2021). *Developing an understanding of translingual writing: A resource for graduate educators* (ED610526). ERIC. https://eric.ed.gov/?id=ED610526

Silverstein, M. (2019). Texts, entextualized and artifactualized. *College English*, *82*(1), 55–76.

Sisco, L. (1995). "Writing in the spaces left": Literacy as a process of becoming in the narratives of Frederick Douglass. *American Transcendental Quarterly*, *9*(3), 195–227.

Sladek, A. (2019). Literacy as threshold concept: Building multiliterate awareness in first-year writing. *Composition Studies*, *47*(2), 108–126.

Soliday, M. (1994). Translating self and difference through literacy narratives. *College English*, *56*(5), 511–526. https://ccdigitalpress.org/book/stories/chapters/bloome/

Steinman, L. (2007). Literacy autobiographies in a university ESL class. *Canadian Modern Language Review*, *63*(4), 563–573. https://doi.org/10.3138/cmlr.63.4.563

Wallace, D. L. (2014). Unwelcome stories, identity matters, and strategies for engaging in cross-boundary discourses. *College English*, *76*(6), 545–561.

White, M. (2007). *Maps of narrative practice*. W. W. Norton.

Williams, B. (2003). Heroes, rebels, and victims: Student identities in literacy narratives. *Journal of Adolescent and Adult Literacy*, *47*, 342–345.

Yang, S. (2013). *Autobiographical writing and identity in EFL education*. Routledge.

Yang, S. (2015). [Review of the book *Translingual practice: Global Englishes and cosmopolitan relations*, by S. A. Canagarajah]. *Iranian Journal of Language Teaching Research*, *3*(1), 145–147.

Yang, S. (2018). Potential phases of multilingual writers' identity work. In Xiaoye You (Ed.), *Transnational writing education: Theory, history, and practice* (pp. 115–137). Routledge.

Yang, S. (2020a). Critical pedagogy for foreign-language writing. *L2 Journal*, *12*(2), 110–127. https://doi.org/10.5070/L212245911

Yang, S. (2020b). Meaningful literacy and agentive writer identity. *MEXTESOL Journal*, *44*(4), 1–15.

Yang, S. (2020c). [Review of the book *Transnational literacy autobiographies as translingual writing*, by S. A. Canagarajah]. *Journal of Second Language Writing*, *48*, 1–5.

Yang, S, & Nong, M. (2019). Making new books in rural middle schools in China: A preliminary exploration of local realities and community-oriented literacy projects. *Asian EFL Journal*, *23*(5), 97–139.

Yang, S., & Reynolds, B. L. (2022). "Even I can do it": Chinese ethnolinguistic minority learners' investment in creative writing and its impact on them. *Chinese Journal of Applied Linguistics*, *45*(3), 340–359. https://doi.org/10.1515/CJAL-2022-0302

Yazan, B., Canagarajah, A. S., & Jain, R. (2021). *Autoethnographies in ELT: Transnational identities, pedagogies, and practices*. Routledge.

You, X. (2010). *Writing in the devil's tongue: A history of English composition in China*. Southern Illinois University Press.

You, X. (Ed.). (2018). *Transnational writing education: Theory, history, and practice*. Routledge.

Zapf, H. (2016). *Literature as cultural ecology: Sustainable texts* (1st ed.). Bloomsbury. https://doi.org/10.5040/9781474274685

Zhang, J. (2019). Composing Da You Shi in English: Chinese EFL students' perceptions and desires to write poetry in English. *Journal of Literature in Language Teaching, 8*(1), 20–39.

Zhao, K. (2014). *Learning, identity and narrative in the late modern age: Towards a theory of reflexive learning*. Zhejiang University Press.

Zhao, Y. (2015). *Second language creative writers: Identities and writing processes*. Multilingual Matters.

4
PEDAGOGICAL TRANSLANGUAGING BEHIND LITERACY AUTOBIOGRAPHICAL WRITING

Shizhou Yang

超语连接你我他，教学语言须细查。
对话探讨得新解，一文多稿叶成花。[1]

超语连接你我他 Translanguaging Links

Promoting a synergic and insider view of multilingual speakers' expansive communicative resources, translanguaging theory has been recognized by language professionals as a viable theory of practice (Canagarajah, 2013; Li, 2018; Poza, 2017; Turnbull, 2019; Velasco & García, 2014). This theory challenges applied linguists, bilingual and multilingual educators, and (not least) TESOL professionals to treat multilingual speakers' communicative resources as a whole and to integrate pedagogical translanguaging in their own classrooms. The purpose is to meet "language-minoritized students' needs to gain equitable education and social inclusion in mainstream society" (Juvonen & Källkvist, 2021, p. 1), an important political vision for translanguaging scholarship in the ESL context.

Recently, scholars have begun to advocate for the use of translanguaging in EFL education to utilize learners' bilingual or multilingual resources (Abdulaal, 2020; Canagarajah & Gao, 2019; Cenoz & Gorter, 2017; Li, 2016; Prilutsakaya, 2021; Turnbull, 2017, 2018; Zhou & Mann, 2021). However, classroom-based studies of pedagogical translanguaging in EFL writing education remain rare. Hence this autoethnographic study on pedagogical translanguaging in an academic writing course that I taught at a Chinese university. In this chapter, I focus on how pedagogical translanguaging informed my interactions with my Chinese–English bilingual students as they wrote their literacy autobiographies (LAs) for the course. Capitalizing on the idea that autoethnography can be both rigorous and artistic at the same time (Ellis et al., 2011), I will spread the four lines of my Chinese poem,

DOI: 10.4324/9781003288756-6

presented at the beginning of this chapter, across four separate headings. My purpose is twofold: to utilize the unique cohering functions of poetry (Gee, 1999) and to decolonize academic writing in English by embedding in it a Chinese-style poem—thus foregrounding "new possibilities and collectivities, new names and identities, new structures of thought and feeling" (Ramazani, 2009, p. 162). Situated within a Global South geographic context, this study provides useful insights on ways to apply pedagogical translanguaging to EFL academic writing beyond the primary level and outside English-speaking countries.

教学语言须细查 Translanguaging Matters

Translanguaging

Translanguaging refers to a synergic use of one's linguistic and other semiotic resources (Li, 2011, 2016, 2018). The term was translated from *trawsieithu*, coined by the Welsh educator Cen Williams to describe the classroom practice of using Welsh as a language of input and English as the language of output, and vice versa (cf. García & Kleifgen, 2020). Extending this pedagogical use of multiple languages, translanguaging scholars are interested in how multilingual speakers use their communicative resources as a whole (Li, 2018). To them, the boundaries between labeled languages such as L1 and L2 are rather fluid. Multilingual speakers can move back and forth between these languages and synergize them to make, communicate, and critique meanings in productive ways (Canagarajah, 2015, 2020; García & Kleyn, 2016). The same is true with mixing modalities of speaking, writing, print, and multimodal resources as provided through modern communication technologies (Canals, 2021; Kusters et al., 2017). As such, translanguaging scholars often adopt definitions of this approach similar to the following: "the act performed by bilinguals of accessing different linguistic features or various modes of what are described as autonomous languages, in order to maximize communicative potential" (García, 2009, p. 140).

However, translanguaging scholars do not merely advocate hybridity; their work is often motivated by an overt political stance. As Wei Li (2011) theorized, translanguaging transcends or goes beyond boundaries in three ways. First, users develop a tendency to go beyond the use of only one language or modality when expressing themselves. Second, translanguaging integrates knowledge from multiple disciplines such as sociology, linguistics, and psychology. Third, translanguaging challenges the dominance of monolingualism and creates new norms for language use. With these three main features, translanguaging may, through its actual practice, "disrupt hierarchies and inequities and build a better and more just world" (García & Kleyn, 2016, p. 26).

Like translanguaging, another similar and widely used term, *translingualism* or translingual practice, also emphasizes hybridity for meaning-making and social justice. Translingual practice was first used by Liu (1995) to describe examples of modern Chinese literature that, through translations from other languages such as

Japanese and Russian, develops features that go beyond the Chinese literary tradition. Composition scholars such as Canagarajah (2013, 2018) used "translingual practice" or "translingualism" to describe flexible uses of languages and modalities by multilingual speakers and writers who move back and forth between communities. In Canagarajah's (2018) own words, translingualism features not only "the languages in contact, generating new forms and meanings in synergy" (p. 42), but also "multiple modalities beyond the visual, and symbols from color, images, objects, and sound" (p. 43). Furthermore, through translingualism, individuals are "transforming established norms and relationships associated with a language" (p. 43). Given these similarities, I use all three terms—translingual practice, translingualism, and translanguaging—as synonyms.

Pedagogical Translanguaging

Pedagogical translanguaging, or "teaching approaches that involve the intentional and planned use of student multilingual resources in language and content subjects" (Juvonen & Källkvist, 2021, p. 1), has been an area of much research interest. Prilutskaya (2021), who reviewed over 200 empirical studies on pedagogical translanguaging published between 2011 and 2021, identified the following benefits: "mediating learners' emotional well-being, alleviating language learning anxiety, reducing negative behaviour, and, importantly, co-construction of emergent bilingual students' identities and promoting social justice through equity in education" (p. 14). However, these benefits mainly concern young learners, as implied by the term "emergent bilingual students," which cannot be used to describe adult learners in the EFL context, especially college students. Through many years of formal education, they have usually already developed a relatively advanced proficiency in both English and their national language.

The case studies in García and Kleyn's (2016) edited book offered concrete examples of pedagogical translanguaging at work in the ESL context with young learners. For instance, Ebe (2016) studied language use in an eighth-grade English class in New York City, where the teacher guided her multilingual students to use translanguaging as a literary device to create their own hybrid cultural texts. Pedagogical translanguaging in this case involved the use of multiple languages, such as Bengali and English, and multiple modalities, such as speaking and writing. Pedagogical translanguaging in this context, as Ebe (2016) concluded, scaffolded students' learning, created a new norm for language use in the classroom, functioned as a literary device, and helped to link home and school languages. In these ways, it serves as an enabling pedagogical condition.

Similarly, pedagogical translanguaging seems to have a positive impact on EFL students' writing as well. Turnbull's (2019) study of 30 Japanese university students' English writing offers an example. He divided the students into two groups, who were assigned to write on one of the two following tasks: an academic writing task concerning the student's personal view about whether "our society is too dependent on technology," or a creative writing task on "advice you would give to your younger self about life and growing up" (p. 7). He then provided three different prewriting translanguaging conditions for the students. Under the *monolingual* condition, the students could only use English for discussion; under the *weak translanguaging* condition, they could use only Japanese for discussion. Under the *strong translanguaging* condition, the students could use both Japanese and English or either language as they chose. All the students were given 20 minutes for prewriting discussion in their own groups and were then to finish their respective writing tasks within 40 minutes. Evaluation of the students' essays, done by three qualified raters using the ESL Composition Profile of Jacobs et al. (1981), found that students who engaged in strong translanguaging scored highest, regardless of the writing task. Turnbull (2019) reasoned that allowing this group to engage in strong translanguaging created ideal conditions for them to "select and suppress some linguistic features in their repertoires" (p. 16) or to be deliberate in their actual writing. This semi-experimental study suggests, at least, that it is necessary to scrutinize the exact forms of translanguaging employed in the teaching and learning of EFL writing.

Indeed, pedagogical translanguaging in the EFL context merits further study for educational reasons. Studies (e.g., in Africa: Kiramba, 2016; Motlhaka & Makalela, 2016; in Asia: Hiller, 2021; Rafi & Morgan, 2021) have revealed both tensions and opportunities that translanguaging brings to EFL academic writing classes. Sharma (2018), for instance, challenged the view that pedagogical translanguaging in itself enables actions and change. He described local translanguaging conditions in Nepal, which has, with dissatisfying educational outcomes for the majority, nonetheless embraced a monolingual, English-only, educational system that punishes the use of other languages in educational settings. Consequently, pedagogical translanguaging in Nepal "becomes distorted—being done in hiding and shame, fear and guilt—and unproductive for teaching and learning" (p. 86). Given complicated scenarios like that in Nepal, the question of whether and how to use translanguaging in EFL writing education requires us to consider critical issues such as the specific historical context and language policies in practice.

Pedagogical translanguaging in the EFL context needs further research for epistemological reasons as well. As several scholars have observed, due to researcher backgrounds and dominant contexts of study, the current knowledge production process concerning pedagogical translanguaging is eschewed. First, geographically, translanguaging scholarship is dominated by studies at the pre-tertiary and tertiary levels (Prilutskaya, 2021) and by scholars from Global North countries (Canagarajah, 2022) where English is the official language, leading to an "imbalance in knowledge production" (Canagarajah & Gao, 2019, p. 1). Furthermore, theoretically, there is a need to broaden the scope of inquiry. As Cenoz and Gorter (2017) suggested, pedagogical translanguaging should entail not only languages but also modalities (p. 320). Lastly, from a methodological perspective, Turnbull (2019) called for further research on "longitudinal effects of a translanguaging approach across an entire semester or year-long course on learners' EFL writing" (p. 16).

In response to these calls, I engaged in autoethnographic research on pedagogical translanguaging and its impact on my Chinese graduate students' LA writing in an academic writing course that I taught from September 2019 to January 2020.

对话探讨得新解 The Translanguaging Context

I adopted an autoethnographic approach, which, as Mirhosseini (2018) observed, is not commonly used in TESOL studies. As a qualitative research method, autoethnography features self-narratives, which draw on both personal memory and external data, to provide insights into the dynamics between self and culture through careful documentation, analysis, and interpretation (Chang, 2008). In particular, I sought to foreground how I used "translanguaging as a resource" (Burton & Rajendram, 2019) to facilitate multilingual students' learning of LA writing within two particular classrooms in China, a Global South context.

The Institutional and Pedagogical Contexts

The study took place in the School of Foreign Languages (SFL) of a culturally and linguistically diverse university in southwest China. Originally founded to train communist cadres for ethnic communities, the university has grown into a comprehensive institution of higher learning and is attended by Han Chinese (the majority group in China), ethnic minority, and international students. The SFL was collocated with a separate department that specializes in the languages and cultures of China's ethnic minority groups. At the entrance to the building, a wall-size poster proudly announced, in Chinese followed by translations into 12 ethnic languages such as Tibetan (Figure 4.1), a promise from clause 4 of the Chinese 宪法

FIGURE 4.1 A Display Highlighting Chinese *Minzu's* Constitutional Right to Use and Develop Their Own Languages and Scripts

Constitution: "Every ethnic group has the freedom to use and develop their own languages and scripts."

The academic writing course was offered through the SFL, which contained three programs: English (BA), Japanese (BA), and Chinese–English translation (BA and Master of Translation and Interpretation, henceforth MTI). It was a required two-credit-hour course for the first-year MTI students and lasted for 18 weeks. I met the students in two separate classes, one with 21 students and the other with 20, once a week for 90 minutes.

My teaching pedagogy was similar to that of Canagarajah's (2020). First, the main writing task was a multi-drafted and autoethnographic research-based literacy autobiography (LA). Second, I adopted a dialogical process approach by frequently inviting my students to interact with me and with each other. Third, I facilitated discussions by preparing handouts, my own LA samples, PowerPoint slides, and an electronic interactive platform for the course where every student could upload documents and make comments. In this way, I hoped to maximize my students' use of the classroom writing ecology as affordances.

In contrast to Canagarajah's (2020) study, though, I made three adaptations. First, I specified the length of each LA as 800 to 1,200 words to encourage concise writing. I also promised that the students' LAs would be included in an in-house publication at the end of the semester, which helped to create a practical need for revision. Lastly, informed by an academic literacies perspective (Lea & Street, 2006), I required my students to observe and reflect on a thesis defense by an upper-class student in the MTI program. Through these adaptations, I intended to develop strategies that could be transferred from LA writing to thesis writing.

The overall teaching activities can be roughly divided into three phases. Phase 1, the first week, introduced the writing task and autoethnographic research to my students. Phase 2, from week 2 to week 15, focused on LA drafting, which I facilitated by having everyone read LA samples and engage in LA-related autoethnographic research. Phase 3 (weeks 16–18) focused on guided revision and copyediting of LA drafts, culminating in an in-house publication, celebration, and reflection (week 18). To me, the in-house publication functioned as an "identity text" (Cummins et al., 2015) enabling my students to develop and display a more complicated and richer understanding of self and others than a mere term paper would. In other words, my ultimate goal was to develop my students' writing identity via LA writing as a social practice.

Data Collection

Following Chang's (2008) advice, I collected two main types of autoethnographic data, featuring my personal recall and external forms of validation, respectively. As the course teacher, I had the advantage of interacting directly with my students. Nonetheless, I collected other types of data to produce a reliable autoethnographic account. These included teaching documents, my weekly fieldnotes, students' writing samples, students' own research data, weekly journals, teacher and peer comments, and a survey using the prompt provided by Belcher and Connor (2001) on multilingual writers' literacy experiences. All these documents were electronically collected and stored on Kingsoft, an online collaboration platform. Some class sessions were audio-recorded and transcribed. At the end of the course, I obtained informed consent from the relevant students to use their course-related archives as research data.

Data Analysis

To analyze pedagogical translanguaging, I adopted the "moment analysis" approach proposed by Li (2011). This approach focuses on significant translanguaging moments that feature "spontaneous, impromptu, and momentary actions and performances of the individual" (p. 1224). As Li (2011) explained further, these moments are important because they impact not only those who translanguage but also those who participate in these moments. Ultimately, through moments like these, classrooms can be turned into spaces where translanguaging becomes the new normal for language use. Therefore, translanguaging moments that stood out for me could potentially be important for the whole class as well. To represent these moments in a less rigid way, I used stories to share my findings and included, as Li (2011) suggested, both "reflections and comments" on my pedagogical translanguaging acts (p. 1234). That is, I told stories of how and why I used translanguaging in my teaching. To facilitate this process, I used texts (such as my fieldnotes and my students' weekly journals), images (such as my students' drawings), and classroom recordings to identify, verify, analyze, and reflect on memorable translanguaging moments. Altogether, I analyzed 30 translanguaging moments termed as vignettes, which are available upon request.

Findings

I used translanguaging in teaching the academic writing course in two main ways. First, I combined the use of Mandarin Chinese and English, although the dominant language of instruction was English. Occasionally, I also used a few words from my dialect Chinese or coined my own expression by joining several languages together. Second, I combined the use of different modalities such as speech, writing, and multimodal objects. Often, I drew on both my linguistic and multimodal resources simultaneously.

In the next three sections, I will present some examples to illustrate three main purposes of pedagogical translanguaging: to demonstrate and guide LA writing, to facilitate understanding about autoethnographic research, and to facilitate revision.

Demonstrating and Guiding LA Writing

Throughout the teaching process, I engaged in LA writing myself and demonstrated how I drew on my multilingual and multiliteracy resources to tell my story. For instance, I wrote about the impact that practicing calligraphy had on me (Vignette 25).

> The character "人," for instance, was used by both my teacher and my father, who emphasized the importance of writing it right. "It should be upright and balanced, standing straight on the two feet!" This was no simple teaching of skill. Rather, it carried a philosophical question of how to be a proper human being: striving for self-reliance and righteous. "字像人形" was frequently used by my teachers, whether they taught Chinese or math or physics, with the ways characters are written becoming an extension of the writer's appearance and a metaphorical manifestation of the writer's internal qualities as well. If you write well, you get praised; if you write poorly, you get criticized. In both cases, your characters are equal to your character, and vice versa.
>
> *(My LA, shared with my students on December 26, 2019)*

In this LA sample, I translanguaged by embedding Chinese characters in my English prose and demonstrated how to interweave cultural interpretation with storytelling. More specifically, I used calligraphy to showcase a Chinese cultural value of writing characters such as "人" in an upright manner.

LA writing inevitably pushes writers to revisit, remember, and articulate their past experiences. To facilitate my students' LA writing, I translanguaged by starting with a drawing activity (Vignette 2). As Kai recounted in his journal:

> When the [writing] class started, we were asked ["in English"] to draw a river on a piece of paper. What's more, Mr. Yang requested us to write ["in English or Chinese or 少数民族话 ethnic languages"] significant individuals or things [who] influenced us around the river. It is really objective model of teaching I praise. When it comes to the most influential person for me, it must be my girlfriend who I met in the university, who imposed me a lot in writing expressions. When I pursued her previously, I [wrote] a growing number of *love letters*, and most of them are from *Shakespeare's tales* with a *little creation by myself*. At that time, I was addicted to describe my *inner voice* for love without any fatigues. From my perspective, the experience of literacy was so pure that [there was] no utilitarianism for scores in the English tests.
>
> *(Journal, September 12, 2019, emphasis added)*

This class literacy event starts with students drawing a river to represent one's reading history and another to represent one's writing history. It then moves to labeling "significant individuals or things." As such, the figurative travel experience was reconnecting the writer with significant others and memories, which, in Kai's case, featured his girlfriend. It also evoked a past image of himself as a creative writer who had composed "a growing number of love letters, and most of them are from Shakespeare's tales with a little creation by myself." It was a literacy endeavor of voluntary investment, qualitatively different from writing "for scores in the English tests." As Kai stated, "I was addicted to describe my inner voice for love without any fatigues." Thus, although the drawing and labeling activities may seem simple or even naïve for adult EFL learners, they can actually be powerful.

66 Shizhou Yang

They began to challenge Kai's formulaic ways of thinking and doing writing. As he wrote in the same journal:

> Influenced by traditional literacy teachers, to be honest, I had aroused some stereotypes for the teacher in front of me. My writing style, to a great extent, is affected by the *template composition* without any freshness or critical thinking. I [was] concerned whether I would exasperate him for my unsatisfied writing assignment last week; nevertheless, all of my worries were redundant in his class. It is so relaxing and considerate that Mr. Yang always encourages our students to read and write with his topics and tasks but *less evaluations about one's level in writing*.
>
> (Emphasis added)

In other words, the translanguaging approach to literacy, including drawing and "less evaluation," countered Kai's negative "stereotypes" of writing teachers and invited him to engage in reading and writing in a different way.

Multiple languages and modalities were involved in this translanguaging approach. Besides the drawing and writing activity, which Kai described in this journal passage, I also asked my students to talk with each other about their drawings and labels. Lastly, a few students were invited to tell their stories to the whole class. Thus, writing and speaking—in both English and Chinese, as the students themselves chose—were involved. The following artifact from Shi, whose LA is presented in Chapter 14, captured her use of both languages to label her reading history and writing history (see Figure 4.2).

Shi used English for most of her text, including the title "My feeling of reading and writing," which was adopted from Canagarajah (2020). However, when giving an example of the contemporary Chinese novels that she read in high school, she wrote it in Chinese: "最小说" (zui novels). Perhaps it was a term that defies translation and is best expressed in Chinese. English and Chinese in the same text thus played different functions.

By inviting my students to articulate their literacy experiences, I translanguaged with them because I believe that each language or modality has its unique affordances as well as limitations. To require my students to use only English or Chinese, or only speaking, or only writing, or only drawing was to waste their expansive resources. Therefore, in my instruction, I included snatches of Chinese, sometimes with their English equivalents, for example, "少数民族话" (ethnic language), thus turning my classroom into a translanguaging space. I further involved my students in a series of translanguaging activities: drawing, labeling (writing short phases), and talking. Through these activities, I wanted to expand my students' vision about (LA) writing, not to treat it as yet another task to be evaluated on language alone. In keeping with my understanding of educational autobiographical writing as a social practice (Yang, 2013), I also wanted to encourage the sharing of social identities and associated stories that would challenge my students' deficit views of themselves and

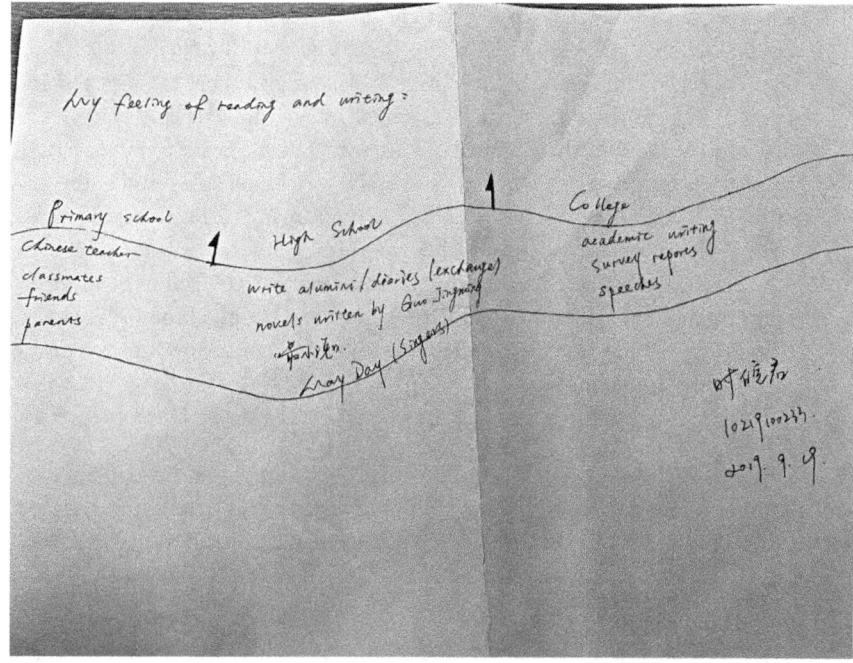

FIGURE 4.2 Shi's Writing History and Reading History

of others as writers. In Kai's case, translanguaging appeared to have allowed such alternative identities and stories to emerge.

Facilitating Autoethnographic Research

Pedagogical translanguaging was also used to facilitate my students' autoethnographic research. For instance, to help my students understand the concept of "external data" in autoethnographic research, I said, "We are going to talk about 'external data' today," thus utilizing the English language in speech. Meanwhile, to ensure that everyone understood, I wrote the words "external data" on the blackboard in white chalk, thus using the modality of handwriting. Additionally, I translated the word into Chinese, saying something like "其他数据," thus using another language. Moreover, I brought real objects such as my diary, graduation certificates, TOEFL score report, and photos to the classroom to illustrate possible resources for autoethnographic research, thus applying multimodality in my teaching.

I then translanguaged in my explanation and teaching of autoethnographic data collection (Vignette 5). My fieldnotes contain this description of the first translanguaging moment:

> First was my recontextualization of Chang's (2008) data generating method: making a list of proverbs important to oneself and ordering them, and making

a list of places important to oneself and ordering them. While in the class, I suddenly thought I could combine this activity with drawing our hands; after all, each hand is unique. So, I gave each student a sheet of A4 paper, and I asked them to trace their hands and then list the proverbs and places. The students then shared their proverbs with each other. I believe this activity is creative and the data generated are themselves generative. As I said at the end of the class, the drawings are "画中有话" (with many words to be said about each of the pictures). Hopefully, they would help my students to travel back to their past and situate their evolving sense of self in the cultural and spatial contexts that shaped them as readers, writers, and people. From this activity, I recall a leading qualitative researcher's comparison of methods to yoga back in 2008 at a conference.

(Fieldnote, October 19, 2019)

In this fieldnote, I recounted a new way of generating autoethnographic data. Instead of just listing proverbs, as Chang (2008) suggested, I began with drawing a hand and filling in each finger with a proverb or saying that had a special significance. I asked my students to do the same thing with regard to important literacy sites in their lives. This translanguaging creativity was invigorating for me as well as for my students.

My second translanguaging moment came when I shared my own proverbs—most of them in Chinese, with my own translation—and related stories, mostly in English, with my students. As I recalled:

> With proverbs like "笨鸟先飞早出林," "吃得苦中苦，方为人上人," "沉默是金," and "Where there is love, there is miracle," I told my students about my experience of struggling to leave the countryside, overcoming my own obstacles in learning English, and preparing to study abroad. Not until I started sharing one of the proverbs and my own life story did I see this indifferent student (who might have used the word "boring" to describe her feelings at the beginning of the class on the 弹幕[2] or the real time streaming) change. I literally saw her face light up. That was a great sight to see!
>
> *(Fieldnote, October 19, 2019)*

My translanguaging in this case—involving speaking in English and Chinese and some translation—was natural. I used whatever was fitting for my pedagogical purpose, which was to illustrate that cultural sayings are impactful. By relating to such sayings, we could situate our autoethnographies within the cultural contexts that have shaped us. Such translanguaging acts had the desired effect on the formerly indifferent student whose face lit up.

My third translanguaging moment came in the afternoon class, when Zhang started sharing her proverbs after I shared mine. She wrote all her proverbs in Chinese (see Figure 4.3).

Two of Zhang's sayings were the same as mine. Four of them emphasize hard work and persistence, particularly in learning—for example, "不劳无获"

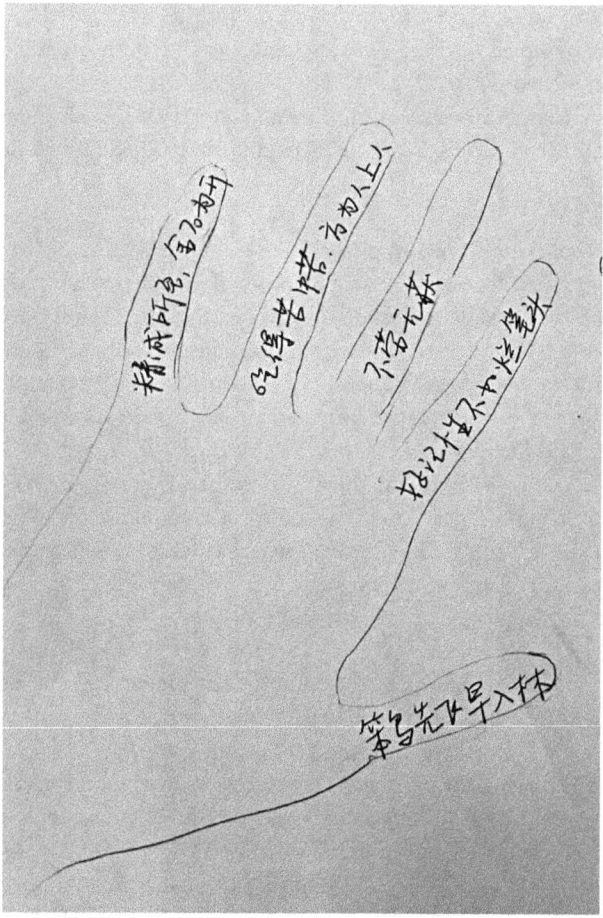

FIGURE 4.3 Zhang's Hand with Five Proverbs

(No pains, no gains). One of them features a distinct literacy practice: "好记性不如烂笔头" (A strong memory is not as good as a simple pen), which encourages learners to take notes as they study lest they forget. Relating to one of her proverbs, Zhang began to recount a difficult time of her life after college:

> To support herself, for reasons she did not specify, she went into teaching but had to sleep [secretly] in the classroom. She became teary-eyed when *retelling the story*, first in *English*, and then in *Chinese*. The class was moved and clapped their hands after she finished her story. I was struck not only by her courage to face life's challenges in her past, but also her courage to tell this story to others. The story deepened my understanding of this student, not just as an MTI student, but as a person, a courageous person.
>
> *(Fieldnote, October 19, 2019)*

While translanguaging served my pedagogical purposes, it was also practiced by Zhang, who combined drawing, writing, and speaking both English and Chinese in her communication.

Although Zhang did not mention translanguaging specifically, her journal that day lent support to the idea that translanguaging had helped her tell her story. She wrote:

> Frankly speaking, sometimes I couldn't catch up with what [Mr. Yang] said [in English] in the class and always answer[ed] the wrong questions which was embarrassing. I appreciated that every time Mr. Yang would make some compliment and further explanation for me [in English or Chinese or both] to deal with this embarrassment. For instance, we were asked to share some proverbs and the stories behind them. I was so nervous and hit by some complicated feelings that I didn't control myself for the most difficult time in my past life. Consequently, I was so embarrassed that my expression was so poor with no logic, organization or a good ending. However, Mr. Yang helped me to deal with what I had worried with his explanation and other topics. I appreciated him very much.
>
> (7J)

For Zhang, this initial sharing of "the most difficult time in my past life" was emotion-laden ("complicated feelings," "so embarrassed") and chaotic ("no logic, organization or a good ending"). Looking back, I felt relieved that I did not adopt an English-only approach in the class. That would have constrained Zhang from articulating her experience and emotions. However, perhaps more important than the language use itself was the impact Zhang's story exerted on the class, which applauded her when she finished sharing. Eleven weeks later, during the final class, Zhang's classmates recalled her story fondly and showed great admiration for her. Pedagogical translanguaging, involving drawing, writing, and bilingual speaking, thus facilitated Zhang and others' research of their own experiences.

一文多稿叶成花 Facilitating Revision

STUDENT [READING A HANDOUT AND TRANSLATING A PHRASE FROM ENGLISH INTO CHINESE]: 个人记忆的数据和其他数据是否同时运用 [Whether personal memory data and other types of data are used].

ME: 对，非常好！或者是说这个作者有没有把个人的数据还有其他的数据用在里面。多种数据的运用是非常好的 [Good, very good. Or maybe we can say whether the writer has used both personal data and other types of data. The use of multiple forms of data is very good. It helps to make our writing more believable.] (Transcript of class interaction, December 19, 2019)

At a glance, this excerpt presents an ordinary dialogue between a student and me, all in Chinese. In reality, it was several translanguaging acts in disguise. As I wrote in my fieldnote:

> Today I focused on helping my students understand ways of evaluating their literacy autobiographies. The students were each given an evaluation form [which was written mostly in English] with specific aspects and questions. They were then asked to discuss the questions in teams of two or three and present their understandings in Chinese. If they had a question related to the form, they were encouraged to ask as well. In the morning class, I spent a great amount of time explaining and illustrating areas where students had questions. The students also had time to do self-evaluation and then evaluate each other's LA drafts.

The translanguaging acts here include, first, the use of Chinese within the title of the evaluation form, "LA 书稿评分标准" (Evaluation Criteria for LA Book Chapters, see Appendix). The same points were used by the peer reviewer. Although we had used "读写自传," a literal translation of "literacy autobiography" several times, LA writing remained a more concise way to refer to the writing task. And since "LA" was already in the title, I did not think it necessary to repeat it in the English title. Similarly, because Chinese do not usually refer to the point system when talking about font size, I switched to the Chinese term "小四号" (an equivalent of 12-point) when instructing my students how to set the font size for their chapters. Thus, through the use of the evaluation form, my students were guided to navigate a primarily English text with some Chinese.

The second main act of translanguaging occurred when my students discussed in "teams of two or three" the meanings of the evaluation form and then presented "their understandings in Chinese." The discussion and translation activated their bilingual competencies as resources for comprehension. The third main translanguaging act took place when the students asked questions in Chinse, as shown in the above excerpt. This can be viewed as a continuation of their presentation. Significantly, their Chinese was not suppressed in any way as they interpreted and discussed the evaluation form. Lastly, this teaching episode or literacy event surrounding the evaluation form qualifies as translanguaging in that it involved the use of multiple modalities, including a double-sided print text, handwritten texts, and speech. This occurred during the 16th week, and we had only two weeks remaining before all the chapters were to be put together in book form. I wanted to ensure that my students knew how to revise their LAs to make them as autoethnographic as possible. I felt a sense of urgency after reading through students' LA drafts, which contained several outstanding problems, including undefined terms, undocumented citations, and lack of analysis from a cultural perspective (Fieldnote, December 19, 2019).

To facilitate my students' revision, I prepared a checklist, summarizing what we had been learning about autoethnographic research. The checklist included three main areas (quality of narrative writing, quality of academic writing, and quality of analytical writing), each with specific aspects to consider. For instance, the first main question was "Is your LA engaging enough?" This prompt guided the class to focus on the use of sensory details, verbs referencing specific actions, proper tenses, and other features to make the literacy narrative engaging. Whereas, in my previous classes, I had been less demanding with regard to whether my students could understand everything I said in English, in the final weeks I wanted to make sure they understood everything I said. Consequently, even though I still prepared the checklist in English, I asked my students to first translate the main questions and descriptions of specific aspects into Chinese to check their understanding. I then would comment in Chinese or English or, as in the case shown above, mostly in Chinese and partly in English. Note that the two languages were not used for the same purpose. For instance, in line 1, students used Chinese to provide their translation of the checklist item. In line 2, I used Chinese to show approval ("对, 非常好!" Right, very good) before moving on to an alternative translation: "或者说 … ." Or it can be said as. The second part of line 2 contains both Chinese and English. The first part provided an evaluation of the use of multiple forms of data as "非常好的" (very good). The second part, spoken in English, explained why.

Drawing on Wu's data, I composed a 50-word poem to showcase the gradual progress of his LA (see Chapter 10).

> *Revision*
>
> My initial writing about literacy
> Was a thin "No" or "Yes."
> Through reading, discussion, peer review …
> I added to my LA—
> Stories about myself being comforted
> By *waipo*'s[3] nursery rhymes
> Scholarly literature
> Argument …
> And strived to see my selves
> From cultures' eyes.
> Academic writing has turned into a how-to-learn process.

Granted, the revisions Wu and other students made cannot be attributed to pedagogical translanguaging alone. Nonetheless, pedagogical translanguaging accompanied the whole process of teaching, learning, researching, and eventually the revisions that the students made.

Discussion

This autoethnographic study reveals that…, I engaged in pedagogical translanguaging in two main ways. First, I combined the use of languages such as English and Chinese; second, I combined the use of modalities such as drawing, speaking, and writing.

Often, my pedagogical translanguaging acts involved the use of both my multilingual and multimodal resources. As such, this study addressed the need to study pedagogical translanguaging beyond linguistic hybridity alone (Cenoz & Gorter, 2017). Using a moment analysis (Li, 2011) approach to sift through my autoethnographic data, I found that my translanguaging acts and those of my students had turned our writing classroom into a translanguaging space (Li, 2011).

However, no empirical evidence suggests that any of these translanguaging acts fits the rosy picture of *"deployment of a speaker's full linguistic repertoire"* (García & Kleyn, 2016, p. 14; emphasis in original). Instead, it seems more reasonable to say that both my students and I utilized our linguistic resources selectively and deliberately in any emergent situation, but never fully in the sense of using everything at our disposal. For instance, even though I had told my students that they could use "少数民族话" (ethnic languages) as well, none of my ethnic minority students actually spoke their own ethnic language in the class. Instead, they resorted to either English or Mandarin Chinese for discussion because these were the two shared languages of the class. Neither did my ethnic minority students write anything in their ethnic language; while attending schools in China, they rarely, if ever, received any education about their heritage language scripts. The external demand or invitation to use a shared language and the internal lack of proficiency in writing in their first language prevented them from using their heritage languages in any meaningful way in the class. This study thus affirms Sharma's (2018) critique that in EFL contexts such as Nepal, we should not assume that translanguaging will automatically enable personal agency and voice but must scrutinize the translanguaging conditions EFL writers face.

Several factors contributed to making pedagogical translanguaging possible in my writing class. Institutionally, there was no English-only policy. Programmatically, studying MTI placed my students in an ideal place of moving between and using multiple languages. Ideologically, I had long rejected "native speakerism" and embraced a translanguaging and translingual orientation. Professionally, I was trained in the West, proficient in speaking, and passionate about writing, and I had published several studies through international channels. These external and internal factors enabled me to translanguage with confidence instead of engaging in shame-filled translanguaging acts, as reported by Sharma (2018).

I found that I used pedagogical translanguaging for three main purposes: to teach LA writing, to facilitate my students' autoethnographic research, and to guide my students' revision of their LAs. In other words, my translanguaging acts were pedagogically motivated. In a nutshell, I wanted my students to produce quality LAs and, through the process of drafting and revising their LAs, to learn academic literacy in an MTI program. This pragmatic goal sets my study apart from existing studies in the ESL context (García & Kleyn, 2016), most of which have a political motivation to challenge a dominant ideology of monolingualism. If my pedagogical translanguaging—as part of my dialogic process and research-oriented pedagogy—has challenged anything, it would be some of my students' fixed and limiting images of literacy, such as treating writing as "template composition" in Kai's case.

My pedagogical translanguaging is perhaps significant in one more way. Studies in the ESL context tend to emphasize how translanguaging addresses social inequality by including nondominant languages in the education process (García & Kleyn, 2016). Although allowing minority learners to use their own languages is definitely important, I am not optimistic that doing so can by itself reverse the trend of "social and educational inequality" (p. 15). This study shows instead that pedagogical translanguaging, as in the case used by Zhang to tell her life story—by first drawing her hand, then writing down her proverbs in Chinese, then telling her story first in Chinese and afterwards in English and with tears—actually contributed to a rich understanding of self and others. As far as I was concerned, that telling "deepened my understanding of this student, not just as an MTI student, but as a person, a courageous person" (Fieldnote, October 19, 2019). Pedagogical translanguaging could thus work together with other aspects of pedagogical design to facilitate such storied views of self and counter negative social views based solely on broad categories such as gender and location.

Two limitations of this study are obvious. In selecting typical pedagogical translanguaging examples from my teaching process, I might have neglected other equally significant ways of using language. For instance, as I listened to recordings of my classroom teaching, I came to realize a pattern of my language use: both in each session and considering the semester as a whole, I tended to speak all English at the beginning but gradually switched to Chinese or translanguaging. However, my use of multimodality—speaking, writing, handouts, and PowerPoint slides—was consistent, even though the specific combinations of modes might vary.

Furthermore, by focusing on my own interpretation alone, I might have missed potentially important insights from my students. The readers should therefore be warned not to read this autoethnographic account as claiming that pedagogical translanguaging is the ultimate solution to all problems faced by writing teachers. For instance, one student, Yue, wrote the following in her journal about the beginning of her first writing class with me:

> My first week as an English [MTI] major student began with an excited mood. I was majored in financial management, to be honest, I'm not confident with myself.
> On Mr. Yang's writing class, I faced my anxiety by introduced my little hobby about Harry Potter, the amazing thing was that my worriment seemed to fade away. I came to realize that my background, as a cross-discipline student, may not be a shortcoming, maybe I can just stay in my character and make the most out of it. (Journal, September 8, 2019).

Yue was not concerned about writing in particular, but about whether she would fit in the new community of translators after changing her major from financial management. Even though no apparent translanguaging was involved in this short classroom interaction, Yue turned a new page by talking about her "little hobby about Harry Potter" (in English). Yue now began to recognize new possibilities: "My background, as a cross-discipline student, may not be a shortcoming; maybe I can just stay in my character and make the most out of it." Thus, teaching, perhaps regardless of the language used, can always impact someone in profound ways. In Yue's case, she changed from being "not confident" because she was coming into this class from a different discipline to hopefulness about the difference as a resource to draw upon.

Despite these limitations, it seems evident that pedagogical translanguaging—albeit selectively presented and illustrated—has played an active role in advancing my students' understanding of LA writing, autoethnographic research, and revision. Future studies can continue to explore how translanguaging can be a pedagogical tool to help teachers accomplish their instructional goals.

Conclusion

This research set out to explore the use of pedagogical translanguaging in teaching an EFL academic writing course, which featured an LA writing project. Using moment analysis (Li, 2011) to analyze my autoethnographic data, I found that I translanguaged mainly through combining languages (English and Chinese) and modalities (drawing, speaking, writing on the board, handouts, and PowerPoint slides). Furthermore, I used pedagogical translanguaging to facilitate my students' LA writing, related autoethnographic research, and revision of their LA drafts. This autoethnographic study thus revealed that translanguaging functioned as a hidden hero behind my students' LA writing.

The findings of this study have three main implications for EFL writing education, particularly concerning the use of LA as a writing task. First, we should relocate pedagogical translanguaging. In the EFL context, and particularly in institutions where multilingual use is already the norm, pedagogical translanguaging is motivated less by a political vision to challenge monolingual ideology than by a pragmatic goal to facilitate learning. Second, contextual studies of LA writing should take into account whether and how pedagogical translanguaging has become a factor shaping students' LAs. Third, given that certain languages (specifically, my own and my students' ethnic minority languages) made virtually no appearance in my teaching process, we may need to adopt a revised notion of pedagogical translanguaging, not as the use of *all* resources. Instead, we may have to consider translanguaging conditions, including program features, pedagogical designs, and the users' proficiency in a particular language. To understand these implications further, future studies could investigate the actual effects of pedagogical translanguaging on students' LA writing and revision more closely. Relatedly, it may be useful to go beyond pedagogical translanguaging and consider classroom writing ecology as a factor in LA writing as a whole. This will be my focus in Chapter 5.

APPENDIX
LA 书稿评分标准 Evaluating Criteria (Part I) (self-evaluation)

Author: _____ Date: 12/18/2019

Chapter title: _____

Question	Observing points	Great	Good	Poor	Outstanding issues
Is the draft engaging enough?	1. whether the story provides enough details to show, not to tell				
	2. whether the chapter has a complete and clear structure				
	3. whether tenses are used appropriately in the context				
	4. whether pronouns have clear referents				
Is the draft autoethnographic enough?	5. whether the content is related to literacy in Chinese and English				
	6. whether personal memory data and other types of data are used				
	7. whether data are analyzed using some relevant theoretical lenses				
	8. whether the chapter title and subheadings show signs that the writer is distilling the theme or essence of his or her own LA				
	9. whether there are signs of the author interpreting self in relation to culture				
Is the LA academic enough?	10. whether there is a clear expression of the argument				
	11. whether relevant and proper terms are used				
	12. whether relevant literature is used or cited in the text				
	13. whether cited literature lends support to or helps advance the writer's argument or expands the significance of a personal story				
	14. whether all cited literature is listed in the references and vice versa				
	15. whether the references are of good quality				
	16. whether literature is cited "properly," i.e., according to the GB-2015 style, both in terms of information (e.g., author name, year of publication) and format (e.g., capitalization, lower case, punctuation, upper case)				

Notes

1 When spreading the four lines in the headings, I adopted a pragmatic approach, providing only the basic meaning. A literal translation of the poem might be: Translanguaging links you, me, and him/her; Worthy it is to study the language of instruction. Dialogic inquiry yields new insights; A text, revised multiple times, is like a leaf turning into a flower.
2 This was possible because I used a free education App in the class, which allowed the students to write on a shared screen anonymously.
3 *Waipo* (外婆) means maternal grandmother.

References

Abdulaal, M. A. A.-D. (2020). A shift from a monoglossic to a heteroglossic view: Metalinguistic Stego-translanguaging lens approach. *Arab World English Journal, 11*(4), 461–473. https://dx.doi.org/10.24093/awej/vol11no4.29

Belcher, D., & Connor, U. (2001). *Reflections on multiliterate lives*. Multilingual Matters.

Burton, J., & Rajendram, S. (2019). Translanguaging-as-resource: University ESL instructors' language orientations and attitudes toward translanguaging. *TESL Canada Journal, 36*(1), 21–47. https://doi.org/10.18806/tesl.v36i1.1301

Canagarajah, A. S. (2013). *Translingual practice: Global Englishes and cosmopolitan relations*. Routledge.

Canagarajah, A. S. (2015). "Blessed in my own way": Pedagogical affordances for dialogical voice construction in multilingual student writing. *Journal of Second Language Writing, 27*, 122–139. https://doi.org/10.1016/j.jslw.2014.09.001

Canagarajah, A. S. (2020). *Transnational literacy autobiographies as translingual writing*. Routledge.

Canagarajah, S. (2018). Transnationalism and translingualism: How they are connected. In X. You (Ed.), *Transnational writing education: Theory, history, and practice* (pp. 41–60). Routledge. https://doi.org/10.4324/9781351205955-3

Canagarajah, S. (2022). Challenges in decolonizing linguistics: The politics of enregisterment and the divergent uptakes of translingualism. *Educational Linguistics*. Advance online publication. https://doi.org/10.1515/eduling-2021-0005

Canagarajah, S., & Gao, X. (2019). Taking translingual scholarship farther. *English Teaching & Learning, 43*(1), 1–3. https://doi.org/10.1007/s42321-019-00023-4

Canals, L. (2021). Multimodality and translanguaging in negotiation of meaning. *Foreign Language Annals, 54*(3), 647–670. https://doi.org/10.1111/flan.12547

Cenoz, J., & Gorter, D. (2017). Translanguaging as a pedagogical tool in multilingual education. In J. Cenoz, D. Gorter, & S. May (Eds.), *Language Awareness and Multilingualism* (pp. 309–321). Springer. https://doi.org/10.1007/978-3-319-02240-6_20

Chang, H. (2008). *Autoethnography as method*. Left Coast Press.

Cummins, J., Hu, S., Markus, P., & Montero, M. K. (2015). Identity texts and academic achievement: Connecting the dots in multilingual school contexts. *TESOL Quarterly, 49*(3), 555–581.

Ebe, A. E. (2016). Student voices shining through: Exploring translanguaging as a literary device. In O. García & T. Kleyn (Eds.), *Translanguaging with multilingual students: Learning from classroom moments* (pp. 57–82). Routledge.

Ellis, C., Adams, T. E., & Bochner, A. P. (2011). Autoethnography: An overview. *Forum Qualitative Sozialforschung/Forum: Qualitative Social Research, 12*(1). https://doi.org/10.17169/fqs-12.1.1589

García, O. (2009). Education, multilingualism and translanguaging in the 21st century. In T. Skutnabb-Kangas, R. Phillipson, A. K. Mohanty, & M. Panda (Eds.), *Social Justice through Multilingual Education* (pp. 140–158). Multilingual Matters. https://doi.org/10.21832/9781847691910-011

García, O., & Kleyn, T. (Eds.). (2016). *Translanguaging with multilingual students: Learning from classroom moments*. Routledge.

García, O., & Kleifgen, J. A. (2020). Translanguaging and literacies. *Reading Research Quarterly, 55*(4), 553–571. https://doi.org/10.1002/rrq.286

Gee, J. P. (1999). *An introduction to discourse analysis: Theory and method*. Routledge.

Hiller, K. E. (2021). Introducing translanguaging in an EAP course at a joint-venture university in China. *RELC Journal: A Journal of Language Teaching and Research, 52*(2), 307–317. https://doi.org/10.1177/00336882211014997

Jacobs, H. L., Zinkgraf, S. A., Wormuth, D. R., Hartfiel, V. F., & Hughey, J. B. (1981). *Testing ESL composition: A practical approach*. Newbury House Publishers.

Juvonen, P., & Källkvist, M. (Eds.). (2021). *Pedagogical translanguaging: Theoretical, methodological and empirical perspectives*. Multilingual Matters.

Kiramba, L. K. (2016). Translanguaging in the writing of emergent multilinguals. *International Multilingual Research Journal, 11*(2), 115–130. https://doi.org/10.1080/19313152.2016.1239457

Kusters, A., Spotti, M., Swanwick, R., & Tapio, E. (2017). Beyond languages, beyond modalities: Transforming the study of semiotic repertoires. *International Journal of Multilingualism, 14*(3), 219–232. https://doi.org/10.1080/14790718.2017.1321651

Lea, M., & Street, B. (2006). The "academic literacies" model: Theory and applications. *Theory into Practice, 45*(4), 368–377. https://doi.org/10.1207/s15430421tip4504_11

Li, W. (2011). Moment analysis and translanguaging space: Discursive construction of identities by multilingual Chinese youth in Britain. *Journal of Pragmatics, 43*(5), 1222–1235. https://doi.org/10.1016/j.pragma.2010.07.035

Li, W. (2016). New Chinglish and the post-multilingualism challenge: Translanguaging ELF in China. *Journal of English as a Lingua Franca, 5*(1), 1–25. https://doi.org/10.1515/jelf-2016-0001

Li, W. (2018). Translanguaging as a practical theory of language. *Applied Linguistics, 39*(1), 9–30. https://doi.org/10.1093/applin/amx039

Liu, L. H. (1995). *Translingual practice: Literature, national culture, and translated modernity--China, 1900–1937*. Stanford University Press.

Mirhosseini, S.-A. (2018). An invitation to the less-treaded path of autoethnography in TESOL research. *TESOL Journal, 9*(1), 76–92. https://doi.org/10.1002/tesj.305

Motlhaka, H. A., & Makalela, L. (2016). Translanguaging in an academic writing class: Implications for a dialogic pedagogy. *Southern African Linguistics and Applied Language Studies, 34*(3), 251–260. https://doi.org/10.2989/16073614.2016.1250356

Poza, L. (2017). Translanguaging: Definitions, implications, and further needs in burgeoning inquiry. *Berkeley Review of Education, 6*(2), 101–128. https://doi.org/10.5070/B86110060

Prilutskaya, M. (2021). Examining pedagogical translanguaging: A systematic review of the literature. *Languages, 6*(4), 180. https://doi.org/10.3390/languages6040180

Rafi, A. S. M., & Morgan, A.-M. (2021). Translanguaging and academic writing in English-only classrooms: A case-study from Bangladeshi higher education. In W. Ordeman (Ed.), *Creating a transnational space in the first year writing classroom* (pp. 17–40). Vernon Press. https://doi.org/10.5281/ZENODO.4539727

Ramazani, J. (2009). *A transnational poetics*. University of Chicago Press. https://doi.org/10.7208/chicago/9780226703374.001.0001

Sharma, S. (2018). Translanguaging in hiding: English-only instruction and literacy education in Nepal. In X. You (Ed.), *Transnational writing education: Theory, history, and practice* (pp. 79–94). Routledge.

Turnbull, B. (2017). Towards new standards in foreign language assessment: Learning from bilingual education. *International Journal of Bilingual Education and Bilingualism, 23*, 1–11. https://doi.org/10.1080/13670050.2017.1375891

Turnbull, B. (2018). Reframing foreign language learning as bilingual education: Epistemological changes towards the emergent bilingual. *International Journal of Bilingual Education and Bilingualism, 21*(8), 1041–1048. https://doi.org/10.1080/13670050.2016.1238866

Turnbull, B. (2019). Translanguaging in the planning of academic and creative writing: A case of adult Japanese EFL learners. *Bilingual Research Journal, 42*(2), 232–251. https://doi.org/10.1080/15235882.2019.1589603

Velasco, P., & García, O. (2014). Translanguaging and the writing of bilingual learners. *Bilingual Research Journal, 37*(1), 6–23. https://doi.org/10.1080/15235882.2014.893270

Yang, S. (2013). *Autobiographical writing and identity in EFL education*. Routledge.

Zhou, X., & Mann, S. (2021). Translanguaging in a Chinese university CLIL classroom: Teacher strategies and student attitudes. *Studies in Second Language Learning and Teaching, 11*(2), 265–289. https://doi.org/10.14746/ssllt.2021.11.2.5

5
THE EMERGENCE OF TRANSLINGUALISM IN AN EFL WRITER'S LA

Shizhou Yang

A literacy autobiography (henceforth LA), also known as literacy narrative, is an individual's narrative of how he or she became literate in one or more languages. Since the 1980s, LA writing has become "a rite of passage or initiation of sorts" in tertiary education in North America (Schmertz, 2018, p. 280). LAs are also important in revealing the identity work of language professionals (Belcher & Connor, 2001) and ESL learners (Canagarajah, 2015, 2018, 2020; Kramsch, 2009; Steinman, 2007). In contrast, LAs are rarely used in the EFL environment (Fujieda & Iida, 2015). With two noticeable exceptions, LAs functioned mainly as data. Fujieda and Iida (2015) analyzed Japanese students' LAs to identify their challenges in English learning. Similarly, Qian (2019) used Chinese students' LAs to identify factors that affected their motivation for L2 academic writing.

Both studies used the EFL learners' LAs as primary data, with little attention to the contextual shaping of these texts and learners' subjectivities. As Canagarajah (2020) observed, "Composition research and pedagogy have not paid close attention to the procedures behind the writing and analysis of literacy narratives. Often the LAs are analyzed as self-standing products without consideration to what motivated their shaping" (p. 37). To rectify this tendency, Canagarajah (2015, 2018, 2020) suggested, based on his studies in North America, that multilinguals' LA writing should be examined ecologically to account for the writers' translingualism (Canagarajah, 2020). Similar studies about LA writing, however, are absent in EFL writing classrooms.

Therefore, more understanding about LAs in EFL contexts is still needed. Pedagogically, such knowledge will help writing teachers to utilize LAs productively and reflectively in their teaching. Theoretically, it will help us to reconceptualize translingualism for EFL writing education. Focusing on one Chinese EFL student Chen, I address the following three questions in this study:

1. How does the EFL classroom writing ecology shape Chen's LA writing?
2. How do transnational experiences motivate Chen's investment in LA writing?
3. How does such investment in turn shape translingualism in Chen's LA writing?

Theoretical Framework

I adopt an ecological theory of writing. Broadly speaking, it means that writing should be situated within its material, social, and historical contexts (Cooper, 1986; Guerrettaz & Johnson, 2013; Syverson, 1999), thus treating "the classroom as only one location within a larger writing ecology" (Lesh, 2019, p. 100). More specifically, a classroom writing ecology entails four main elements: (1) the *participants*, such as writers themselves and their peers; (2) *processes* such as drafting and revision; (3) *structure*, such as curriculum and institutional policies; and (4) *artifacts*, such as textbooks and students' writing (Canagarajah, 2020, pp. 102–104). To further contextualize classroom LA writing, we can map transnationalism, translingualism, and investment onto the classroom writing ecology.

For some critical literacy educators, transnationalism captures the contemporary life and literacy realities of multilingual writers, which include both increased ease of movement and information flow (Canagarajah, 2018, 2020; You, 2018). Canagarajah (2020, p. 5) claimed that multilingual writers today reside in a "transnational space" with diverse ties beyond national borders. Transnationalism can be experienced directly through relocation as well as exposure to "translocal resources through media, texts, and technology" (Canagarajah, 2020, p. 5). Therefore, theoretically speaking, a transnational lens should apply to EFL writers as well.

Canagarajah (2020) argued that by inhabiting a transnational space and engaging in LA writing, multilingual writers can redefine their identities. Instead of viewing themselves solely in terms of their ethnic origins or citizenship status, they can engage in a "trope of becoming" to refashion their preferred sense of self that features their transnational "footing" (p. 33). Canagarajah's own study of proficient ESL writers also found that "diverse historical, social, environmental, and rhetorical factors" shaped both these authors' LA writing and their identities, and that importantly, the pedagogical process is open to intervention (Canagarajah, 2020, p. 37). A pedagogy embracing translingual writing may encourage multilingual student writers to adopt a transnational stance and to textually perform their emergent translingual subjectivity.

Translingual writing contrasts with conventional writing in both its radical intention and hybrid textual features. Canagarajah (2016) defined it as "a form of situated literate practice where writers negotiate their semiotic resources in relation to the dominant conventions of language and rhetoric" (p. 266). In a classroom, translingual writing is jointly accomplished by the teacher and the students. It requires the teacher to model a *translingual orientation*, or "a perspective on languages as always in contact and generating new grammars and meanings out of their synergy" (Canagarajah, 2016, p. 266). It also challenges students to "draw from their repertoires to strategically negotiate their interests contextually"

(Canagarajah, 2016, p. 266). For the process to succeed, teachers need to affirm the following stances: (1) that a translingual orientation informs translingual writing; (2) that translingual writing results from writers' negotiation of dominant norms with their own semiotic or communicative repertoire; and (3) that writing teachers can adopt pedagogical practices that nurture their students' translingual orientation and engagement with translingual writing.

A similar term in a Chinese EFL context is productive bilingualism, which was proposed by Gao (2001, 2002) to capture a synergic cultural vision and language use resultant from bilingual proficiency. Gao (2001, 2002) defined productive bilingualism as "the command of the target language and that of the native language positively reinforce each other; deeper understanding and appreciation of the target culture goes hand in hand with deeper understanding and appreciation of the native culture" (see Gao et al., 2005, p. 40). An example statement for productive bilingualism goes as "With the improvement of my English proficiency, I can better appreciate the subtleties in Chinese" (Gao et al., 2005, p. 46). Gao's (2001, 2002) research revealed that productive bilingualism, succinctly expressed as "1+1>2," is not only a shared feature of "best foreign language learners" (Gao, 2001, 2002); it is also widely reported by Chinese college students, suggesting that productive bilingualism is achievable by common foreign language learners as well (Gao et al., 2005). Productive bilingualism and translingualism are thus similar in that both seek to transcend the limit of only one language or culture.

The two terms, however, differ in their theoretical orientations. Productive bilingualism features a psychological state, a desirable state of being a bilingual, in which one's heritage language and culture have formed a reciprocal relationship with an additional language and culture. In contrast, translingualism emphasizes language use as a social practice (Canagarajah, 2013). Furthermore, translingual scholars take a political stance against monolingualism (Horner, 2017; You, 2018), regarding translingualism as one of the "good myths" or language ideologies that affect language use (Canagarajah, 2020, p. 50). Canagarajah (2020) further suggested the notion of "rooted translingualism" to describe a multilingual writer's "appropriation of diverse semiotic resources, with a clear grounding in [their] own heritage community and its interests" (Canagarajah, 2020, p. 108). Through this grounding, translingualism goes beyond simply mixing languages or scripts for exotic "linguistic tourism" (Matsuda, 2014, p. 484) and performing "superdiversity" in Internet-mediated interactions (Blommaert, 2015) or "metroethnicity" in relating to diverse cultures in contemporary living (Maher, 2010), all of which promote playful and free-flowing meshing. An example of rooted translingualism is a Japanese student taking "ownership of Japanese" in her final LA drafts (Canagarajah, 2020, p. 116). More succinctly put, productive bilingualism emphasizes an enlarged vision through synergy without having to distinguish which culture dominates. In contrast, translingualism, especially rooted translingualism, seeks to foreground one's heritage identity in a context of hierarchical relation with the dominant English language. Therefore, translingualism seems more politically invested.

The concept of investment was first introduced to TESOL by Norton (2000) in her diary study of five immigrant women in Canada. It is relevant here because it can capture multilingual writers' writing-mediated identity work within the broad sociocultural context. As Norton (2000) argued, learners invest their resources in learning a language for the potential gain of becoming members of some *"imagined community."* Such desired memberships, which Norton called *"imagined identities,"* significantly shape learners' ways of learning, depending on their perceived relevance to the learners. From this perspective, becoming a translingual subject can be considered an imagined identity, which affects whether and how learners mobilize their diverse communicative resources in their language use.

Darvin and Norton's (2015) expanded framework reinforces this connection between investment and ideology. They contended that ideologies, defined as "dominant ways of thinking," interact with factors such as mobility to allow individuals to exercise "greater agency and capacity for resistance" (Darvin & Norton, 2015, p. 44). Interpreted from this framework, translingual writing is but one form of symbolic capital, the value of which may fluctuate when it enters a new context. Thus, it should be studied contextually.

This ecological theory of writing—merging transnationalism, translingualism, and investment—provides additional complexity and possibility. Transnationalism emphasizes multilingual writers' resources and "liminal identity" through their connections with "imagined and virtual communities" outside the immediate classroom context (Canagarajah, 2018, p. 42). The transnational space can then be seen as an extension and influencer of the classroom writing ecology. Translingualism points to the normalizing power of structure, which entails "dominant ideologies, policies, and norms in particular educational contexts" and which influences both the writing teacher and the students (Canagarajah, 2020, p. 104). Lastly, investment ties together the *who* (participants), *what* (artifacts), and *how* (processes) in any given writing activity. It highlights multilingual writers' writing as guided by a particular ideology, powered by particular imagined identities, and influenced by their affiliations with a particular transnational space. More importantly, it always involves the writers' agency in negotiating the value of their background within a particular sociocultural context. In this study, I approached my participant's LA writing and evolving subjectivity from such an ecological perspective.

The Study

Context

This study took place at a culturally and linguistically diverse university in southwest China, within a Master of Translation and Interpreting (MTI) program. The students were 41 first-year graduates majoring in Chinese and English translation, who took Intermediate Writing for Translators, a required course, 90 minutes a week for 18 weeks in their first semester. The students met with me, the instructor, in groups of 20 and 21, respectively.

I adapted Canagarajah (2020) ecological principles in teaching this course by introducing a multi-staged autoethnographic LA production as the main writing task. To necessitate revision and editing, I instructed the students to write their individual LAs as if each one would become a chapter of a self-published book. To inform their LA writing, I introduced three books: *Reflections on Multiliterate Lives* (Belcher & Connor, 2001), *Autoethnography as Method* (Chang, 2008), and *Transnational Literacy Autobiographies as Translingual Writing* (Canagarajah, 2020). For illustration, I also wrote my own LA and shared it with my class. Furthermore, I adopted a dialogical multi-draft pedagogy to encourage LA-centered interactions and revision. To facilitate peer interactions after class and for ease of collecting data, I used a paid version of a collaborative writing website, Kingsoft, and gave each student a folder in which they should upload their own documents and comment on each other's documents. These electronic portfolios would later become the primary research data, after written consent was granted.

Method

Teacher/researcher positionality: My evolving language ideology and theoretical positions have inevitably informed my teaching and shaped the data I collected. By the time I was teaching the course, I had debunked English monolingualism and regarded all languages and vernaculars as valuable communicative resources. I further endorsed translingualism for its communicative and pedagogical functions, even though I believed that within an EFL context, writing teachers still need to meet students' needs for standard written English. As a compromise, I adopted a process and translingual approach in teaching and allowed my students to use their multiple languages in their oral and written communication. However, I acknowledge that the resulting text should still feature standard written English.

Data collection: To capture LA writing within its classroom writing ecology, I adopted an ethnographic case study approach (Heath & Street, 2008). Data from the class included course artifacts, LA drafts (coded as D1, D2, etc.), weekly journals (J1, J2, etc.), interviews, an end-of-semester survey (S), teacher comments (TC), and peer comments (PC). A written interview used the 27 questions suggested by Belcher and Connor (2001), such as "How would you describe the education and literate [sic] activities (reading and/or writing) of current and preceding generations of your family?" It was completed at the beginning of the semester. Follow-up interviews were conducted via email correspondence. To facilitate triangulation and data interpretation, I kept weekly fieldnotes (F1, F2, etc.) to record my observations of and reflections on my teaching. To minimize negative influences of my role as both the writing instructor and the researcher, I did not start the study until all students had already received their course grades.

Case study participant: Chen was chosen as the case study participant because she was an instance of special interest. Even early in the program, she struck me as highly proficient in both Chinese and English and as possessing a rich family literacy experience, making her an informative subject on language-related issues.

Chen came from "a typical Chinese middle-class family" (D4) in a city in central China. Her parents work in hospitals and "are compulsive readers with good reading tastes and hobbies" (D4–D7). Her final LA featured her talent and accomplishments in learning to read and write in both Chinese and English, as supported by her parents and "commended" by many of her teachers. It effectively showcases the potential for EFL students' LA writing within a classroom context. I contacted Chen one year after the course ended. When she learned about the study, she gladly gave written consent for me to use all her course-related data and to conduct further interview.

Data analysis: My analysis was guided by both my research questions and theoretical framework described earlier. It was further facilitated by contextual approaches to analyzing autobiographical data (Pavlenko, 2007) and discourse (Gee, 1999; Pihlaja, 2018). The analyzing process thus involved the following steps: (a) analyzing Chen's LAs sentence by sentence for signs of transnationalism and translingualism; (b) comparing similarities and differences between Chen's LAs; (c) examining intertextual relationships between Chen's LAs and the specific texts and interactions in the classroom; (d) identifying ways in which Chen's LAs were shaped by "cultural models" or social norms (Gee, 1999, p. 59) of literacy; (e) identifying ways in which Chen's investment in LA writing was shaped by her identities and ideologies; (f) triangulating textual realities present in Chen's LAs through other data such as survey, interview, and classroom artifacts; and (g) member checking by integrating feedback from Chen.

Findings

The Influence of the Classroom Writing Ecology on Chen's LA Writing

The classroom writing ecology shaped Chen's LA writing in significant ways. Chen herself, of course, played the central role as an autoethnographic researcher and writer. She actively invested in LA-related activities: researching her own life and literacy experiences, reading recommended books, collecting and analyzing her data, and drafting and revising her LA. Chen's active investment was evidenced by her portfolio, which contained seven LA drafts, one survey response, seven self-selected references, six peer feedback artifacts, two drawings with labels, and 12 journal entries.

As the course instructor, I guided Chen's research and writing process. Chen had a very vague notion of LA writing and autoethnographic research at the beginning (interview, January 2, 2020). Her early drafts, including those composed outside class, were often short, at times ambiguous or incomplete. Her later drafts gradually took shape as scaffolded by my explanation of LAs and the materials I shared with the class. As Chen recalled:

> At first, you [the teacher] explained the meaning of LA, which set the foundation for our later LA writing. Then, when I was writing my LA, I read your LA and the documents you uploaded many times, which was really helpful in organizing the structure and content of my LA. Once I decided the

different sections and headings, I selected the experiences I wanted to include in my LA. I then summarized some theories that could be used to explain my experience, related to them, and completed my LA.

(Interview, September 4, 2020; my translation from Chinese)

Chen also found that the teacher was guiding the class's autoethnographic writing week by week, fulfilling the steps outlined in the course syllabus, until the individual stories culminated in a complete project (interview, January 2, 2020).

Mediated by the online platform accessible to everyone in the class, I influenced Chen's revision through my feedback. Chen's earlier drafts were merely storytelling. In her LA draft 3, for instance, she recounted a teacher's influence on her:

> She [The middle school English teacher] always commended every progress I made in English writing and read the compositions I wrote in front of the whole class. … she really cared and have [sic] a high expectation on me. Ever since then, I have never read comic books in her class, in order not to fail her.
>
> (D3)

In the margin of her text, I commented: "What an interesting story of how a teacher influenced a student's investment in English learning! Might be possible to relate to the concept of 'investment' in a poststructuralist theory" (TC, October 24, 2019). These comments and my emphasis in class about the need for theories contributed to Chen's adoption of the term "investment" in her later drafts to summarize her middle-school teacher's impact on her English learning: "Hence, my investment in English learning in junior and senior high school was greatly fueled by her commendations and encouragements" (D4, D5, D6).

Additionally, Chen's peers played a supporting role. Although Chen claimed that "I didn't exchange ideas with my peers when I wrote my LA, I just wrote it alone" (email, November 1, 2020), she did actually share her draft with one classmate during a class peer review session (artifact, December 18, 2019). Three main questions were asked in the peer feedback form: "Is the draft narrative enough?" "Is the draft autoethnographic enough?" and "Is the LA academic enough?" The responding classmate marked all three areas and related subdimensions as "great." Therefore, the feedback did not cause her to make any changes.

Nonetheless, the multi-draft process helped Chen's LA to gradually take shape. Chen's early drafts were rather short and general. For instance, her first draft, which used my suggested title "My Feeling about Chinese and English Writing," had only three paragraphs, no in-text citations or references, and virtually no support for her opinions. In her first paragraph she wrote, "Little difference do I feel in the Chinese and English writing." She then contrasted the two: "It is typical of people to making an assumption before the deduction, giving the result before analyzing the reasons, which is the complete opposite of the Chinese writing and is quite worthy of our attention." In her second paragraph, she juxtaposed Han Yu, a Chinese poet from the Tang Dynasty, with Hemingway, stating that they had a similar literary style, which is also her preferred style for writing: "Every word you write should carry meanings, flowery but empty words should be omitted in the processing of writing" (D1). She then concluded: "As for my feelings about Chinese and English writing, so long as you develop a suitable prose style for yourself, you can find both of them very entertaining" (D1).

Benefiting from the multi-stage writing process, Chen's later drafts began to take on additional autoethnographic features. Important details were added to make her story interesting. Her initial mention of an English teacher now grew into several paragraphs featuring the teacher's appearance, character, ways of teaching, and impact on her. Several scholarly references were added, compared to none in drafts D1 through D3, to make her narrative more academic. Additionally, she adopted the department's preferred reference style, as introduced in the writing course. Cultural analysis and interpretation were incorporated to qualify her LA as an autoethnographic narrative. For instance, in her early draft, Chen merely named literary works that had influenced her, without making any connection with culture (D1). In contrast, her later drafts articulated the cultural influences more clearly; D6 used the words "culture" and "cultural" seven times. As she wrote, "Actually, my literacy is deeply rooted in Chinese culture." This added cultural analysis might have been facilitated by the class activity of each student sharing five proverbs and sayings that had influenced him or her (artifact, October 17, 2019).

Furthermore, the artifacts, including textbooks, writing samples, and handouts, facilitated Chen's LA writing. Besides the three books mentioned earlier, some class handouts featured my own literacy experiences, cultural interpretations, and connections with academic publications. Other handouts were designed to deepen the students' understanding of autoethnographic research and writing conventions used in the department. Some lessons were aimed to help the students to "identify features in written texts that make them academic" and "integrate similar features in [their] own revision" (lesson plan, week 7).

Lastly, the program structure positioned Chen culturally while also familiarizing her with MTI academic writing. It includes the requirement to take Intermediate Writing for Translators in the first semester, writing a thesis based on translation practice, and milestone activities such as a proposal defense and thesis defense. Taking an academic literacies perspective (Lea & Street, 2006), I required my students to observe and reflect on one proposal defense. From this activity, Chen learned three important lessons about how translation students should engage in academic writing in the department: avoiding excessive quotation, attending to details, and emphasizing theory (J4), all of which were also introduced in the writing course. With regard to details, Chen wrote:

> It is the details that really count. The details that students should pay their attention to comprise punctuation marks, case sensitivity and proper names of various places, etc. Teachers fixed their eyes on those details, once you neglect them, criticism will be heaped on.
>
> *(J4)*

Thus, the classroom writing ecology—which involves important participants such as the instructor and the peers, artifacts such as handouts, processes such as drafting and revision, and structure such as curriculum—played an important role in shaping Chen's LA writing.

Chen's Investment in LA Writing as Motivated by Transnationalism

Transnationalism manifested in Chen's reading of foreign literature, as initially guided by her mother. During her first library trip, her mother recommended two American books: Helen Keller's *Three Days to See* and Mark Twain's *The Adventures of Tom Sawyer* (D7). Chen's earlier drafts also revealed how her subjectivity and literary tastes were influenced by foreign literature. For instance, she wrote:

> At that time, I am very much into reading such fantasy and adventure novels as *Harry Potter, Tom Sawyer* and the science fictions written by Jules Verne, for they opened a decidedly fresh new world to me, and made me believe that though we human beings are shackled to the earth, some of us can still look at the stars. *Influenced by these books, I have a taste for the prose style that is concise, scientific and accurate, instead of flowery but empty words.*
>
> (D2, emphasis mine)

Foreign literature has not only introduced to Chen a broad transnational space, but also motivated her to write with "the prose style that is concise, scientific and accurate."

Foreign literature provided Chen with a way to interpret her experience. One example illustrates well the profound impact foreign literature has had on her:

> Pavel Korchagin, protagonist of *The Making of a Hero*, got a hurt in his eyes in a brutal war. When he recuperated, the writer goes like this, "he sees this world as if he saw it for the first time." It also applies to me; I feel like a new-born who see the world for the very first time through reading every new book, without which my world will still be in a chaotic state with no sunshine.
>
> (D7)

Here, Chen did not stop at describing the Russian character Korchagin's experience by quoting him. She went further by elaborating, "I feel like a new-born … without which [every new book] my world will still be in a chaotic state." She was thus using a foreign writer's words as a springboard for her own voice about the importance of reading. Therefore, although Chen's transnational reading experience did not in itself lead her to compose her LA, when such an opportunity presented itself in the writing course, she was able to draw on her transnational reading experience as a resource to inform her LA writing.

Similarly, Chen also expanded her communicative resources through her extensive exposure to transnational music, that is, "pop music in English and western rock." As she explained,

> I'm really interested in pop music in English and western rock. They helped me with both my pronunciation and English writing. After I listened to English songs, I would remember some expressions unconsciously and use them in my English writing in middle school and high school. My English teacher praised me for that.
> *(Email, February 3, 2021, my translation from Chinese)*

Although I cannot identify ways in which this transnational relationship motivated Chen's LA writing, her *autobiographical self* or habitus-like sense of self rooted in her past literacy experience (Ivanič, 1998) inevitably influenced her LA writing.

Transnationalism, however, indirectly motivated Chen's investment in LA writing. As her writing instructor, I have brought into the writing class a plethora of transnational relations such as a transnational family, training in English-speaking countries, and most tangibly, books and theories, as well as the idea of LA writing, from North America. Furthermore, Chen wrote her LA in English at a time in Chinese history when transnational connections were treated more favorably than in some earlier times. It would have been less likely for her to write her LA in this way during the Great Cultural Revolution period (1966–1976), when even the learning of English was discouraged. At any rate, her own prior transnational reading experiences and external transnational influences informed her in her investment in LA writing and shaped her translingual subjectivities. Even though Chen has never crossed the national border, she has developed a transnational vision and translingual orientation through reading foreign literature, learning English, listening to western music, and investing actively in writing her LA in the class.

Investment and Rooted Translingualism

Chen's sustained investment in LA writing and related research within the classroom context allowed her to revisit and revise her initial articulations about her literacy experiences. Her final LA draft (D7) told her story of becoming literate first in Chinese and then in English. It situated her literacy experiences—mostly positive—in relation to her parents, teachers, and friends. Even though Chen never used the term "translingualism" herself, her final draft seemed to show multiple strong signs of translingualism, and possibly "rooted translingualism" (Canagarajah, 2020). For example, she concluded by stating that "as Chinese people, our voice rooted in Chinese culture must be manifested in our writings." Rooted translingualism seemed also evident in her appreciative stance of Chinese culture:

> Actually, my literacy is deeply rooted in Chinese culture, "One has to convey in a language that is not one's own the spirit that is one's own. ... We cannot

write like the English, we should not" (Raja Rao, 1938). Hence, if used properly, I believe my Chinese thinking pattern, cultural background and unique Chinese rhetorical devices will add to my writings' literary grace, like special oriental spices added into western food, chemistry will be produced between my L1 and L2.

(D7)

In her statement, "my literacy is deeply rooted in Chinese culture," Chen expressed her agreement with the Indian writer Raja Rao's position, "We cannot write like the English, we should not." Importantly, Chen used the metaphor of mixing "special oriental spices" with Western food to suggest that her "Chinese thinking pattern, cultural background and unique Chinese rhetorical devices" can actually "add to [her] writings' literary grace." This implies that she did not consider her Chinese heritage a problem, but a resource, which could enrich her English writing. However, it may be too hasty to suggest this is definitely a sign of rooted translingualism. After all, English remains the dominant language in her LA and Chinese is only added as "spices." It is therefore safer to suggest this to be a case of translingualism or productive bilingualism.

This translingual trait or productive bilingualism also appeared in Chen's discussions on Chinese classics. According to her LA (D4–D7), two Chinese classics, 《菜根谭》 (*Tending the Roots of Wisdom*) and 《曾国藩家书》 (*Home Letters from the Marquis Zeng Guofan*), especially "shaped my view of the world." Her "parents' favorites," these books "contain plain yet sophisticated ancient philosophical thoughts of Chinese people." She then cited three quotations from the first classic, followed by her own translation. One of them was presented as follows:

"肥辛甘非真味， 真味只是淡； 神奇卓异非至人， 至人只是常" (Real flavour does not lie in refined liquors or sumptuous dishes; only plain food gives forth a pure taste. The man who has attained the realm of perfect virtue is not the wonder maker who stands out from all his fellows. He is found among the run-of-the-mill).

(D7)

These Chinese classics taught Chen about "plain" and "pure" tastes, as well as "the realm of perfect virtue." More importantly, they have shaped her identity. They "have cultivated my moral character and enabled me to have a clearer vision of the world, of who I am, and of my position in this world" (D4). In view of this profound impact of Chinese classics on her, Chen fittingly described Chinese culture as the "root" and "soil" of her literacy in English (D7).

Another sign of Chen's translingualism or productive bilingualism can be found in her alignment with "an unadorned style" in writing, which she first developed through her literacy experiences in Chinese. At first, Chen attributed its formation to reading a Chinese contemporary writer, Lu Yao (D4), but in a later draft, she traced it further back to a Tang poet, Han Yu:

During my high school years, I have developed a taste for an unadorned style of writing after I took a class about Han Yu, a famous poet of mid-Tang-dynasty, who claims that writings should be meant to convey ideas and ethics. To put it in another way, every word you write should carry meanings, flowery but empty words should be omitted in the processing of writing. This taste has been embodied in my L2 writing, too. I like Ernest Hemingway, who is famous for his concise and informative writing style, which has also exerted a positive influence on my writing.

(D7)

Chen practiced translingualism or productive bilingualism because even before she applied the "unadorned style" in her L2 writing, and before she encountered Hemingway's writing style, she had already embraced the style as advocated by Han, a Chinese poet. At any rate, Chen displayed consistently through her story that her sense of self is rooted in Chinese culture and its literary traditions.

Discussion

This study has considered an EFL student's LA writing from a writing classroom ecology perspective. As in Canagarajah's (2015, 2020) study of ESL students' LA writing, Chen's LA writing was shaped by *participants* in the writing course, a dialogical and multi-draft *process* of teaching and a concurrent *process* of autoethnographic research, *artifacts* of the writing class, and *structure* such as the course curriculum and the department's preferred reference style. It provides empirical evidence about the complex and dynamic interactions between LA writing and writing ecology (Canagarajah, 2020; Syverson, 1999) in an EFL context, yielding new insights about transnationalism and translingualism.

Transnationalism featured in Chen's LA and literacy experiences through her extensive exposure to foreign literature and "pop music in English and western rock." Later, within the classroom writing ecology, she was exposed to and encouraged to integrate theories from transnational sources. It confirms the claim that, even within an EFL context where language learners have not physically crossed national boundaries, transnationalism is still pertinent through "transnational space" and "translocal resources" (Canagarajah, 2020, p. 5), which "complement their English verbal resources" (p. 97). This recognition can support writing scholars as they counter monolingualism through transnational writing education (You, 2018). Chen's story provides a glimpse into EFL student writers' unique transnational spaces (Canagarajah, 2020). It showcases the role of EFL writing classrooms as fertile *contact zones* (Pratt, 1991) for hybrid practices and subjectivity reformation, as mediated by LA writing. As other studies have shown, multilinguals do not have fixed deficit-featuring identities; their identities can be re-imagined along storylines featuring their bilingual and multilingual resources (Pavlenko, 2003), transnational affiliations (Yazan, et al., 2021), and emergent translingual orientation (Canagarajah, 2020).

The theme of translingualism (Canagarajah, 2020, p. 108) and "productive bilingualism" (Gao, 2001) was prominent in Chen's later LA writing. It was shown through her mixed use of Chinese and English (languages and literary values) in her final LAs and her expressed need for all Chinese—English bilinguals to develop a "voice rooted in Chinese culture." However, it is questionable whether Chen's case can be interpreted as evidence to counter the "English+" bias in translingual scholarship (Canagarajah & Gao, 2019, p. 1). It is further questionable whether Chen's unique metaphor in her final LA, that is, "like special oriental spices added into western food" can be interpreted as rooted translingualism per se. After all, Chen was a unique case from a privileged family background, which had already prepared her for transnational affiliations and translingual writing. It was possible that her extensive exposure to and expertise in Chinese—English literacy have already equipped her to marshal and synergize her bilingual resources in her LA writing. The classroom writing ecology, as assisted by a dialogical, multi-draft, and autoethnographic approach to teaching LA writing, contributed but some nurturing effects to facilitate Chen's revisit and reappreciation of the resources that she had already accumulated. Thus, her case should not be taken as representing other EFL learners, including those in her class. Instead, she is more comparable to Kyoko and other ESL students in Canagarajah's (2020) study, who have already achieved advanced language proficiency to attend a graduate program in a leading university in the USA. The dynamic nature of multilingual writers' identity work (Shuck, 2010; Yang, 2013, 2018), with due attention to their biographical histories, can thus go hand in hand with the malleable nature of LA writing to shape multilingual writers' translingual contours (Canagarajah, 2020), resulting in productive bilingualism (Gao, 2001).

Chen's investment in LA writing is worth pondering. Beyond the initial impact of her upbringing, it was partly related to the symbolic capital (Darvin & Norton, 2015) of Chinese and English, the two dominant languages in contemporary China, and partly to her imagined identity. However, Chen's investment did not seem to point to imagined identities that feature native speakers, L2 learners, or L2 users, as found in an early study (Pavlenko, 2003). Instead, her imagined identity as a writer influenced both her early investment in L1 writing and her later investment in L2 writing. Moreover, it was significantly shaped by her personal ideology of reading as life-enriching and self-revealing, enabling her to "have a clearer vision of the world, of who I am, and my position in this world" (D7). Similarly, she saw writing as long-lasting: "Only through writing can we leave an indelible imprint on the world" (D4–D7). This personal ideology shaped her willing investment in and positive attitude toward L1 and L2 writing. As she wrote, "Never in my life have I thought writing is a drudgery, and I have maintained a positive attitude for both Chinese and English writing since then" (D6). Chen's story thus supports Darvin and Norton's (2015) framework that considers investment alongside capital, ideology, and identity. However, even this framework can be expanded to include still another factor: a writer's level of enjoyment when engaging in literacy activities. In Chen's case, writing was a natural outgrowth from reading: "I really enjoy the process of weighing each word. If I have to trace some origin, I think it is because I have read and accumulated enough to enjoy writing" (email, February 3, 2021; my translation from Chinese).

Conclusion and Implications

Ecological explorations of LA writing are rare within the EFL context. This classroom-based case study thus contributes important knowledge. It reveals the profound impact exerted by the classroom writing ecology on an EFL student writer's LAs. It further reveals the writer's investment as motivated by her transnational literacy experience both during and prior to the writing course. Last, it reveals the writer's translingualism (Canagarajah, 2020) or productive bilingualism (Gao, 2001, 2002), as exemplified by her statement "like special oriental spices added into western food," was influenced by her active investment in LA writing, privileged prior literacy experiences in Chinese and English, and supported explorations of these experiences. These findings confirm the insight that, LA writing, situated within a nurturing classroom writing ecology, can facilitate multilinguals' identity work in progress (Canagarajah, 2015, 2018, 2020).

Teacher researchers who are motivated to expand pedagogical use of LA in their own contexts are strongly encouraged to read and adapt Canagarajah's (2020, pp. 141–153) syllabi and activities. In addition, the following list of actions may serve as a quick reference because it summarizes my adaptations:

1. Provide a rationale for and description about LA writing;
2. Create a need for revision (e.g., writing for publication);
3. Integrate autoethnographic research;
4. Engage the class in reading and discussing other multilinguals' LA;
5. Make it dialogic;
6. View learners' languages and literacies as resources;
7. Write and share your own LA with your students.

Last, teachers who want to study LA writing in their own classrooms may consider using online folders to facilitate data collection and group interactions. However the LA is used pedagogically, as writing teachers, we should design our classroom writing ecology to encourage, model, and nurture effective ways of drawing upon our life, language, and literacy resources.

The findings of this case study concerning translingualism, however, should not be generalized to other EFL contexts uncritically. Readers interested in this topic should note three tensions that I have wrestled with in adopting a translingual approach in my particular EFL context. First, there seemed to me a mismatch of functions. The translingual scholarship in the ESL context is often politically motivated to challenge the dominant monolingual ideology in educational institutions. In contrast, such an ideology was not apparent in my institution, which did not mandate English as *the* language of instruction and my students, majoring in Chinese and English translation, were already moving back and forth between the two languages.

Second, depending on the languages in use, translingualism seemed to favor a selected few, such as Chen in the current study. Growing up in a privileged family with rich transnational literacy experiences, Chen deployed her Chinese and English linguistic and literacy resources effectively in LA writing, particularly her later drafts. In contrast, although I had encouraged my ethnic minority students to integrate their heritage languages and scripts in their LAs, none of them did. The absence of non-English and -Chinese scripts in my students' LA writing is worth pondering. One reason is that they actually did not know how to write in their own languages, which take a relatively marginal status in Chinese educational system. Translingualism within this particular EFL context thus encounters a thorny issue: not all languages are equal in their actual use. Whether a language makes its way into a translingual text depends on many factors, including, for instance, the language's current sphere of influence and the user's proficiency and literacy level in that language. These factors suggest that similar pedagogical explorations of translingualism in the EFL context may need further localization and require additional pedagogical support. Possibly, a less politicized pedagogical goal such as *productive bilingualism* (Gao, 2001, 2002) should be promoted more in the EFL context instead. This is especially true in the case of rooted translingualism, which, if used to promote the interests of ethnic minority communities, may be interpreted by authorities as the students or the teacher taking a political stance against official ideologies.

The third tension concerns standard written English and deviations in the EFL context. Although in my teaching practice, especially in class interactions and my students' early LA drafts, I was largely tolerant of their grammar and spelling mistakes, I saw it as my duty to teach them standard written English valued by the local institution. I adopted two strategies for this purpose. One strategy was requiring my students to observe a thesis defense in the department, which exposed my students to ways academic writing was commonly evaluated. As Chen recorded: "Teachers fixed their eyes on those details [such as punctuation marks], once you neglect them, criticism will be heaped on" (J4). The other strategy was to arrange revision workshops, which included activities such as providing guided peer feedback and studying sample theses from the department, in the latter part of the semester to facilitate the use of standard written English. To me, the teaching of translingual writing has to go hand in hand with the teaching of standard written English to really serve these EFL student writers. Otherwise, a translingual pedagogy may do a disservice to these writers as they engage in high-stake academic writing such as their graduation thesis.

References

Belcher, D., & Connor, U. (2001). *Reflections on multiliterate lives*. Multilingual Matters.
Blommaert, J. (2015). Commentary: Superdiversity old and new. *Language and Communication*, *44*(1), 82–89. http://dx.doi.org/10.1016/j.langcom.2015.01.003

Canagarajah, A. (2013). *Translingual practice: Global Englishes and cosmopolitan relations*. Routledge.
Canagarajah, A. S. (2015). "Blessed in my own way": Pedagogical affordances for dialogical voice construction in multilingual student writing. *Journal of Second Language Writing, 27*, 122–139. https://doi.org/10.1016/j.jslw.2014.09.001
Canagarajah, A. S. (2016). Translingual writing and teacher development in composition. *College English, 78*(3), 265–273.
Canagarajah, A. S. (2018). Transnationalism and translingualism: How they are connected. In X. You (Ed.), *Transnational writing education: Theory, history, and practice* (pp. 41–60). Routledge.
Canagarajah, A. S. (2020). *Transnational literacy autobiographies as translingual writing*. Routledge.
Canagarajah, S., & Gao, X. (2019). Taking translingual scholarship farther. *English Teaching & Learning, 43*(1), 1–3. https://doi.org/10.1007/s42321-019-00023-4
Chang, H. (2008). *Autoethnography as method*. Left Coast Press.
Cooper, M. (1986). The ecology of writing. *College English, 48*(4), 364–375. https://doi.org/10.2307/377264
Darvin, R., & Norton, B. (2015). Identity and a model of investment in applied linguistics. *Annual Review of Applied Linguistics, 35*, 36–56. https://doi.org/10.1017/S0267190514000191
Fujieda, Y., & Iida, A. (2015). Literacy autobiography in EFL contexts: Investigating Japanese student language learning experiences. In D. Shaffer, & M. Pinto (Eds.), *Embracing change: Blazing new frontiers through language teaching (proceedings of the KOTESOL/KAFLE International Conference)* (pp. 97–104). Korea TESOL Organization.
Gao, Y. (2001). *Foreign language learning: 1 + 1 > 2*. Beijing University Press.
Gao, Y. (2002). Productive bilingualism: 1 + 1 > 2. In W. C. D. So, & G. M. Gary (Eds.), *Education and society in plurilingual contexts* (pp. 143–162). VUB Brussels University Press.
Gao, Y. G., Cheng, Y., Zhao, Y., & Zhou, Y. (2005). Self-identity changes and English learning among Chinese undergraduates. *World Englishes, 24*(1), 39–51. https://doi.org/10.1111/j.0883-2919.2005.00386.x
Gee, J. P. (1999). *An introduction to discourse analysis: Theory and method*. Routledge.
Guerrettaz, A. M., & Johnson, B. (2013). Materials in the classroom ecology. *Modern Language Journal, 97*, 779–796. https://doi.org/10.1111/j.1540-4781.2013.12027.x
Heath, S. B., & Street, B. V. (2008). *Ethnography: Approaches to language and literacy research*. Teachers College Press.
Horner, B. (2017). Teaching translingual agency in iteration: Rewriting difference. In B. Horner, & L. Tetreault (Eds.), *Crossing divides* (pp. 87–97). University Press of Colorado.
Ivanič, R. (1998). *Writing and identity*. John Benjamins.
Kramsch, C. (2009). *The multilingual subject*. Oxford University Press.
Lea, M., & Street, B. (2006). The "academic literacies" model: Theory and applications. *Theory into Practice, 45*(4), 368–377. https://doi.org/10.1207/s15430421tip4504_11
Lesh, C. N. (2019). Writing workshops in the public turn. *Composition Studies, 47*(2), 87–107.
Maher, J. C. (2010). Metroethnicities and metrolanguages. In N. Coupland (Ed.), *The handbook of language and globalization* (pp. 575–591). Wiley-Blackwell.
Matsuda, P. K. (2014). The lure of translingual writing. *PMLA, 129*(3), 478–483.
Norton, B. (2000). *Identity and language learning: Gender, ethnicity and educational change*. Pearson Education.
Pavlenko, A. (2003). "I never knew I was a bilingual": Reimagining teacher identities in TESOL. *Journal of Language, Identity & Education, 2*(4), 251–268. http://dx.doi.org/10.1207/S15327701JLIE0204_2

Pavlenko, A. (2007). Autobiographic narratives as data in applied linguistics. *Applied Linguistics*, *28*(2), 163–188. https://doi.org/10.1093/applin/amm008

Pihlaja, S. (2018). Discourse analysis. In P. Seargeant, A. Hewings, & S. Pihlaja (Eds.), *The Routledge handbook of English language studies* (1st ed., pp. 379–391). Routledge. https://doi.org/10.4324/9781351001724-26

Pratt, M. L. (1991). Arts of the contact zone. *Profession*, *91*, 33–40.

Qian, Y. (2019). Motivation to English academic writing: Chinese students' literacy autobiography. *Theory and Practice in Language Studies*, *9*(5), 530–536. http://doi.org/10.17507/tpls.0905.06

Rao, R. (1938). *Kanthapura*. George Allen & Unwin.

Schmertz, J. (2018). Writing our academic selves: The literacy autobiography as performance. *Pedagogy*, *18*(2). 279–293. https://doi.org/10.1215/15314200-4359197

Shuck, G. (2010). Language identity, agency, and context: The shifting meanings of multilingual. In M. Cox, J. Jordan, C. Ortmeier-Hooper, & G. G. Schwartz (Eds.), *Reinventing identities in second language writing* (pp. 117–138). NCTE.

Steinman, L. (2007). Literacy autobiographies in a university ESL class. *Canadian Modern Language Review*, *63*(4), 563–573. http://doi.org/10.3138/cmlr.63.4.563

Syverson, M. A. (1999). *The wealth of reality: An ecology of composition*. Southern Illinois University Press.

Yang, S. (2013). *Autobiographical writing and identity in EFL education*. Routledge.

Yang, S. (2018). Potential phases of multilingual writers' identity work. In X. You (Ed.), *Transnational writing education: Theory and practice* (pp. 115–137). Routledge.

Yazan, B., Canagarajah, S., & Jain, R. (Eds.). (2021). *Autoethnographies in ELT: Transnational identities, pedagogies, and practices*. Routledge.

You, X. (Ed.). (2018). *Transnational writing education: Theory, history, and practice*. Routledge.

6
VOICE CONSTRUCTION BEYOND TRANSLINGUALISM

Shizhou Yang

金箍套身心，落笔书伤痕。
作者有新声，超语资源论。

Diary #1: March 5, 2022. (Bangkok time)

    The task of analyzing, interpreting, and writing about literacy autobiographies (LAs) by 11 EFL writers, including my own, with a focus on translingualism feels like preparing for international travel during COVID-19—a mission impossible. About an hour ago, I took my family for a COVID-19 antigen test so that we can fly from Thailand to Hawaii tomorrow. We are still waiting for the results as I type this sentence. Similarly, moving translingualism from its center in the Global North to its periphery in the Global South, as necessary as that may be (Canagarajah, 2022; Canagarajah & Gao, 2019), is a trans-Atlantic intellectual journey filled with its own uncertainties. Although the destination is set, I struggle with both content and form, both texts and their boundaries, and—not least—with practices of the Global North and realities in the Global South. Adding to the complexity is the need to view these LAs in their contexts (Canagarajah, 2020; Pavlenko, 2007). Nonetheless, as an autoethnographic researcher, I must embrace these tensions and negotiate translingualism on my own terms. To turn my marginal place into a vantage point, I will use the four lines of my Chinese poem, introduced at the beginning of this chapter, and combine it with letters, diaries, and poetic inquiry to argue that we should reconceptualize translingualism in understanding EFL writers' literate identities, as constructed and revealed through their LAs. By doing so, I hope to join other Chinese writing scholars who regard personal writing such as narrative and the ancient style of *sanwen* 散文 (scattered writings) as a critical subcurrent in Chinese composition history (You, 2010).

金箍套身心 Spellbound to a Master

Diary #2: March 5, 2022 (Bangkok time)

The COVID-19 antigen test results finally arrived at noon, in an email. "Bravo! All negative!" We are now sitting in a row at our gate, waiting to fly to Bangkok in two hours. It's so ironic that our travels have become so dependent on a single test. COVID-19 has become a dominant narrative of our time since early 2020. Strangely, in composing LAs, I felt that both my students and myself have been confined to something invisible, yet truly powerful.

> *Spellbound*
>
> I am like the Monkey King
> Abnormally born
> Out of a stone
> Hairy and speaking like other monkeys in the mountain
> —"Southern Barbarians"—
> Cursed and confined under the Great Wall of civilization.
> A monk rescued me
> To follow his cause of a great mission.
> His Buddhist spell binds
> My skull.

In my LA, which I first composed with my students, I did not dare to share some parts of my family history. For instance, I did not mention that my grandfather was killed by the government, which first labeled him a "landlord" and then executed him based on false accusations. Although he was absolved of his "crime" about 50 years after his death, the physical violence of the powerful other and its lasting pain on my family could not be healed easily. LA writing, like other self-narratives, is political in the Chinese context, with the authorities demanding that any personal storytelling must fit into their master narrative. In this case, the narrative—told and retold in songs I sang, TV shows I watched, history books I read, even the slogan I saw every day on the wall of my elementary classroom—features the ruling party as the savior. Any dissonant expression concerning this official storyline, be it about language, literacy, or (more recently) COVID-19, means trouble.

Likewise, my classroom teaching was not autonomous. My colleagues and I all knew—from meetings we attended and news on the WeChat messages that we read—that several Chinese professors had been sacked because of saying something radical or ideologically problematic when teaching. Having been educated in the West and having embraced a Christian faith, I was kindly warned to be careful, particularly about sharing my faith. Therefore, in writing my LA and demonstrating how it could be written, I was inevitably practicing self-censorship to fashion and refashion my multidimensional realities (Pavlenko, 2007), just to stay safe. At times, I felt like the Monkey King in the Chinese classic 西游记 (*Journey to the West*), spellbound by his Buddhist master. As a descendant of the "南蛮"

(Southern Barbarians)—a term used by Han historians of the Tang Dynasty (618–907) to refer to the mountain dwellers, yak riders, and others living in southwest China (Southeast Asia Program, 1961)—I needed someone to civilize me. First, I needed to get rid of my dialect and avoid my mother's Naxi language. I needed to "说普通话, 做文明人" (speak Mandarin; be civilized), just as a slogan on my university campus, as well as in my children's Chinese school, decreed. Second, I needed to improve my substandard English and, ideally, write like an American. That was, at least, part of my journey as recounted in Chapter 2. Thus, I composed my LA under the influence of dominant cultural narratives in China.

The same is true with my students' LAs. Pavlenko (2007) suggested that, in analyzing autobiographical data, we should attend not only to the written but also to the unwritten content. About this kind of sociocultural shaping, silence often speaks louder than words. Going through my students' LAs, coding them paragraph by paragraph with the qualitative analysis software ATLAS.ti 9, and then turning to poetic inquiry to capture what my students did not mention, I noticed some interesting absences.

Absences

Not a single word of
Religion
—a forbidden subject
— in today's Communist China.
Nor any trace of critique or doubt
About the many signs in public, "Please speak Mandarin!"
Even the Christian student I know
Wrote only,
"I was inspired by my girlfriend
Shakespeare's poems
And Second Language Acquisition (SLA)."

Diary #3: March 5, 2022

The flight to Bangkok was smooth. Soon after my family checked into our hotel, everyone went straight to sleep, except me. Like me, my students in China have been spellbound in our storytelling; the government's ideology shapes not only what we do not write in our LAs, but also what we do write. Recall Chen's LA in Chapter 5, which articulates a voice "rooted in Chinese culture." This personal embrace of Chinese culture echoes the central government's call for its citizens to embody "文化自信" (cultural confidence) in China's 5,000 years of traditions and, more recently, in the Communists' revolutionary and socialist culture (Xi, 2016). That invisible spell is the official and therefore power-filled discourse of the ruling party—an "authoritative discourse," or some truth-sounding statement from powerful others that makes negotiation impossible (Bakhtin, 1981, p. 343). On one hand, it legitimizes expressions of obedience, agreement, and loyalty; on the other hand, it condemns expressions of dissonance, disagreement, and disloyalty.

Therefore, Chen wrote her LA under the weight of that invisible ideological spell. So did my other students and myself.

Another invisible spell concerns the form of writing, particularly the institutionally transmitted norms. Wang Y. wrote: "My writings have not been improved much because I continue to use the same model as I used in middle school. Exam-oriented writing templates make me have no time thinking [sic] about what writing really is" (80:1 ¶ 1 in Weekly Journal#16_Wang Y). Similarly, Shi wrote in her LA:

> Meanwhile, as most of the teachers in China who only focused on the imparting of writing skills but ignored the development of our writing interest and ability, seldom did my writing teacher guide us how to write essays step by step. He just provided us with writing temples [templates] to fight against exams, which was a test taking strategy helping us improve scores quickly, but impeding the "cognitive development" (Ferris & Hedgcock, 2005) for us to acquire.
>
> *(128:8 ¶ 6 in LA_Shi WJ)*

These instances reveal the dominance of a mechanical approach to EFL writing education that features the use of templates to produce essays suitable for passing exams. Therefore, although my students have not suffered any physical violence, as my grandfather did, through this kind of template-based writing education they are victims of a type of "symbolic violence." Bourdieu (2001) defined symbolic violence as "a gentle violence, imperceptible and invisible even to its victims, exerted for the most part through the purely symbolic channels of communication and cognition (more precisely, misrecognition, recognition, or even feeling)" (pp. 1–2). Through reflection partially mediated by LA writing, my students have begun to narrate the lasting and ill effects that these invisible spells have exerted on them through formal education.

落笔书伤痕 Writing the Wound

Diary #4: March 8, 2022

No two foreign language learners learn the same way—that is, with the same intention, under the same conditions, and with the identical outcome. A few months ago, our first son started to learn Japanese by himself, using Duolingo. As linguists who encourage multilingualism, his mother and I gave him two books on the Japanese language to celebrate his birthday. He has already become a fluent speaker of both Chinese and English. He has also learned some Thai and developed a positive attitude toward language learning. However, the situation can be very different for my students, and even for myself, as we mainly learned the dominant languages through formal education.

My student Li L. provides an example. Like me, Li L. is Naxi (one of the 55 officially recognized ethnic minority groups in China), and she grew up in the countryside. Whereas I never learned more than a few words of the language,

Li L. spoke Naxi as her first language. However, this experience was associated with pain for her. In her survey response as well as her multiple LA drafts, she described a traumatic memory. Once she was trying to tell her Chinese-speaking cousin from the city, "This is a *persimmon*," but all she said was "tao zu," a Naxi word. Her cousin misunderstood her as saying *taozi* ("peach" in Chinese), and she felt "ashamed" of her inability to speak Chinese.

Why was Li L. ashamed of not knowing Chinese? Why shouldn't her cousin have felt ashamed of not understanding Naxi? Li L.'s story reflected a general social attitude toward minoritized languages, revealing the degree to which formal education in the dominant language has been inflicting psychological wounds on learners from minority backgrounds due to their limited proficiency in the dominant language and literacy (Wang, 2016; Wang, et al., 2012; Yang, 2013). Such a negative attitude can be expressed in the form of a disbelief in minority students' ability to learn. As a retired professor once told me, when he decided to found an English department for minority students in southwest China, his Han Chinese colleagues in the north remarked, "They can't even speak Mandarin Chinese. How can they learn English?" The attitude can also be expressed through some teachers' public ridicule of minority students' substandard Mandarin, strong accents in English, and flawed expressions—a ridicule that I witnessed a few times at university. Being a "少数民族" (ethnic minority) in China is similar to carrying some institutionalized ways of labeling language students as ESL learners (see a critique in Bordonaro, 2020; Harklau, 2000; Ortmeier-Hooper, 2008). That's the wound that society and education have often inflicted on the marginalized, just as the government's label of "landlord" once justified its mistreatment of my grandfather. If learners can't speak the dominant language (be it Chinese or English), they are deficient. This equation can be internalized. In fact, Li L. used the word "deficient" to describe herself in her first writing class with me:

> [Mr. Yang] let us use one word to express oneself and share with classmates. I became nervous, and my mind went blank. Finally, I chose "deficiency." Actually, I am a lack of confidence [*sic*]. I dare not express myself because I am afraid of making mistakes. … Yeah, my oral English need to improve, and other areas also need improvement. … I will keep my passion of learning, and make my deficiencies fewer and fewer.
>
> (Li L., J1)

Despite the multiple grammar mistakes in the paragraph, we can understand Li L.'s overall meaning and recognize that deficiency has thus become a defining feature of Li L.'s linguistic identity. Learning is for her a process of reducing her "deficiencies." A contact zone (Pratt, 1991), whether experienced in a private encounter with a Chinese-speaking cousin or in a graduate writing classroom, may thus evoke a sense of inferiority in language learners from minoritized backgrounds. For them, the move from home to school is not a rosy path.

Similarly, critical pedagogues (Canagarajah, 2021) caution against a romanticized notion of mobility, as if geographical relocations, particularly transnational ones, constitute upward social mobility. In the EFL context, mobility within one's national boundaries may also incur losses and wounds, which can then become raw material for LA writing. I now present a poem drawing on words and ideas from Wang Y.'s LA (see Chapter 8) and related data to feature her wounds from within-the-country relocations and her parents' preference for her to learn the two nationally and internationally dominant languages: Mandarin and English.

A Rootless Lily Pad

I am—
A rootless lily pad …
My parents, moving to Guangdong,
Tucked away their dialects
And shielded me from Cantonese
By sending me to a (Mandarin-English) bilingual boarding school.
My English writing is stuck
In a three-paragraph rut.
Now a graduate in Kunming[1]
I learn its dialect to fit in.

Wang Y.'s stories showed me that EFL writers can engage in profound identity work, especially in relation to their lost heritage. Wang Y.'s quest for identity continues in the midst of multiple languages and cultures. As she wrote in her LA, "I have been influenc[ed] by my mother's Dai culture and my father's Han culture, and hesitating between Chinese and English." LA writing has provided for her, as with proficient ESL writers in North America (Canagarajah, 2015, 2020; Tso, 2020), a textual home to resolve her ontological crisis that accompanies her geographical relocations and multilingual connections.

作者有新声 Re-voicing the "I"

Diary #5: March 9, 2022

My wife and I were taking a walk in the morning, as is our daily routine. Around us, palm trees stood still, minas chirping.

"Can I challenge my American students, who already have a B.A. in linguistics, to be teaching assistants for the other students from Myanmar?" she asked.

In about two months, she would start teaching in the same international college where I began my second career. A Caucasian linguist committed to training others to research minority languages, she constantly thinks about the best way to engage her students without patronizing or marginalizing any of them. I have a similar concern.

Relating to my research on LA writing, I responded, "We need to re-voice the 'I.'"

I went on to explain that we need to change the default and unidirectional information flow from the allegedly more knowledgeable Global North to the less knowledgeable Global South. I felt as if Freire (2000) were speaking through me about turning farmers into teachers on farming matters. In EFL literacy education, this repositioning might involve a similar epistemological "I" shift. Each individual in the Global South, including my students and myself, has a story to tell from a first-person perspective. Each of us needs to occupy the irreplaceable place of living our own lives, making sense of our own existence, and processing others' representations of ourselves (Bakhtin, 1981). Autoethnographic writing, born of struggles for a cultural and linguistic identity in contact zones (Pratt, 1991), is the cross on which we hang our shame of being a member of the uncivilized tribe in some barbarian land. But it is also the crown with which we claim our treasured identities along hopeful storylines such as transnational belonging (Ramazani, 2009), productive bilingualism (Gao, 2001, 2002), and translingual subjectivity (Canagarajah, 2013, 2015, 2020).

Traditionally, students, especially ethnic minority students, have been marginalized from this kind of epistemological process. First, they tend to be positioned only as *learners* of the dominant language and literacy. As in the case of Li L. discussed above, their local knowledge doesn't count, nor do their minority languages, life experiences, and aspirations. These learners are "deficient" because of their limited proficiency in or deviations from the dominant language and literacy. Fortunately, this myth has been challenged by a poststructuralist perspective, which recognizes both ESL learners (Norton, 2000; Pavlenko, 2001) and EFL learners (Teng, 2019) as agents who embody multiple, changeable, and conflicting identities. Second, language learners are often treated as data providers. Following the established Western protocol of research ethics, language learners often remain anonymous, faceless, voiceless. If they told stories in a narrative study, they would not actually own the stories (Pavlenko, 2002). Third, through the common but misleading advice not to use first-person pronouns in academic writing, as observed and critiqued by Hyland (2002) with regard to academic writing in a Hong Kong university, English language learners are denied the multiple identity options associated with "I," especially the most powerful form of standing as an author (Ivanič, 1998; Tang & John, 1999). Thus, the great wall of epistemological process has blocked language learners from contributing new knowledge in their own names. To disrupt such a lopsided process, we need to re-voice the "I" and unleash its full epistemological potential.

When I refer to re-voicing the "I," I envision a more radical epistemological process that entails three steps. First, the writing course should provide students with a space where they can tell their stories in their translingual manners. Recall the case of Zhang in Chapter 4, whose telling of her painful life experience was mediated by a series of translingual acts: drawing, writing of proverbs in Chinese, explaining the personal significance of one of these proverbs, telling her story first in English and then in Chinese, with teary eyes. The stories shared in this way may not be coherent from a standard English or standard Chinese perspective, especially at first. Nonetheless, these (initially crude) articulations or expressions may serve as a powerful critique of dominant storylines that tend to lock learners in deficiency-saturated ways of conceptualizing the self. From a narrative practice perspective, these dominant storylines claim a status of absolute truth and deny individuals rich identity options that honor their preferences, desires, and values (White, 2007). Therefore, if one senses pain due to not knowing the dominant language, as Li L. did, let the pain be exposed and let its root causes be revealed. If it is an achievement, let it be recognized, celebrated, and extended in the writing classroom. After all, our sense of self as a reader and writer, in our first as well as in subsequent languages, emerges and evolves with our life and literacy experiences in both formal and informal settings (Cox et al., 2010; Ivanič, 1998; Lam, 2000; Zhao, 2015).

Second, we should explore ways of representation that allow our participants to speak with their voice. Poetic inquiry, which embeds participants' words in a poem, can be an approximation (Richardson, 1993; Wiebe, 2015). Let us consider Shi as an example. Her collection of data features her early multilingual exposure, reading experience, and literary success. Most importantly, it also foregrounds her unceasing pursuit of language art, especially writing. Her stories inspired me to write the following poem:

> *A Girl Passionate for English*
>
> Operas of my grandpa's troupe
> Taught me Jiangsu dialect, Hokkien, Cantonese, and Mandarin.
> "Tang Poems" nurtured my literary literacy.
> I then fell in love with Guo Jingming's novels
> And published my Chinese school writings.
> A lover of languages
> Mistakenly enrolled in administration;
> English—my soul passion,
> Writing—my lasting companion.

This kind of re-voicing—first through her LA, presented in Chapter 14, and then through my poem—showcases as much an individual pilgrimage as a class experience. It involves identity making through the writer's active and deliberate investment in LA writing. By foregrounding the backgrounds, aspirations, and preferred identities of EFL writers, poetic inquiry can help us avoid misrepresenting them or reifying any deficit imagery associated with them.

Third, we should involve our students as co-researchers and co-producers of new knowledge, as some critical literacy educators (Duckworth & Tett, 2019) have advocated and demonstrated. Coupled with a dialogical pedagogy that emphasizes in-class interactions and autoethnographic research that stresses personal experience and data-informed insights, her storytelling efforts eventually led to deepened understandings of self. As Shi reflected in her journal at the end of the writing course:

It is the first day of 2020. Amazingly, it has been four months since I set out to keep writing. Time moves fast but leaves profound mark every day. I reviewed some of the diaries in my file. It was interesting, and all those words remind me of the past days, unfolding like a scroll of life stories with various feelings emerging unexpectedly. To tell the truth, I do learn a lot during these days. I even cannot imagine how can I write so many journals, drafts, and finally finish my [literacy] autobiography. Academic writing is a process of speculative thought; in my case it is absolutely not an easy or relaxing process. More challenge to me, as a non-English major student, I got few chances to write in English in such a systematic way over the past years, let alone write academic articles. Even if I have been improving, how much time I need to catch up with those people with a solid foundation in English writing is a question I have always been pondering for. I know I have a chance now, but whether I can make it depends on how I use it. I know nothing about tomorrow, but what I can do is to move step by step. Nevertheless, I sense something has been changed after a semester of hard work. It is not the aspiration of the success that can stimulate me anymore, instead, it is enjoying the processing itself that pushes me forward.

(Shi, 18J)

Although this journal starts with a recognition of prior lack of opportunity (e.g., "few chances to write in English in such a systematic way over the past years"), it continues to foreground Shi's subjective wealth—including her actual use of an opportunity provided by the writing course, her sustained "hard work," and eventually embracing her preferred storyline as a writer who learns to enjoy "academic writing [as] a process of speculative thought."

Unless EFL writers have developed such stories to tell about themselves as readers and writers, they will remain an object of being authored without entering the critical "self-authoring" space in which they wrestle with and orchestrate multiple voices (Holland, et al., 2001, p. 178). Without this kind of critical self-authoring, literacy education will most likely continue to dehumanize our learners. As Wei Li (2022) reminded us, translanguaging as a political stance to decolonize English language education is a systematic project, in which

> the rich and diverse and social experiences and practices of the English language learners should be mobilized to provide alternative points of reference, horizons, and perspective for knowledge production and at the same time to transform the subjectivities of the learners.
>
> *(p. 179)*

Otherwise, we will continue to marginalize language minorities through English language education.

超语资源论 Reconceptualizing Translingualism

> **Dear Translingual Scholars**
>
> Please tolerate me [Shizhou] for writing to you in the forms of letters and diaries (with an informal style), rather than a straight academic discourse, on so important a subject as translingualism in the EFL writing classroom. If I'm not mistaken, successful translingualism involves negotiation, thus requiring both sides to give and take. Moreover, to decolonize academic writing through translingualism requires our engagement with epistemologies of the Global South (Canagarajah, 2022), which, to me, includes uncommonly used forms of written communication as well.
>
> Like you, I believe that social justice is important in the teaching of English (writing) in a global context; that language is a dynamic, situated, and negotiated social practice; that multilingual speakers' or writers' language use should not be judged solely by the standard of standard (written) English; and that translingualism, alternatively known as translanguaging, can index bilingual speakers' and writers' creative expressions (Canagarajah, 2013; Horner, 2017; Horner & Alvarez, 2019; Li, 2018; Yang, 2022; You, 2016; You, 2018). Like you, I am sorely aware that the center of translingual scholarship remains in the Global North and fails to properly take into account both local realities and non-Latin scripts in the Global South (Canagarajah, 2022; Canagarajah & Gao, 2019). Hopefully, this autoethnographic study based on an extensive pool of classroom data, with 333 documents, in an EFL writing classroom can speak to that void to some extent. In particular, I want to invite you on a journey of relocating translingualism in the EFL context that I have worked in.

Diary #6: March 10, 2022

Yesterday, I went through Zhang's (see Chapter 13 for her LA) folder, a collection of 39 documents, and wrote memos on every entry. I was not searching for codes and themes per se; to do so would run the risk of "generating theories and practices that are out of kilter with our intuitive experience of being in the world" (Wiebe, 2015, p. 152). Instead, I engaged in poetic inquiry, embedding the participant's own words in the form of a poem (Richardson, 1993, 1997) to recapture her lived experience and to politicize the personal (Faulkner & Cloud, 2019). I further limited each poem to exactly 50 words, a practice adopted by both creative writing educators (Hassall, 2006) and academic communities such as TESOL, which sometimes require the authors to submit 50-word abstracts. With words taken from her LA drafts, survey responses, and journals, I composed the following poem:

A Girl from "an Ordinary Family"
Playing an animal game with my elder brother

Opened a door for me to Chinese characters.
Listening to my father's tapes of popular songs
And practicing calligraphy taught me more Chinese
And its cultural values:
hard work, perseverance, and filial piety—
Eternal themes in my Chinese poems and literacy autobiography.

Diary #7: March 11, 2022

Writing the poem based on Zhang's words has been instructive for me. In fact, ever since she told the class her experiences of hardship while in college, which I did not include in the poem above, I have been pondering: How does this story relate to literacy? It is certainly a life story, but it does not contain any specific literacy content except this brief description: "I opened the computer to lighten [sic] for preparing teaching materials which was a particular English reading and writing. I persisted although it's very tough for me because it's my duty to make a good lesson for all the students" (Zhang, LA). If a narrative is a performance of one's identity, rather than a faithful reflection of some lived experience (Coffey & Street, 2008), then Zhang, by telling her hardship story, must be performing an identity of someone who perseveres through adversities and as a responsible teacher.

Why is it important to recognize Zhang's performed identity? What can we learn from her story and the many stories shared by me and my students through our LAs? In what ways do they differ from LAs produced by ESL students (e.g., Canagarajah, 2020), who reside in some Inner Circle countries such as the United States, or transnational scholars who wrote their stories of shuttling between communities and negotiating new literacy norms (Belcher & Connor, 2001; Yazan et al., 2021)? In what ways are our stories addressing the theoretical foreignness about translingualism? The more I thought about these questions, the more I was convinced that we need to reconceptualize translingualism from a Global South perspective by first examining the concept of investment.

Certainly, investment, featured in a poststructuralist theory of learner identity, has provided a powerful way to interpret language learning. In proposing this theory, Norton borrowed from Bourdieu (1986), who expounded on two forms of capital: *material* (e.g., money) and *symbolic* (e.g., a language). Norton then drew on Anderson's (1991) concept of an imagined community to magnify the symbolic value of languages, suggesting that language learning is a process of pursuing memberships in imagined communities or *imagined identities*. Learners are then agents insofar as they may *participate in* or *resist* a particular language activity in keeping with their imagined identities.

A more recent articulation of this theory (see Darvin & Norton, 2015, 2018) situated investment at the intersection of capital, ideology, and identity. As Darvin and Norton (2018) explained, capital features learners' backgrounds, which are valued differently across social spaces. Ideology features imposed and accepted norms that inform individual actions and language use. Identity features who the learners are by virtue of their backgrounds, who they want to become by virtue of imagination, and who they can be, even if temporarily, by virtue of pedagogical design. Meeting at the conjunction of these three shaping forces, learners' investment thus foregrounds their agency through both participation in and resistance of a given practice. At least, this is what poststructuralists such as Darvin and Norton (2018) seem to suggest: although all resources can be capital, their values shift in different contexts. It is thus both the teacher's and learner's responsibility to (re)discover and negotiate the values of the learners' suppressed resources. Yet what values do we bring to the discussion that may affect our ways of assigning values to things, activities, and practices? To address this question, I'm afraid I'll have to detour.

Diary #8: March 12, 2022

It's Saturday morning. After enjoying a toasted English muffin with butter and fresh avocado, I debated in my mind: "Should I do my writing now, or exercise, or do some chore for my host family in Hawaii?" Growing up in China and having been instructed by numerous cultural sayings to cherish the value of time, I am often time-conscious. In the end, I decided to clean the windows in the kitchen, which then continued on to cleaning all the bathrooms.

As I performed these simple chores, it dawned on me that I was investing my time not in writing my chapter but in housework, a service that I delighted in. Although this seemed to have nothing to do with LA writing, the more I thought about it, the more I began to see connections. I grew up doing housework of all kinds—sweeping, cooking, feeding pigs, cleaning pigsties, doing laundry, and hoeing cornfields. Because my mother was paralyzed, each child needed to do more. Housework taught me to appreciate others' service, obey my parents, collaborate with my siblings, and persevere until a task was completed. Overall, my pursuit of a desired personhood, that is, being a proper person in a Chinese cultural sense, powered my willing investment in chores. Therefore, my investment in cleaning seemed to support the poststructuralist perspective that one's imagined identity impacts one's investment in a given language and literacy practice (Darvin & Norton, 2018; Norton, 2000). Equally important, I was investing in a relationship; through service, I showed my appreciation for my Hawaiian host family and strengthened my bond with them.

LA writing is similar. Although people tend to think of writing as a solo activity, within the classroom context my students and I have turned LA writing into a social practice. We did it because we were all members of the same class, Intermediate Writing for Translators. As the instructor, I invited my students to participate, writing a little bit at a time, during and after class, week after week. They responded, each one in their own way, with a shared hope that their writing would eventually become part of a self-published book. Due to the unbalanced teacher-student relationship, their investment is semi-compulsory, not voluntary. Nonetheless, I served my students by inviting them into the project, by guiding and encouraging them, and eventually by celebrating with them. I created an alternative space in which everyone had a chance to participate, not just the privileged few who were already proficient in reading and writing in dominant languages. In return, my students served me by sharing their stories, bit by bit, tentatively, reluctantly, and incoherently at first, but eventually confidently and coherently. Their participation and stories challenged and deepened my understanding of LA writing and of myself as an EFL writing teacher and researcher. It was a power-filled, diffusing, and generating process of teaching and learning, researching, and co-researching.

The same social principle applies to translingualism. Through my translanguaging moments in teaching LA writing and autoethnographic research (see especially Chapter 4), I turned my writing classroom into a translanguaging space where my students also participated in translanguaging in their own way, but with similarities. For example, my hybrid language use, such as embedding Chinese poems in my LA (see Chapter 2), was mirrored by some of my students, such as Zhang. My reflection on my dialect was echoed as some students, such as Shi and Wu, engaged with their own native languages in similar ways. By sharing my LA with my students, together with other LAs as part of an explicit translingual orientation (Canagarajah, 2020; Kuboto, 2000; Tso, 2020), I normalized translingualism, at least for LA writing, in my writing classroom. Pedagogical translanguaging as part of the classroom writing ecology (see Chapter 4) thus provided opportunities for the class to revisit, reassign, and negotiate values for non-English languages and dialects through their actual use.

However, we may need to consider a different conceptualization of translingualism. In the Global North, translingualism or translanguaging is often defined as

> a process by which students and teachers engage in complex discursive practices that include *all* [emphasis added] the language practices of all students in a class in order to develop new language practices and sustain old ones, to communicate and appropriate knowledge and to give voice to new sociopolitical realities by interrogating linguistic inequality.
>
> *(García & Kano, 2014, p. 214)*

This definition paints an idealized picture of translanguaging that I failed to see in my students' LAs or in my classroom reality. For instance, despite my multiple invitations, none of my ethnic minority students used their ethnic script in their LAs. If translanguaging involves the use of "all the language practices," then Li L.'s writing can qualify only as partial translingualism. Furthermore, the above definition fails to mention modality, as if modality were optional. In reality, I found modalities to be primary rather than secondary. In teaching my students LA writing and autoethnographic research, I used multiple modalities such as speech, drawing, and writing. My messages were always embodied in some modalities. They were an indispensable part of my pedagogy, which shaped my students' understanding as well as subsequent LA writing. In addition, the collection of EFL writers' LAs challenged me to view repertoire as entailing native genres such as games, nursery rhymes, and opera. These native genres are the very resources that have been suppressed by monolingual ideologies. Therefore, re-activating them is the key to addressing linguistic injustices in English literacy education. Nonetheless, these resources are not fixed. They are expansive and can still be expanded through life and learning experiences. Accordingly, I redefine translingualism or translanguaging as the act and synergic effects of bilingual or multilingual speakers selecting, deploying, and orchestrating features from their expansive and still expanding repertoire that can be conveyed in multiple modalities, as well as namable languages, dialects, and (native) genres from these linguistic backgrounds. I believe this new definition helps us to capture the Global South reality more accurately.

We should consider two kinds of normalizing conditions, one external and the other internal. Again, I will turn to a mundane example from house cleaning. When I cleaned windows as a child, in my rural home in China, I used a rag, some soapy water, and the most conveniently available old newspapers. This was the normal practice given the materials and limited money we had. But when cleaning the windows of my host family's residence in Hawaii, I used dish detergent, a sponge, clean water, and paper towels, since these were the materials provided to me. Obviously, materials are important; they normalize or at least help to normalize a practice. They are external normalizing conditions. Looking back at my writing classroom, the material conditions included the following:

- The MTI program as a bilingual context
- A blackboard and a projector in the classroom
- An online collaborative writing platform
- Access to the Internet and smartphones
- Availability of hard-copy MTI theses, handouts, and eventually self-published books
- Last but not least, the face-to-face contact time during 2019, which was still normal practice prior to the COVID-19 pandemic

These external conditions made it convenient for my students to write notes on the handouts I provided, to discuss the meanings of the texts in the handouts, to draw pictures, and to share their ideas in Chinese or English or both. Translanguaging was externally enabled.

We should also attend to internal normalizing conditions, especially concerning ideologies. When I was a child, cleaning was a daily activity. I had to use two kinds of brooms: a bamboo broom for the courtyard and a sorghum broom for inside the house. Why? Because that's what my parents (the power figures in my family) told me to do. Or I saw them do it. Or I understood, through their explanation and my own reflection, why one tool was reserved for one purpose and the other tool for a different purpose. These reasonings underlying the designated use of brooms, once internalized, become my ideology of cleaning. Any cleaning activity I have done since then is informed and shaped by this ideology.

Likewise, ideologies have informed and influenced my own and my students' language use. These are not singular, nor variants of one another per se, but diverse ideologies that compete for normalizing status (Darvin & Norton, 2018) within the classroom context. Some ideologies I have identified in my data are as follows:

- Major-lingualism, which succumbs to the dominant status of a language and measures one's own worth solely or primarily in terms of one's proficiency or lack thereof in that language. Within this particular EFL context, such major languages include not only English, in particular the reified standard of written English, but also Chinese, in particular the reified Mandarin. Li L.'s shame over not being able to say the Chinese word for "persimmon" exemplifies this tendency. The same applies to literacy. The writer considers his or her own worth solely or primarily in light of his or her inability to write in the major language in an error-free manner. Alternatively, this normalizing ideology may be called a deficiency discourse, which neglects or tends to marginalize the writer's knowledges, proficiencies, and literacies in a minor language, be it a dialect or an ethnic minority language. Hence the following poem captures Gui's triumph over the major languages:

A Triumphant Country Man

I grew up in a mountain,
Startling my illiterate mother one day,
By saying something in Mandarin—
A language of the educated.
I dropped out of high school after my father's business
Failed.
All I have gained since then,
I taught myself:
BA in Chinese, novel writing, English tutoring …

- Bilingualism, which considers it normal to be competent in two major languages—in this case, Chinese and English. The writer is motivated to use and become proficient in one language at a time, with each language reserved for certain domain or functions, like the two different cleaning tools I used in my old house. From a bilingual perspective, proficiency in dialects and ethnic languages is often perceived as a hindrance to learning a major language and thus to be avoided, as in the case of Wang Y.'s parents.
- Multilingualism, which considers it normal to be competent in three or more major languages—in this case, Chinese, English, plus another foreign language such as Japanese. Similar to bilingualism, each language has its own designated functions and domains of use and they should not be mixed.
- Translingualism or translanguaging, which considers it normal for languages, including minor languages such as dialects and ethnic languages, and modalities to mingle in hybrid fashion and create synergic effects of $1 + 1 > 2$ (Gao, 2001, 2002) or $1 + 1 + 1 > 3$. It emphasizes deliberate acts of contemporary communication that feature creative design and reconfiguration (The New London Group, 1996). My LA and the sample LAs we read as a class all demonstrated clear features of translingualism. This practice defies major-lingualism, bilingualism, and multilingualism by creating texts that

- invite a similarly translingual response, through which translingualism is further normalized within a given social space.
- Scientificism, which considers it normal that academic writing should rigorously follow the writing conventions of scientific reporting, including the avoidance of first-person pronouns. Feedback given at the thesis defense of graduate students in that MTI program, which I required my students to observe, take notes on, and reflect on, sometimes reflects this type of discourse. As the dean of the School of Foreign Languages, where I taught the writing course, once commented at a thesis defense, MTI students' translation reports should adopt features of "理工科论文" (research reports by science and technology majors) (personal communication, 2019). Consequently, most MTI students would use "the translator" or "the author" to refer to themselves.

Diary #9: April 14, 2022

We are at the airport again, now waiting to fly back to Thailand. Still one hour before boarding our plane, I find myself wondering what a trip to Hawaii has done for me and my family and how poetic inquiry informed by thematic analysis of my students' data has affected my understanding about transnationalism, translingualism, and investment. I am again reminded that like Canagarajah (2001) and many other translingual scholars, I am a "fortunate traveler" with resources and connections, at the same time as people in Shanghai are going through a massive lockdown due to COVID-19 surges and the central government's zero-COVID policy. Next to me, passengers are chatting lively in Hawaiian, mingling with the airlines' "Aloha" and "Mahalo" announcements. Even the bathroom signs are decorated in Aloha shirts with vibrant palm leaf patterns. If transnationalism is the phenomenon of people and information moving and connecting across national boundaries (Canagarajah, 2020), its manifestations are always locally situated and individually experienced. In contrast to the strong presence of the local culture and language in Hawaii, I notice different configurations in my students and myself, especially the absence of ethnic language in my students' LAs.

Wouldn't it be great if their LAs could include a heritage script, like Tamil in Canagarajah's (2020) LAs? Wouldn't that make these students' LAs perfect examples of rooted translingualism? But even for Tso (2020), a Tibetan student, a return to her heritage was only partial. Granted, it included her stated lament regarding her loss of her Tibetan language; it also involved her reevaluation of the Tibetan legends she had heard as a child, along with other efforts, such as visiting monasteries and reading books on Tibetan literature, to reclaim her heritage culture. But as far as the published LA itself was concerned, no Tibetan scripts were used. Like Li L. and myself, Tso has not learned to write in her heritage language and cannot do so in a short time either. LA is not "a trope of becoming" (Canagarajah, 2020) in itself; it only mediates LA writers' evolving relationship with the world, an important part of which concerns their ever-complicating language ideologies. This is then a shared reality that many EFL learners must face: the presence of a heritage language, be it an ethnic language or a dialect of an official language, in one's repertoire not as a written language but only as a spoken one. Can something like this really be turned into a resource under the translanguaging framework? To answer this question, we have to not only consider language use as fluid but also adopt a more fluid view of boundaries between texts and contexts, between translanguaging and the surrounding conditions. Pragmatically rather than ideally, we can create the optimal conditions to allow our students to translanguage in different ways at different times through different combinations. For instance, a writing task may have within it a component of researching in one's heritage language, and the final LA would then, in some way, foreground knowledge and understandings based on such firsthand research.

We should also caution against adopting a fixed view of heritage culture when talking about translingualism. Translingualism does not seem to favor either the major language or the minor language, either the standard version or the dialect, either one mode or culture or another. However, rooted translingualism is different. It seems to favor one's heritage culture. The benefit of this favoritism, at least theoretically, is clear. If monolingualism (or the major-lingualism I have observed in the EFL context) seeks to advance the interest of the dominant English language, rooted translingualism can counteract this imbalanced relationship by promoting one's heritage culture's interest. However, the reality is more complex. One can develop multiple relationships with one's heritage culture and the culture of the other. More specifically, one can embrace some aspects of a heritage culture while rejecting other aspects, and one can do the same with the other's culture. Therefore, I feel that the concept of translingualism is sufficient. Similar to productive bilingualism (Gao, 2001) and global souls (Li, 2007), translingualism challenges living and being that adopts only one cultural perspective. More precisely, it seeks a synergic cultural vision, as mediated by the merged use of both major and minor languages. If there is a root for such language use and subjectivity behind translingualism, the root should reach to the underground water and soil of culture or cultures that are less marked than scholars and politicians would like. In fact, we could lump everything together and define the water and soil as human culture and all its potential forms.

Diary #10: March 17, 2022

In this final entry, I reflect on my use of autoethnography to study my students' LAs and their multiple contexts. I want to especially consider three essential questions in approaching the epistemological imbalance between Western and Eastern assumptions, or between the Global North and Global South: Are my ways of inquiry and representation contributing to decolonization? What kind of decolonization is it? Are there any unresolved tensions?

I believe the answer to the first question is positive, if we take decolonization to entail empowering alternative ways of representation (Swadener & Mutua, 2008) that depart from the Western scientific discourse so as to enable the formerly silenced parties to have a voice, as feminist scholars have done (Ellis, 2009; Richardson, 1997). I have decolonized my writing classroom by approaching academic writing in English through LA writing that features translingualism. Furthermore, I used a Chinese classic style of poem to introduce and organize my chapter. I have also used a creative form of autoethnography, encompassing diary, poetry, and letter writing, to critically examine issues of power, oppression, and representation in international academic communication. Moreover, I responded to the call to reconceptualize a Global North concept (de Sousa Santos, 2014), that is, translingualism, to match with the Global South reality. Finally, if decolonization implies a shift of positioning of the subjects of research as researchers themselves or co-researchers (Zavala, 2013), I took this step by inviting, guiding, and helping my students to draft and revise their LAs while simultaneously engaging them in learning about and carrying out related autoethnographic research.

Did I use too much metaphorical language in this chapter? Perhaps. I am reminded of the comments I received on a paper about 20 years ago, when I was a master's student in the United States: "You used too much metaphorical language! In academic writing, you need to use more citations." I will not apologize, though, because I have learned to embrace metaphorical language as part of my repertoire for making meaning, just like the dialect of Chinese I grew up speaking and the snatches of the ethnic Naxi language that I know. The problem is not whether my students and I can translanguage. Instead, it's a matter of pedagogical design and the extent to which translingualism is applied to enable all members of the writing class to participate in making meaning in productive ways. That responsibility concerns not only heritage language but also heritage genres, and even experiences that may seem only remotely related to literacy from a Global North perspective. Essentially, it's a matter of creating, recognizing, and orchestrating external and internal translanguaging conditions so as to involve EFL writers as co-producers of knowledge about them and their literacies.

Note

1 Kunming is the capital city of Yunnan in southwest China.

References

Anderson, B. (1991). *Imagined communities: Reflections on the origin and spread of nationalism* (rev. ed.). Verso.
Bakhtin, M. M. (1981). *The dialogic imagination: Four essays* (M. Holquist, Trans.). University of Texas Press.
Belcher, D., & Connor, U. (2001). *Reflections on multiliterate lives*. Multilingual Matters.
Bordonaro, K. (2020). From ESL to EAL: Moving from a deficit framework to an asset framework. *Journal of English Learner Education, 11*(1), 33–53.
Bourdieu, P. (1986). The forms of capital. In J. Richardson (Ed.), *Handbook of theory and research for the sociology of education* (pp. 241–258). Greenwood Press.
Bourdieu, P. (2001). *Masculine domination* (R. Nice, Trans.). Polity Press.
Canagarajah, A. S. (2013). *Translingual practice: Global Englishes and cosmopolitan relations*. Routledge.

Canagarajah, A. S. (2015). "Blessed in my own way": Pedagogical affordances for dialogical voice construction in multilingual student writing. *Journal of Second Language Writing, 27*, 122–139. https://doi.org/10.1016/j.jslw.2014.09.001

Canagarajah, A. S. (2020). *Transnational literacy autobiographies as translingual writing*. Routledge.

Canagarajah, S. (2021). Rethinking mobility and language: From the Global South. *The Modern Language Journal, 105*, 570–582. https://doi.org/10.1111/modl.12726

Canagarajah, S. (2022). Challenges in decolonizing linguistics: The politics of enregisterment and the divergent uptakes of translingualism. *Educational Linguistics*. Advance online publication. https://doi.org/10.1515/eduling-2021-0005

Canagarajah, S., & Gao, X. (2019). Taking translingual scholarship farther. *English Teaching & Learning, 43*(1), 1–3. https://doi.org/10.1007/s42321-019-00023-4

Coffey, S., & Street, B. (2008). Narrative and identity in the "language learning project". *The Modern Language Journal, 92*(3), 452–464.

Cox, M., Jordan, J., Ortmeier-Hooper, C., & Schwartz, G. G. (Eds.). (2010). *Reinventing identities in second language writing*. National Council of Teachers of English.

Darvin, R., & Norton, B. (2015). Identity and a model of investment in applied linguistics. *Annual Review of Applied Linguistics, 35*, 36–56. https://doi.org/10.1017/S0267190514000191

Darvin, R., & Norton, B. (2018). Identity, investment, and TESOL. In J. I. Liontas (Ed.), *The TESOL encyclopedia of English language teaching* (pp. 1–17). John Wiley & Sons.

de Sousa Santos, B. (2014). *Epistemologies of the South: Justice against epistemicide*. Routledge.

Duckworth, V., & Tett, L. (2019). Transformative and emancipatory literacy to empower. *International Journal of Lifelong Education, 38*(4), 366–378. https://doi.org/10.1080/02601370.2019.1574923

Ellis, C. (2009). *Revision: Autoethnographic reflections on life and work*. Left Coast Press.

Faulkner, S. L., & Cloud, A. (Eds.). (2019). *Poetic inquiry as social justice and political response*. Vernon Press.

Ferris, D. R., Ferris, D. R., Hedgcock, J. S., & Hedgcock, J. S. (2005). *Teaching ESL composition* (1st ed.). Routledge. https://doi.org/10.4324/9781410611505

Freire, P. (2000). *Pedagogy of the oppressed* (30th anniversary ed). Continuum.

Gao, Y. (2001). *Foreign language learning: 1 + 1 > 2*. Beijing University Press.

Gao, Y. (2002). Productive bilingualism: 1 + 1 > 2. In W. C. D. So & G. M. Gary (Eds.), *Education and society in plurilingual contexts* (pp. 143–162). VUB Brussels University Press.

García, O., & Kano, N. (2014). Translanguaging as process and pedagogy: Developing the English writing of Japanese students. In J. Conteh, & G. Meier (Eds.), *The multilingual turn in languages education* (pp. 258–277). Multilingual Matters.

Harklau, L. (2000). From the "good kids" to the "worst": Representations of English language learners across educational settings. *TESOL Quarterly, 34*(1), 35–67. https://doi.org/10.2307/3588096

Hassall, P. J. (2006). Developing an international corpus of creative English. *World Englishes, 25*(1), 131–151.

Holland, D. C., Lachicotte, Jr., W., Skinner, D., & Cain, C. (2001). *Identity and agency in cultural worlds*. Harvard University Press.

Horner, B. (2017). Teaching translingual agency in iteration: Rewriting difference. In B. Horner & L. Tetreault (Eds.), *Crossing divides* (pp. 87–97). University Press of Colorado.

Horner, B., & Alvarez, S. (2019). Defining translinguality. *Literacy in Composition Studies, 7*(2), 1–30. https://doi.org/10.21623/1.7.2.2

Hyland, K. (2002). Authority and invisibility: Authorial identity in academic writing. *Journal of Pragmatics, 34*(8), 1091–1112. https://doi.org/10.1016/S0378-2166(02)00035-8

Ivanič, R. (1998). *Writing and identity: The discoursal construction of identity in academic writing* (Vol. 5). John Benjamins Publishing Company. https://doi.org/10.1075/swll.5

Lam, W. S. E. (2000). L2 literacy and the design of the self: A case study of a teenager writing on the Internet. *TESOL Quarterly*, *34*(3), 457–482. https://doi.org/10.2307/3587739

Li, W. (2018). Translanguaging as a practical theory of language. *Applied Linguistics*, *39*(1), 9–30. https://doi.org/10.1093/applin/amx039

Li, W. (2022). Translanguaging as a political stance: Implications for English language education. *ELT Journal*, *76*(2), 172–182. https://doi.org/10.1093/elt/ccab083

Li, X. (2007). Souls in exile: Identities of bilingual writers. *Journal of Language, Identity, and Education*, *6*(4), 259–275.

Norton, B. (2000). *Identity and language learning: Gender, ethnicity and educational change*. Longman.

Ortmeier-Hooper, C. (2008). English may be my second language, but I'm not "ESL". *College Composition and Communication*, *59*(3), 389–419.

Pavlenko, A. (2001). "In the world of the tradition I was unimagined": Negotiation of identities in cross-cultural autobiographies. *International Journal of Bilingualism*, 5(3), 317–344.

Pavlenko, A. (2002). Narrative study: Whose story is it, anyway? *TESOL Quarterly*, *36*(2), 213–218. https://doi.org/10.2307/3588332

Pavlenko, A. (2007). Autobiographic narratives as data in applied linguistics. *Applied Linguistics*, *28*(2), 163–188. https://doi.org/10.1093/applin/amm008tr

Pratt, M. L. (1991). Arts of the contact zone. *Profession*, *91*, 33–40.

Ramazani, J. (2009). *A transnational poetics*. University of Chicago Press. https://doi.org/10.7208/chicago/9780226703374.001.0001

Richardson, L. (1993). Poetics, dramatics, and transgressive validity: The case of the skipped line. *Sociological Quarterly*, *34*(4), 695–710.

Richardson, L. (1997). Skirting a pleated text: De-disciplining an academic life. *Qualitative Inquiry*, *3*(3), 295–303. https://doi.org/10.1177/107780049700300303

Southeast Asia Program. (1961). *The Man Shu (Book of the Souther Barbarians)* (G. P. Oey, Ed.; G. H. Luce, Trans.). Cornell University.

Swadener, B. B., & Mutua, K. (2008). Decolonizing performances: Deconstructing the global postcolonial. In N. Denzin, Y. Lincoln, & L. Smith (Eds.), *Handbook of critical and indigenous methodologies* (pp. 31–44). Sage. https://doi.org/10.4135/9781483385686.n2

Tang, R., & John, S. (1999). The 'I' in identity: Exploring writer identity in student academic writing through the first person pronoun. *English for Academic Purposes*, *18*, 23–39.

Teng, M. F. (2019). Learner identity and learners' investment in EFL learning: A multiple case study. *Iranian Journal of Language Teaching Research*, *7*(1), 43–60.

The New London Group. (1996). A pedagogy of multiliteracies: Designing social futures. *Harvard Educational Review*, *66*(1), 60–93. https://doi.org/10.17763/haer.66.1.17370n67v22j160u

Tso, B. (2020). Rediscovering heritage identity through literacy. In A. S. Canagarajah (Ed.), *Transnational literacy autobiographies as translingual writing* (pp. 175–180). Routledge.

Wang, G. (2016). *Pains and gains of ethnic multilingual learners in China: An ethnographic case study*. Springer.

Wang, G., Tsung, L., & Ki, W. (2012). The pains of becoming trilingual in China: An ethnographic case study of a Naxi college student. *The Asia-Pacific Education Researcher*, *21*(2), 257–266.

White, M. (2007). *Maps of narrative practice* (1st ed.). W. W. Norton & Co.

Wiebe, S. (2015). Poetic inquiry: A fierce, tender, and mischievous relationship with lived experience. *Language and Literacy*, *17*(3), 152–163. https://doi.org/10.20360/G2VP4N

Xi, J. P. (2016, July 1). *在庆祝中国共产党成立95周年大会上的讲话* [Xi Jinping's speech to the conference commemorating the 95th anniversary of the founding of the Chinese Communist Party]. Xinhuanet. http://www.xinhuanet.com//politics/2016-07/01/c_1119150660.htm

Yang, S. (2013). *Autobiographical writing and identity in EFL education*. Routledge.

Yang, S. (2022). Using a translanguaging approach to capture emergent bilingual creativity. *International Journal of Virtual and Personal Learning Environments, 12*(1), 1–12. https://doi.org/10.4018/IJVPLE.295303

Yazan, B., Canagarajah, A. S., & Jain, R. (2021). *Autoethnographies in ELT: Transnational identities, pedagogies, and practices*. Routledge.

You, X. (2010). *Writing in the devil's tongue: A history of English composition in China*. Southern Illinois University Press.

You, X. (2016). *Cosmopolitan English & transliteracy*. Southern Illinois University Press.

You, X. (Ed.). (2018). *Transnational writing education: Theory, history, and practice*. Routledge.

Zavala, M. (2013). What do we mean by decolonizing research strategies? Lessons from decolonizing, indigenous research projects in New Zealand and Latin America. *Decolonization: Indigeneity, Education & Society, 5*(1), 55–71.

Zhao, Y. (2015). *Second language creative writers: Identities and writing processes*. Multilingual Matters. https://doi.org/10.21832/9781783093014

PART III
Student's Literacy Autobiographies

Introduction

This section contains 10 students' LAs, which were the results of these student writers engaging in autoethnographic research, multiple revisions, and related classroom interactions. These LAs illustrate that even though these students are all EFL learners who have not crossed national boundaries, mobility, transnationalism, and translingualism remain relevant to them as they work out their individual literate identities in a contemporary time.

Chapter 7 features the literacy journey of Chen from a "typical middle-class" Chinese family. Her experiences with learning to read and write in Chinese and English were largely positive and supported by her parents and teachers. The chapter showcases Chen's transnational reading experiences, ideologies of reading and writing, and ways of voice construction across her multiple drafts of literacy autobiography, with an embrace of a personally preferred second-language writing style rooted in Chinese culture and literary traditions.

Chapter 8 by Wang Y. recounts her experience of learning Mandarin and English from an ethnically mixed Han and Dai family that relocated frequently within China. It contains her reflection on how culture and language, including dialect Chinese, are interconnected and how her sense of self is situated in her experiences of learning English in several contexts (bilingual school, test-oriented teaching, and after-school training) and reading and writing in Chinese. It concludes with the insight that "I will continuously find my culture identity in language study since learning is a cyclic process and I will figure [develop] a new identity in each cycle."

Chapter 9 retells Gui's experience of language learning in his home village, where he spoke a Chinese dialect but soon discovered the esteemed Mandarin Chinese and the importance of *dushu* (studying) to become a member of "the well-educated." His literacy journey features his personal aspirations and agency.

DOI: 10.4324/9781003288756-9

Through the Chinese higher education examination program for the self-taught learners, he gained his first degree in Chinese literature and then also "conquered" English by studying New Concept English, a series of English textbooks imported from Great Britain. After that, he became a graduate student majoring in translation and an English teacher in a training school. Gui's story provides insight into upward social mobility in contemporary China, as shaped by two dominant languages and the dynamic relationship between them: "It is my Chinese literacy that helps me understand English better and it is English that has given me a very much better life."

Chapter 10, by Wu, provides an account of growing up in "an average family" where the Wu dialect was spoken and Mandarin Chinese was learned only at school. Having his grandmother as a caregiver when he was very young, Wu recalls children's nursery rhymes from his grandmother, reading classics in Chinese, reading and writing as influenced by examination, exposure to Western literature, and creative writing on the QQ, a popular Chinese social media platform. His reading habits greatly influenced his writing style.

Chapter 11, by Li J., presents a journey of exploring and gaining literacy in Chinese and English mainly through schooling. In her account, she reflects on her failures in writing in both Chinese and English. She also analyses cultural and social factors that shaped her writing style and her "secret" for achieving high grades on writing exams. English gradually changes from fun "game time" to "a monster" that involves much rote learning of vocabulary, texts, and grammar rules. However, even rote learning provided a foundation for Li J.'s later literacy development. Moreover, her English writing style is an extension of the style she had already formed in Chinese. Meta-linguistically, Li J. begins to recognize the diversity and situatedness of academic writing as contingent not only on cultural ways of thinking, but also on social factors.

Chapter 12, by Li L., reflects on her journey of becoming multilingual and multiliterate. As an ethnic Naxi student who grew up in a village speaking Naxi as her first language, she recounted an experience of feeling "ashamed" due to not knowing the Chinese word for persimmon. Without qualified teachers to teach English in her elementary school, she did not start learning English until middle school. Fortunately for her, that English teacher was encouraging and had confidence in every student. Li L.'s story offers a revealing glimpse of formal education in China's rural ethnic minority areas.

Chapter 13 tells Zhang's experience with literacy. Her Chinese learning began with playing games such as Chinese chess with her elder brother. Toy money also taught her basic numerical literacy. She was exposed to more advanced literacy in Chinese through practicing calligraphy and listening to songs on her father's tape recorder. Being praised by her teacher and winning a poetry contest boosted Zhang's confidence. She then recounted and reflected on her most unforgettable experience of writing in English, i.e., when she was working as a teacher and had to prepare for her lessons by living in the classroom. The chapter provides rich insights regarding cultural influence on self-development, especially as a literate subject, and personal agency in overcoming adversity, as again rooted in Chinese cultural values.

Chapter 14, by Shi, recounts her experience of growing up in the eastern China countryside, in an "ordinary working-class family" but with "open-minded" parents who bought books for her beginning in her early childhood. Her initial contact with Chinese literacy and multiple languages (Chinese, Hokkien, and Cantonese), however, came through music, including traditional opera introduced by her grandfather. Although test-oriented writing prompts at school dampened her interest in writing, she began to develop a passion for words through reading the works by Guo Jinming, a contemporary Chinese novelist. Shi began to write for contests and her school newspaper. That same passion for language learning persisted even while she studied a "boring" major chosen by her parents, eventually leading her to choose translation as her field of graduate study. This chapter highlights an ongoing passion for language learning as intertwined with cultural art forms and transnational learning experiences.

Chapter 15 features Zhao, who grew up speaking a Henan dialect similar to Mandarin Chinese. Her early exposure to Chinese literacy came through learning to sing opera with her grandfather. Her first successful writing a Chinese composition was facilitated by her mother, a teacher. She managed writing in English for examinations by imitating "good sentence structures in others' writing" but gradually developed her own writing style. This narrative account provides insights concerning language, culture, and one's attitude toward becoming a literate subject.

Chapter 16 focuses on Wang X., who grew up in the countryside as a left-behind child with her grandparents. An object of neighbors' ridicule, Wang X. gradually developed an inferiority complex. However, with her parents' and teachers' encouragement, she began to make progress in her English writing, which gave her more confidence.

7
MY LITERACY ROOTED IN CHINESE CULTURE

Guo Chen (陈果)

Though I started English learning at a tender age, it was not until I was in grade 2 of junior high school that I really entered the world of English reading and writing, with the help of my beloved English teacher in junior high school, Chen Shumei, who has bolstered up my confidence and interests in English learning by providing me with a positive L2 learning experience. As Norton Peirce (1995)[11] paraphrased Gardner (1985) by saying, "self-confidence arises form positive experiences in the context of the second language." By contrast, I have immersed myself in reading classic Chinese novels and classic foreign novels translated into Chinese since I was a little kid and always savor every moment of reading with great relish. As a result, I found my English, as a late-comer in my own reading and writing experiences, has been inevitably influenced by my Chinese in terms of writing and reading, this is the so-called language transfer, which refers to the use of L1 in the acquisition of L2 (Odlin, 2001). After all, as my mother-tongue, Chinese has shaped my thinking mode and linguistic habit, which will definitely have an impact my L2 writing and reading. Therefore, I found my reading and writing development is deeply rooted in the soil of Chinese culture, which will be reflected in all my writings throughout my whole life. Below will I illustrate at length my L1 and L2 literacy development by using some relevant theoretical lenses.

Childhood Memories of Reading

I was born into a typical Chinese middle-class family. My father is a doctor and my mother is an accountant at another hospital, both of whom are compulsive readers with good reading tastes and hobbies. My mother told me that when she was pregnant with me, she had read the Four Classics over and over again, just to kill time. While my father, who is a taciturn and seemingly cold person, got first place in the university entrance exam in his village and then became a doctor when he was only 20.

Both of my parents enjoy reading and have bought a lot of books of various genres, and in the study of our house there are three big bookshelves full of books dating from the 1960s to the present day. My mother got me a library card and would also buy me children's books after her business trips. Books that have remarkably influenced me include *Three Days to See* written by Helen Keller and *The Adventures of Tom Sawyer*, they are the books recommended by my mother when I first went to the library. Apart from these two books,《菜根谭》(*Tending the Roots of Wisdom*) and《曾国藩家书》(*Home Letters from the Marquis Zeng Guofan*) have also shaped my view of the world, they are my parents' favorites, both of which contain plain yet sophisticated ancient philosophical thoughts of Chinese people, for instance, "肥辛甘非真味，真味只是淡；神奇卓异非至人，至人只是常" (Real flavour does not lie in refined liquors or sumptuous dishes; only plain food gives forth a pure taste. The man who has attained the realm of perfect virtue is not the wonder maker who stands out from all his fellows. He is found among the run-of-the-mill), "君子之心事，天青日白，不可使人不知；君子之才华，玉韫珠藏，不可使人易知" (The heart of a real gentleman is as clear as the blue sky and the broad daylight, so others may never misunderstand it, but he seldom revels his talents, which are a jade hidden in a jadestone). These books have taught me how to conduct and improve my life and enabled me to have a clearer vision of the world, of who I am, and my position in this world. Therefore, I can reach an inner peace and stay immune from opinions that lack objectivity, hence becoming a person of independent mind.

Besides, when I was a primary school student, I used to spend my winter vacations in my aunt's house nestling in the countryside, a place my mother spent her younger days and so left loads of books in there, including many comic books and *Gushuhui* or *Anthology of Stories*, and many Greek and Chinese mythologies and fairy tales. These books may not seem to be very useful, however, they are interesting enough to arouse a kid's interest in reading and hence prompt her to read more.

Through reading, I also got a friend, that is Lily, a smart little girl who regards reading as an indispensable part of her life. She has helped me to develop a good habit of reading. Back in 2006, a year when cellphone use was not all-pervading, we used to kill time in the library every summer vacation, reading novels shoulder to shoulder on the bench and then exchanging books we fancied with each other. Lily's father is a rigorous orthopedic surgeon, who wouldn't permit her to read any fiction and comics he thought were useless, whereas Lily's enthusiasm for reading didn't wear off, she kept on reading and began to write essays after reading and would share her essays with me, through which she showed me a little girl's inner world that is of sheer beauty, curiosity, and purity, the same world reading showed me.

Pavel Korchagin, protagonist of *The Making of a Hero*, got an eye injury in a brutal war, and when he recuperated, the writer recounted: "he sees this world as if he saw it for the first time." It also applies to me, I feel like a new-born who sees the world for the very first time through reading every new book, without which my world will still be in a chaotic state with no sunshine.

Writing to Leave an Indelible Mark on the World

I have been constantly praised for my compositions since I was in primary school, nearly all my Chinese teachers like me, as much as my math teachers hate me. Of course, I owe it to my parents' positive roles in encouraging me to read real classics, and reading has so motivated me to write something, for I want to show other people what I have got and depict the world in my perspective.

When I was in junior high school, I began to write diaries as a way to express my feelings and picture the world in my eyes, which I thought was quite interesting, for I felt like a painter who colored the world with my own crayons. Hence never in my life have I thought writing is a drudgery, and I have maintained a positive attitude for both Chinese and English writing since then.

During my high school years, I developed a taste for an unadorned style of writing after I took a class about Han Yu, a famous poet of the mid-Tang dynasty who claimed that writing should be meant to convey ideas and ethics. To put it another way, every word your write should carry meaning, and jazzy lines should be omitted in writing. This taste has been embodied in my L2 writing, too. I like Ernest Hemingway, who is famous for his concise and informative writing style, which has also exerted a positive influence on my writing.

I used to consider choosing writing as my future career, for my compositions often received commendations from my Chinese teachers, and I think this is a world where a man's death will only be lamented for a day, and then he will be forgotten forever, with his body decayed, whereas his thoughts written down will be remembered forever. Thus, only through writing can we leave an indelible imprint on the world. In other words, writing is the only way for humans to reach immortality. Though now my dream has shifted, I still assume writing to be a substantial part of my life, without which I will be unable to build a peaceful inner world.

My L2 Literacy Development

I began learning English when I was around 9 or 10 years old. At first, I thought English studying was boring and I didn't do well in it. The reasons hidden behind it are as follows:

First, when I was in primary school, my life had nothing to do with English. There was not a single English speaker in my life. Nor did I listen to English songs or watch English movies at that time.

Second, my English teacher in primary school cared about nothing but money; he asked us to attend his after-school classes, and of course we must pay for them. Somehow, the fee-based after-school classes made me tired of English learning.

Last but not least, what I received in English class is not comprehensible input, which is described as "one level above that of the learners if it can only just be understood … can be understood by listeners despite them not understanding all the words and structures in it" (Krashen, 1982). Without enough illustrations, I found it hard to concentrate in English lessons.

However, things changed when I entered junior high school, for I met one of my favorite English teachers, Chen Shumei, who could speak decent English and was always considerate and encouraging with her students. Moreover, her class was really interesting, for she would teach us English songs and let us watch English movies.

Mrs. Chen also cared about me as much as my own parents. She always said to me: "You are a quick-witted girl who is really gifted for English studying and I want you to be a top student in English." At that time, I was depressed for I was too poor at math. However, Mrs. Chen built up my confidence. She would commend every progress I made in English writing and read the compositions I wrote out aloud in front of the whole class. Hence, my investment in English learning in junior and senior high school was greatly fueled by her commendations and encouragement.

Therefore, I made "incredibly fast progress" in English (this is what my math teacher told Mrs. Chen). The first semester Mrs. Chen taught me English I got the highest score in the mid-term English examination in the whole school, with a score of 118 out of 120. According to Gardner (1985), "Self-confidence … develops as a result of positive experiences in the context of the second language and serves to motivate individuals to learn the second language" (as cited in Peirce, 1995)[18]. This is the conclusion that can be drawn from my L2 literacy development in school.

Speaking of my L2 literacy development in college, something interesting occurred to me. All my English teachers in junior and senior high school liked me a lot, and none of them ver criticized me for my English writing, all I heard were commendations. The first time I was "criticized" was when my English writing teacher said to me:

> Yes indeed, you have a large vocabulary, the words you use in your composition is advanced, your structure is clear, but I noticed that seldom did you use attributive clause in your composition, and somehow your English writing is strongly influenced by your Chinese thinking pattern and cultural background.

Since then, I have tried my best to write more attributive clauses and avoid the so-called Chinese thinking patterns and culture in my compositions. It was until I began to read Ernest Hemingway's works that I came to realize that I should try to write simple and informative sentences just like Hemingway, otherwise those attributive clauses will make your writing awkward and lack clarity. Actually, my literacy is deeply rooted in Chinese culture: "One has to convey in a language that is not one's own the spirit that is one's own. … We cannot write like the English, we should not" (Rao, 1938)[4]. Hence, if used properly, I believe my Chinese thinking pattern, cultural background, and unique Chinese rhetorical devices will add to the literary grace of my writing, like special oriental spices added to Western food, chemistry will be produced between my L1 and L2.

Conclusion

In the light of my literacy autobiography, my acquisition of reading and writing is a process shaped by the environment I live in, the education I received, and the people I meet. From my perspective, what counts most in this process is the build-up of self-confidence in, and the developing of, interest for reading and writing. In addition, as Chinese people, we can just integrate the beauty of Chinese into our English writing. After all, to reach cultural diversity and prosperity, Chinese and Western cultures must interact with each other. That means, as Chinese people, our voice rooted in Chinese culture must be manifested in our writing.

References

GARDNER R C, 1985. Social psychology and second language learning[M]. London: Edward Arnold.
KRASHEN D S, 1982. Principle and practice in second language acquisition[M]. New York: Pergamon Press.
ODLIN T, 2001. Language transfer—cross-linguistic influence in language learning[M]. Shanghai: Shanghai Foreign Languages Education Press.
PEIRCE N B, 1995. Social identity, investment and language learning[J]. TESOL quarterly, 29(1): 9–31. https://doi.org/10.2307/3587803
RAO R, 1938. Kanthapura[M]. London: George Allen & Unwi. 4.

8
A LEARNING CYCLE OF READING AND WRITING IN ENGLISH AND CHINESE

Yuejia Wang (王粤佳)

Learning is a cyclic process that integrates concrete experience, reflective observation, abstract conceptualization, and active experimentation (Althof & Brooks, 1979). The process never ends; it constantly moves back upon itself to go forward. When I look back at my learning process of reading and writing English and Chinese, I find that it is a cycle and I begin to figure out who I am and reclaim something cultural that I ignore, which improves my understanding of expressions in English and Chinese. Language, according to Sapir, is the historical product and is closely related to the history, customs, and beliefs of a people. Language learners form their language habits unconsciously (Yang, 2018). I believe that language as a part of culture influences thought or our way of thinking. As Sapir put it, "Language and our thought-grooves are inextricably interwoven, are, in a sense, one and the same" (Sapir, 1921)[232]. My personal literacy journey in English and Chinese traces how different language environments influenced my thought process and how I gradually developed my writing style.

The Influence of Different Language Environments on My Thought

Born in Guangdong Province where schools attached more importance to English education (than other parts of China), I started English early when I was four years old. However, I cannot be defined as a Cantonese for I am unable to speak Cantonese but I follow the local lifestyle habits. My father and mother come from different provinces and have different lifestyle habits and values. To make it easier to educate me, they uniformly communicated with me in Mandarin only. Therefore, my home language is Mandarin. My mother, a Dai, comes from Yunnan province where people like sour and spicy food, whereas my father who comes from Guangxi province and eats food with lighter flavors, which represents two ways

DOI: 10.4324/9781003288756-11

of thinking in cultivating me. The thought that knowledge can change fate is the educational objective advocated by my mother, but my father supports that there is nothing more precious than to be happy. Following my mother's will, I went to a bilingual primary school in Guangdong where learning English was attached great importance, and the journey of learning English was formally begun.

After I transferred to the schools in Wuhan city where English was also significant, I was forced to acquire knowledge ahead by taking training classes that inevitably included English. This was the toughest part of my learning process. Having Chinese and English as two independent subjects did not help me to learn English. I could not immerse myself in the language environment (Fan & Ning, 2006) and so I ignored the context of English and cultural differences during my middle and high schools.

Unexpectedly, going to Dianchi College in Yunnan province dropped me into an "identity crisis" which generated my interest in reclaiming Chinese, in particular the Kunming dialect which is my mother's second language. I went to school in three cities. Three kinds of experiences have had three kinds of influence on my reading and writing in English and Chinese, and I divide them into three phrases.

Becoming a Bilingual Language Leaner

My first phrase started when I went to the kindergarten as a four-year-old in Guangdong province. It was my first contact with English. The teachers taught us the 26 letters and some simple words like "father" and "mother." I was curious about and interested in that strange language for the tones and pronunciations of English differed from those in Mandarin. Somehow, at that time, I was happy to experience anything and everything different.

After entering elementary school (2003–2009), I had two English courses with two English teachers. One taught English in Chinese and English, and the other one taught English only in English. I feel so fortunate that I used to get the chance to be in the two language environments which developed my language sense and helped me know how to express the same meaning through other languages (linguistic signs). My first L2 teacher, Miss Yang, who liked to use heuristic education, taught us through the elicitation method. She liked to organize competitions about writing. I had participated in making vocabulary books with drawing pictures and hand-copied newspaper. She drew many cards to make us remember the equivalent information in English; she played the video or sang English songs to guide us to know the themes of the units; she would prepare gifts to exchange when Western festivals came, which helped me know Western cultures and their customs. In contrast, my L1 teachers in primary school taught us using models, for example, how to skim the articles, construct a paragraph by describing peoples' actions, dialogues, minds, and so on, and how to describe scenery. However, I was not good at describing so I practiced the model again and again until I got recognized by my Chinese teacher. I regarded this teaching model as the standard and did not ask why I should write in this way until I was older.

With my keen interest in English, I really enjoyed becoming a bilingual learner. Learning a new word is like twisting a kaleidoscope. Through this, I expose myself to a foreign country, speaking their way, feeling their way, and thinking their way. In other words, it seems that I was travelling by taking the "English" Airline.

Different Cultures Have Different Languages

The second phrase corresponds to the six years from middle school to high school. When my parents' jobs required transfers, I followed them to Wuhan city in Hubei province where learning content was more difficult and the teaching process was quicker. Adapting to the new study environment shaped my tough personality. Since my English foundation was weak, I attended English training classes, learning *New Concept English* to catch up. I began to know the writing styles of narration and argumentation in English which are different from those in Chinese. Li (2012) stated that "different cultural traditions and ways of thinking between English and Chinese speakers determine their respective modes of information transmission. Chinese speakers attach importance to the formal structure, whereas English speakers attach importance to the semantic logic link." For example, "敲打"和"一打鸡蛋". There is no mark indicating the parts of speech in Chinese. The part "打" can only be recognized in the context. However, there are specific verbs and measure words in English.

As hard as I tried, I never received any good result from my writing in English. Finding it difficult to transfer my meaning and feelings into English, I turned my attention to Chinese writing. In middle school, I was fond of reading romance novels like *Class K of Three Years* and some books written by Guo Jingming. Compared with the tedious reading practice in my workbook, I preferred to read light-hearted love stories and read some famous literary works such as *The Shadow Thief* and prose in Chinese, especially Xi Murong's works in high school. Influenced by these works, my writing style changed from straightforward narration to specific description. However, exam-oriented education did not allow us to write as we wished, and I gradually believed that all types of writing have their own standards. Teachers in middle and high school asked us to do lots of reading practice in politics, business, culture, society, technology, and so on. And they taught us to write short narrative compositions about life and argumentation in accordance with the requirements of the exam.

My learning passion died out quickly at this time. No matter how willing I was, I could not choose the way to learn. Studying English was not a delight anymore and became a burden. I thought to myself, "If I do not pick it up, it will be my stumbling block in my future."

My Cultural Identity Changes with Context

My third phrase began with my college. I was admitted to Dianchi College in Kunming, Yunnan province which is my second hometown. I majored in English and many things were about words, grammars, culture, news, and so on of English. Chinese was almost put to the side. To enhance our language and cultural competence, teachers in the university encouraged us to read and analyze British and American literature. My writing teacher, Mrs. Wang, focused on teaching us argumentation in English. Her classic principle is "san duan shi" (三段式, divide your writing into three parts)—indicating your attitude on a problem and promoting your thesis statement, proving your point, and making a conclusion. She also advocated using diverse and detailed examples while proving the point, and using parallelism and metaphor in your statements as much as you can. The way I express and think was influenced by English. Sometimes I would forget how to express myself in the Chinese way.

At that time, I first had an idea to go abroad for further study after graduation as a second language learner, but when I found out how incredibly difficult it is to write in idiomatic English or put Chinese into idiomatic English, I suffered a breakdown. Adapting to life with my relatives and receiving treasured affection from them, I became intent on remaining in Kunming for I longed to belong to somewhere and find a place where I could settle. I was tired of moving around as it confused my cultural identity. "When it comes to choosing a language, we subconsciously choose a language that is closer to the traditions and habits of the culture" (Yang, 2019)[231–232]. I started to learn to speak Kunming dialect from my relatives last year. When I was learning, I tried to express myself in a more local way through their idioms, which enlightened my English learning methods and reading and writing habits. I found that I should pay more attention to the relationship between language and culture and the common ground between Chinese and English. For instance, Kunming dialect has some idiomatic expressions: "mie mie sa sa (咪咪撒撒)," an interjection, is equivalent to "天啊" (oh my) in Mandarin; "zheng na yang (整哪样)," an interrogative, is equivalent to "在干嘛" (What are you doing?) in Mandarin. This way is applicable for the transformation of some words or sentences between Chinese and English. By memorizing idiomatic expressions, I found it easier to engage in English L2 writing. Similarly, by familiarizing myself with the ethnic and national cultures, I can effectively and fairly decently express myself in different language environments. Gao et al. (2002) considered that the process of learning is a process of identity construction. Learners will selectively combine the knowledge they already possess and the knowledge taught by teachers, based on their own experiences. At present I choose the most comfortable language environment that is like a cradle. I reclaim Chinese under the dialect context.

Conclusion

Language and culture influence each other. In terms of the influence of culture on language, culture influences the spread, cognition, and evolution of language, and cultural habits can also influence people's choice and preference for language. In terms of the influence of language on culture, language can carry the cultural characteristics of its corresponding culture. Bilingual study helps me know the diversity of languages and understand people in the world differ in cultural thought patterns and the use of languages. According to Sapir (2011), nations and cultures do not always coincide. For instance, China is a country where multi-nationalities have lived and where multi-cultures have existed. I have been influenced by my mother's Dai culture and my father's Han culture, and hesitated between Chinese and English. Of course, I will continuously find my culture identity in language study. To me, language learning is a cyclic process and I will develop a new identity in each cycle.

References

ALTHOF E J, BROOKS E S, 1979. Enriching the liberal arts through experiential learning[M]. San Francisco, CA: Jossey-Bass.
范文静 [FAN W], 宁玉洁 [NING Y], 2006. 英语语境与写作能力的培养[J] [English context and the development of writing ability]. 石家庄职业技术学院学报 [The journal of Shijiazhuang vocational college], 18(5): 120–122.
GAO Y, LI Y X, LI W N, 2002. EFL learning and self-identity construction: Three cases of Chinese college majors[J]. Asia journal of english language teaching, 12(1): 95–119.
李靖民 [LI J], 2012. 英汉语形合和意合研究中的几个问题[J] [Some questions regrding the research on hypotaxies in English and parataxis in Chinese]. 外语研究 [Foreign language research], 2: 47–50.
SAPIR E, 1921. Language:An introduction to the study of speech[M]. New York: Harcourt, Brace and Company.
爱德华•萨丕尔 [SAPIR E], 2011. 语言论[M] [Language]. 商务印书馆 [The commercial press].
杨辉 [YANG HUI], 2019. 在英语通用语背景下重新认识语言与文化的关系[J] [Reconsidering the relationship between language and culture against the context of ELF]. 当代教育研究与教学实践 [Contemporary education research and teaching practice], 231–232.
杨艺 [YANG YI], 2018. 论萨丕尔的语言观——爱德华•萨丕尔《语言论》解读[J] [Sapir's language perspective: A guided reading of Edward Sapir's *Language*]. 四川民族学院学报 [Journal of Sichuan University for Nationalities], 27(5): 74–79.

9
MY BILINGUAL JOURNEY

Li Gui (桂粒)

The effect of language learning is related to how you regard the target language. As a boy, I had a strong desire for Mandarin and as a young man I wanted to learn English.

Interest in Mandarin

I was born into a farming family in a small, isolated village in Yunnan with no one at that time speaking Mandarin, let alone English. Villagers all used Wenshan language, a dialect of Chinese, when communicating.

One day, on the way to a corn field in a mountain, I exclaimed: "我们要上天了!" (We're going up towards the sky). Hearing this, my mother cried: "You are speaking Mandarin, my son!" "What is Mandarin?" I asked. She just told me that Mandarin was a wonderful language only spoken by well-educated people such as teachers.

"Language is important as a means by which access to networks is regulated: If you do not speak the right language, you do not have access to forming relationships with certain people or to participating in certain activities" (Norton, 1995)[12]. Despite the backwardness of the village, some people attached great importance to their children's education. Among them was my father who always repeated a famous saying, "万般皆下品, 唯有读书高" (Studying is superior to all other trades). The repetition sowed the seeds of *dushu* (studying) in my mind. When I was six, a villager got a black-and-white TV set, attracting waves of visitors filled with curiosity to his house. Through the TV for the first time in my life, I saw a scene depicting a student *dushu*ing in a strange language totally unfamiliar to me.

"Putonghua (i.e., Mandarin) is too difficult to understand," complained TV goers. It was due to the scene that for a long time, Mandarin was associated with *dushu* which was "better than anything else." I made a big decision to master the language which I thought could provide me with access and communicate with a well-educated society.

Exposure to Mandarin

One year later, my school life began in a mixed-grade class in which there were three grades studying together. Much to my disappointment, our teacher, who taught the grades all subjects in turn, did not speak Mandarin at all. As a result, Mandarin remained a mystery to solve. When I entered grade four, I at last had a few teachers who spoke Mandarin with a strong Wenshan accent; they could not even pronounce the second tone. In spite of this, I gradually became an awkward Mandarin speaker, which was a significant achievement for me.

Literacy Improvement

After becoming a sixth grader, I began to engage in non-course books, from which I gained a great deal of so-called "irrelevant knowledge." During that time, my reading activity consisted mainly of *Journey to the West*, stories from *Romance of the Three Kingdoms* and *Stories*, a-then famous magazine, which enlightened me a lot. Exactly at that time my composition writing in Chinese improved. Two years passed before I became a middle school student studying in a very small town, where I had a great interest in martial arts novels by Louise Cha (whose penname is Jin Yong), who wrote 14 books known to nearly all Chinese people. These novels at one time gave me the illusion that I was a swordsman doing justice to those treated unfairly.

Exposure to English

In the same grade, I began my English learning which seemed very difficult for me. I spent the three years struggling with English to no avail. Since then, I thought it a mission impossible for me to master English, so I gave it up and turned to Chinese study.

Ten years later I got a self-taught diploma in the Chinese language and literature. I also published a short story in a purely literary magazine, but English remained a lion in my way. "Language acquisition device, like other biological functions, works successfully only when it is stimulated at the right time" (Lenneberg, 1967) (as cited in Yang & Yang, 2015)[171]. "Motivation, attitudes, and set of beliefs, about learning the language are among the determining factors that can influence efficiency of the students in language classes" (Oroujlou & Vahedi, 2011)[994]. When I wanted to go further in my studies, English turned out to be a terrible obstacle. I was left with no choice but conquer it. A famous English book series, *New Concept English* by Alexander and He Qixin (1997), became the only textbook I invested almost all my spare time in. Language transfer plays a significant role in acquisition of a second language (Yang & Yang, 2015). To my surprise, it was my Chinese literacy and meta-linguistic awareness obtained during the process of studying Chinese that shed light on English.

In 2010, one year after my English learning began, I tried to write on my QQ-zone an English novel-like composition titled *A Trip to Wenshan*, a story about a fictional man who drives into a city. On the way, he is stopped by a beautiful young woman asking for a free ride. On the journey they flirt with each other, making the hero believe that she loves him. Just as she gets out, he is disillusioned by the fact that she refuses to tell him her phone number. I sent the writing to an English major who described it as "fairly good." Imagine how I was feeling when I got such feedback. I was very excited and encouraged. Considering that I had just learned English, it is a satisfying one for me, despite the faults.

Progress in English

Last year I passed the graduate entrance exams with a high score of 423 and got admission to Provincial University (pseudonym). English seems to have become something conquered by me, to a degree. Since last year I have been an amateur English teacher, teaching basic English to adults who need self-improvement. Now I have drawn a conclusion that both the Chinese and English languages are powerful. It is my Chinese literacy that helps me understand English better and it is English that has given me a much better life. In hindsight, I should have started it earlier. To sum up, what I want to express is that English provides me with another way to recognize the world. English as a global language is not only a tool but a way of thinking differently to Chinese.

Conclusion

Though one learns a specific second language for certain reasons, becoming bilingual involves innovation, L1 literacy, and a positive attitude toward the two languages.

References

亚历山大 [ALEXANDER L G], 何其莘 [QIXIN H E], 1997. 新概念英语[M] [New concept English]. 北京: 外语教学与研究出版社 [Foreign Language Teaching & Research Press].
LENNEBERG E H, 1967. Biological foundations of language[M] New York: John Wiley & Sons.
NORTON B, 1995. Identity and language learning[M]. Hartlow: Pearson Education. 12.
OROUJLOU N, VAHEDI M, 2011. Motivation, attitude, and language learning[J]. Procedia: Social and behavioral sciences, 29: 994–1000.
沈阳 [YANG SHEN], 贺阳 [YANG HE], 2015. 语言学概论[M] [Introduction to linguistics]. 北京: 外语教学与研究出版社 [Foreign Language Teaching & Research Press].

10

A LITERACY HISTORY OF MY EARLY TWENTY YEARS

Jian Wu (吴坚)

In this chapter, I first describe my personal profile before the literacy story. I then respectively present the Chinese and English reading and writing journey during my first 20 years, which had a great influence on my life. Finally, my own expectation for the future during my childhood is unfolded. Based on the above, I come up with some ideas and thoughts about my life. This chapter explicates the theories of literacy autobiography writing and demonstrates my own literacy experiences in Chinese and English to prove that there is a close link between reading habits and the development of writing. Meanwhile, culture also plays a vital role in the process of my literacy.

I was born into an average family in the east of China. It was a place where many people spoke Wu dialect (吴语), which is quite different from Mandarin. For as long as I can remember, my parents always spoke in dialect. Thus, my first language is the Wu dialect, pronounced quite differently in Mandarin. As I grew up, I was sent in 2002 to an elementary school where the medium of instruction was Chinese. From that time, the door to developing both Chinese and English literacy was opened.

Childhood Nursery Rhymes

My grandmother (外婆) played a significant role during my childhood. Even now the lines "摇呀摇，摇到外婆桥。外婆请我吃年糕，糖一包，果一包，我是外婆的好宝宝"[1] often linger in my mind. When I was four years old, I used to cry when it was time for bed. My grandmother often sang "天黄黄，地皇皇，我家有个夜哭郎。每天念上三百遍，一夜困到大天亮"[2] when I cried to refuse to sleep. After hearing these rhymes, I would stop crying and go to sleep. My grandmother is illiterate, but she taught me a lot including honesty, politeness, kindness, and so on.

Mi states (2019) that nursery rhymes, as a traditional form of art, develop children's language abilities. Thus, nursery rhymes exerted an intangible influence on me. Now, I cannot remember many early nursery rhymes, but I did spend a carefree time during my childhood immersed in nursery rhymes.

Early Journey of Reading

According to Hull and Schultz (2002), most people tend to believe that literacy development ties in with schooling. Children develop their reading and writing abilities mainly in school. My first lessons learning reading and writing must have begun at kindergarten when I was five. I myself could read words with pinyin and wrote some phrases. However, influenced by the dialect, I could not distinguish "ing" and "in." But for me now, it is still an obstacle and difficulty. I was quite happy because games occupied my class time and snacks were always provided for us. Although I had never learned anything before entering elementary school, I experienced a pleasant time during my childhood.

At school, the basic and main aim of reading and writing was to pass different exams and be admitted to a university. However, as time went on, I found that my life was not just exams, but many other interesting things filled daily life. Thus, I began to read and write for fun. I started to select books I was interested in to read and I wrote some thoughts and poems in my diary.

When I began to attend school, my father brought me a lot of books including "The Four Classics of Chinese Literature," that is, *Romance of the Three Kingdoms*, *Water Margin*, *Journey to the West*, and *Dream of the Red Mansion*, in simplified versions. On my birthdays, my parents gave me books and novels as my gifts. Simultaneously, my elder cousins also presented me with plenty of books they had read. Ferris and Hedgcock (2004) argue that reading may actually make a more significant contribution to writing proficiency than the practice of writing, particularly when reading is self-initiated or self-selected. In my case, I got a lot from these books and novels. And I got high scores in Chinese examinations especially in Chinese writing during my elementary school time. However, when I was in junior high school, I was crazy about comic books and romantic fiction. I often spent pocket money my parents gave on these books, which lead to my setback in grades. So, I was criticized by both my teachers and parents. They said that it was a waste of time and I would lose my chance to get a high score in exams and finally my opportunity to go to high school and college. Since then, I reduced my time reading these books and spent more time studying. Although I thought carefully about my future, I just went to an ordinary high school.

I had not read English classics and novels until I went to college. When I was in my third year of university in the course *British and American Literature*, I was forced to read many Western masterworks and poems such as *Tess of the D'Urbervilles*, Shakespeare's *Sonnet* and *Pygmalion*, and so on. From then on, I had my first understanding of Western works and poems. In addition, I learned a lot of idiomatic expressions in English that were always applied to my English compositions.

Writing Experiences

Although I read many books from an early age, I can now rarely write good compositions in Chinese due to my limited vocabulary. My English compositions were really terrible. I could never write a composition like native people write.

Both my Chinese and English teachers introduced and analyzed the structure of one article and found the main sentence of the article. Then they asked us to follow the structure and write a similarly structured composition. Under such circumstances, students' test performance should improve but their cognitive and affective development might be hampered because they do not receive meaningful and relevant pedagogical resources (Erickson, 1984)[530]. Our main aim was to get a high score instead of producing a thoughtful and reflective composition.

Later, I encountered the Internet in high school. At that time, I registered with QQ and was nicknamed "世界是我的" (The world is mine). I started to post my articles and many comments and suggestions were received. At the same time, I knew the deficiency and weaknesses of my articles. Mendonca and Johnson (1994)[746] suggested that "students can re-conceptualize their ideas in light of their peers' recreations." The process of revising my articles according to my peers' advice helped improve my language and expand my ideas. Most importantly, we shared our feelings and thoughts with each other on the Internet. Meanwhile, I began to contact web words such as 7456 (气死我了) for being so mad and 88 (拜拜) for "Bye Bye," and so on.

During my senior high school time, I sometimes wrote poems and informal essays in my spare time, which made me more relaxed under high stress. Gao (2015) suggested that quotes make a difference in forming good habits and emphasizing ideals. Besides, my teacher let us write quotes and post them on the desk. I wrote the lines "书山有路勤为径, 学海无涯苦作舟" (Diligence is the only way out of the mountain of books; perseverance is the only boat through the sea of learning), which drove me until the end of the college entrance examination.

A Vision of the Future

When I was 14 years old, I hoped that one day I would become a famous novelist. I read many Kung fu novels and romantic novels and admired these writers greatly. Then, I was determined to write a novel and tried my best to be a well-known novelist. However, when I wrote the beginning, I gave up. I found it too difficult to write the whole story. Now, when I look back, I believe I could still be successful if I persevered at that time.

Now, I have to think about my future career. I hope to be an English teacher at a junior high school, so good reading and writing skills are a must for me to possess. From now on, I must force myself to read more Chinese and English books and communicate with others to enhance my English and other capabilities.

Conclusion

The literacy process is truly a priceless gift for me, during which I have learned quite a lot. I will never stop reading and writing, for they are always the treasure that can be manifested in one's speeches and deeds and that cannot be stolen by anyone else. Simultaneously, my literacy autobiography demonstrates that there is a close link between reading habits and the development of writing and good reading habits may facilitate the improvement of writing.

Notes

1 Row, row, row the boat,
  Row all the way to Grandma's bridge.
  Grandma treats me to rice cake.

  She gives me some fruits,
  She also gives me some candy.
  I am her baby.
2 Heaven King, Earth Queen
  Hear a child cry in my house
  Late every night.

  Read every day
  These very words—three hundred times.
  Sleep well through the night.

References

ERICKSON F, 1984. School literacy, reasoning, and civility: An anthropologist's perspective[J]. Review of educational research, 54(4): 525–546.
FERRIS D R, HEDGCOCK J S, 2004. Teaching ESL composition: Purpose, process, and practice[M]. New York: Routledge.
高长亭 [GAO CHANGTING], 2015. 名言警句在高校学生素质教育中的作用[J] [The roles of mottos and proverbs on character development among university students]. 湖北函授大学学报 [Hubei open education university journal], 32(2): 34–35.
HULL G, SCHULTZ K, 2002. School's out: Bridging out-of-school literacies with classroom practice[M]. New York: Teachers College Press.
MENDONCA C O, JOHNSON K E, 1994. Peer review negotiations: Revision activities in ESL writing instruction[J]. *TESOL quarterly*, 28(7): 745–769.
宓阿敏 [MI AMIN]. (2019). 用童谣促发展: 浅谈金典童谣在幼儿语言发展中的应用[J] [Using nursery rhymes to facilitate development: The use of classic nursery rhymes in children's language development]. 课程教育研究 [Curriculum education studies], 7(2): 25–26.

11
A JOURNEY OF READING AND WRITING IN CHINESE AND ENGLISH

Jinling Li (李金玲)

When it comes to thinking patterns, many people mention Robert Kaplan's idea that culture shapes one's mind to a large extent and that Chinese is spiral while English is linear (Kaplan, 1966). The Chinese, who are shaped by their oriental culture, may experience conflict when they learn English. I believe that cultural patterns influence Chinese learners' English learning, English writing in particular, but there are more factors beyond it. It is a fact that the individual is not static but dynamic, which means that one keeps his subjectivity so that he can selectively accept external influences. My personal Chinese and English learning experiences show how my writing style developed into what it is today. It also traces different factors that can contribute to a different literacy journey.

Exposure to the Literacy World

I was born in Yanjin county of Zhaotong city in the northeast of Yunnan province. I could only speak the Zhaotong dialect before I entered elementary school in my hometown, for my parents and all the people around me only really speak the local language. I started learning *Pinyin* and Chinese characters in the first grade of elementary school, a language that I could speak fluently, but couldn't write particularly smoothly. Whether you admit it or not, speaking Chinese is like using chopsticks to eat, it seems an "innate" skill of Chinese people. I was forced to write it over and over until I could write it correctly. Once, my father taught me to write Chinese characters by hand, but I suddenly got angry: "Not the same, not the same, what we wrote is different from what printed in my book," and then I threw away my pen and textbook. In fact, the reason was that my handwriting was too bad. I suffered from the character barriers in that I couldn't distinguish the use of some characters like "的、地、得," which tested my patience. Through practice day after day, I mastered *pinyin* well and knew some Chinese characters so that reading story books became one of the greatest pleasures in my childhood (the other is watching TV). I bought one Andersen story book every time I went to the bookstore with my mother. She'd happily give me 5 or 10 yuan to do this, for she is not well educated due to poor conditions in her childhood, but she clearly understood the importance of reading. So I knew that the ugly duckling could become a white swan with effort, that Thumbelina is so tiny that she just sits on a green stem, that the little girl who lights a match again, sees her grandmother's smile finally. These fairy tale books enriched my childhood and my inner world.

I made my "Chinese writing debut" in the third grade of elementary school. I still remember that I wrote one sentence as a paragraph in order to finish faster than my deskmate. My Chinese teacher corrected me that one sentence couldn't be a paragraph. So the first Chinese writing in my life ended in failure.

At the same time, English appeared in my school life as a new language. English class was "game time" for me then. The English teacher only taught us simple letter like "A, B, C, D…" or numbers like "one, two, three, four…" or words related to our personal life, such as "father, mother, teacher, doctor." Then she told us stories using those simple words. All in all, no English test was yet part of my primary school life.

Hit by the Monster, Struggle with the Monster

I went to middle school when I was 11, which was a painful but critical stage in my literacy journey.

After the "forced" study in elementary school, I have been able to write those Chinese characters fluently, like speaking them. But new barriers occurred and I couldn't recite the long ancient Chinese poems; I was confused by the mysterious classical Chinese like *LI SAO (The Lament)*; I was also puzzled by the connotation of Chinese, like the lily symbolizes purity at first. Fortunately, I crossed these barriers by reading in the morning, self-study class every day, and absorbing my Chinese teacher's explanation. Gradually, I have known the military strategist Zhuge Liang and his story of "borrowing the enemy's arrows"; I have learned about the miserable life of Xiang zi in Rickshaw Boy; I have also appreciated the spectacular natural beauty by the lines "It is torrent dashes down three thousand feet from high, if the Silver River fell from azure sky." I have to say that reading helped me a lot in my Chinese learning. Similar to Lai: "My reading preferences in turn shaped my writing style" (Lai, 2020)[219]. Some beautiful sentences, especially poems, would pop into my mind when I was writing a Chinese composition, which rescued me from my debut writing failure.

For English, only god knows how hard it was for me to learn English in junior high school. I found that English was no longer a "game paradise" for me. Instead, there were inexhaustible words, complicated grammars, numerous English readings that couldn't be fully understood. At that time, I was terrified. The strict middle school teacher was so enthusiastic about rote learning that she forced us to memorize words every day, and did plenty of exercises according to the grammar she taught. Moreover, it was a normal pattern for us to recite the text or grammar points. What I couldn't understand most was that she would punish us if we made mistakes in exercises. I thought English was a monster who was threatening me. Just like studies have shown, excessive anxiety can directly affect the effect of second language acquisition; the more anxiety, the lower the learning efficiency (Bai, 2016), which applied to me very well. I was so nervous that I couldn't think in English exams. Thus my English teacher seldom noticed me because of my poor performance.

One day, she picked some good pieces titled "My favorite person in my life" and showed them in class. Unexpectedly, one of them was mine! It was the experience of being praised by her for the first time that inspired my passion for English writing.

It has to be acknowledged that teaching methods and the attention students receive have an impact on their learning process and results (Peng, 2019). Because of her strict teaching methods and little attention to me, I was too nervous to follow her class well. But in the same way, the encouragement and affirmation of a teacher will greatly enhance the students' enthusiasm and creativity in study (Peng, 2019). It was this inadvertent encouragement that lightened my heart to pick up my confidence in English learning. I was so grateful for that encouragement even though she may have forgotten it. I gradually struggled with the monster with the belief that if others can, you also can, and sometimes you are the "other" to others.

During the struggle, I have suffered word barriers like a fence which stopped me. I tried to cross the fence by memorizing word lists, but I forgot the words quickly. Then I started to memorize words in reading, which is an easier way for me to learn these new words. I not only memorized the word itself, but also knew its collocation. In L2 acquisition, semantic collocation is an important part of language ability. Correct semantic collocations can eliminate Chinese English in language output (writing or speaking) so that learners can master idiomatic expressions. Learners' collocation input in and out of class will help their second language development, and they should learn, use, and accumulate collocations to improve writing skills (Wu, 2017). So memorizing words was my first step to struggle with the monster. Besides, I have faced incomprehensible grammar, which was like thorns that frightened me. I couldn't analyze the syntactic structure to know the meaning correctly. My way was to do some exercise with grammar books. Of course, I have been also puzzled by some cultural words. For example, "You are a white elephant" in English means "you are useless" rather than "you are an animal." I had to accumulate these special words and learned more about foreign cultures. Interestingly, I slowly became friends with the monster during the fight. In retrospect, this rote teaching model isn't the best way of teaching, but it is undeniable that this way lays sound foundation for most zero-based English learners in China.

Hold the "Secret" of Reading and Writing

I took the high school entrance examination and began my high school life in 2012. Like most Chinese students, countless knowledge points, practices, and exams crowded my last year of high school. Gradually, it seemed that it was easy to master the exam-based writing, both in Chinese and English. As Lai (2020)[219] wrote in her own literacy autobiography, I also learned several organizing strategies from my high school teacher. More specifically, "Kai men jian shan (开门见山)" features a straightforward approach to an argument, "Zu zhang xian zhi (卒章显志)" delays the thesis to the end of a passage, and "Jie wu yan zhi (借物言志)" uses events and objects to convey a hidden theme. Besides, I tried to write to the evaluation standards that my teachers used: write grammatically, choose the right words, and transition well (Lai, 2020)[222]. I always got good grades in Chinese and English tests by this secret method.

New Attitude to Reading and Writing

In 2015, I entered the Province University (pseudonym) with excitement as an English translation major student. As a university student, I seldom read or wrote in Chinese. To be frank, I was like most freshmen in China, who are birds escaping from their cage after they finishing a long and draining third year of high school. I was no longer motivated to learn to enter college. However, I gradually found that I couldn't keep up with my big university family.

The writing template wasn't a savior anymore. Besides grammar and limited words, my thinking model shaped by Chinese culture also hindered my English writing. Different thinking modes determine different forms of language expression. English is a linear pattern, which means one should get straight to the point, but my original pattern is shaped by oriental cultures where background and modifiers are needed before the point in writing (Kaplan, 1966)[2]. The reason is that the Chinese respects the Confucian doctrine and emphasizes the Doctrine of the Mean or *Zhongyong*. Therefore, when writing articles or expressing opinions, the Chinese do not directly show the theme, but first "beat around the bush," which is called spiral thinking mode. The British are influenced by ancient Greek and Roman philosophy, especially Plato-Aristotle's thoughts, so they tend to get straight to the point (Luo & Zhang, 2016). While culture shapes the mind, the mind also shapes writing style. "Chinese thinking mode + English grammar" bothered me a lot in English writing.

Then I changed my learning attitude and followed teachers' requirements. When I endured the pain that English brought to me, I also enjoyed the pleasure it brought to me. In the past four years, I have known the Anglo-Saxons who were from a different time and place; I have known the Mayflower that carried 102 people to pursue their liberty; I have also known the Elizabeth Bennet who dares to love and hate in *Pride and Prejudice*. Besides, I have known that study is not a duty, but self-improvement. And I have enjoyed reading *The Diary of Anne Frank*, *Jane Eyre*, *Pride and Prejudice*, *Wuthering Heights*, *Twelve Years a Slave*, and so on, which influenced my English writing potentially. I won't completely abandon my original writing style. Instead, I will integrate my original writing style into a new one under the influence of the expressions in English novels.

March Forward

Now, I have continued to major in English translation in the Province University. I have gradually realized that my major largely influenced me to ignore Chinese, and to stay at the level of spoken language. English, whether I learn it actively or passively, I am in contact with it every day. But these two languages are of equal importance and have their own unique charm. One of the roles of translators is to convey the meaning and style of the source language, and I have already experienced that the lines of the source language are so graceful, but I couldn't find suitable words in the target language to translate them. So there are more things to consider than thinking patterns and culture.

Conclusion

As the only child in my family, no older sibling can set an example for me to follow in my study. My father doesn't often talk with me about school things after class. My mother, a less-educated woman, can take care of me well except study. So the main explorer of my journey of reading and writing in Chinese and English is me. It doesn't mean that I am the only character in this journey, but it means that I am the master and I subjectively accept the external factors.

When I recall my academic study years, there were factors outside of thinking patterns that influenced my writing and reading. When I was a blank page (the time I started school), I was dotted by the regular education system which forced me to follow the standard writing style to get high scores. Later, I developed my own taste for writing. I believed that good writing should express deep meanings with elegant language and poetry. Now, I change my "elegant" style while in higher education, which tells me that writing is diverse according to different purposes. For example: can I use rhetoric and poems in legal text writing? No! Can I use "I" in my graduation paper? No! Can I use "I think" in academic writing? Yes, of course in literacy autoethnography! So writing can be influenced by social environment, teachers, peers, writing genres and purposes rather than only thinking patterns. Figuring this, we can create an acceptable writing style rather than follow others all time.

References

柏涛 [BAI TAO], 2016. 浅谈个体差异因素对二语习得的影响及其教学启示[J] [On individual differences, their impact on second language acquisition, and teaching implications]. 海外英语 [Overseas english], 7: 7–8.

KAPLAN R B, 1966. Cultural thought patterns in intercultural education[J]. Language learning, 16(1): 1–20.

LAI J, 2020. Negotiating contrasting languages and rhetorics[M]//Canagarajah S. Transnational literacy autobiographies as translingual writing. New York: Routledge. 218–227.

罗娇 [LUO JIAO], 张娇 [ZHANG JIAO], 2016. 中英议论文写作模式的文体分析——浅析文化思维模式对英汉写作模式的影响[J] [Genre analysis of Chinese and English argumentary writing: The impact of cultural thinking modes on English and Chinese writing]. 亚太教育 [Asia Pacific education], 13: 103–104.

彭操红 [PENG CAOHONG], 2019. 教师态度对学生学习投入的影响研究[J] [Teachers' attitudes and their impact on students' investment in learning]. 学周刊 [Weekly journal on learning], 36: 62–63.

伍桂媛 [WU GUIYUAN], 2017. 英语搭配习得与中国学习者二语写作水平发展的有效性研究[D] [A study of the efficacy of English collocations and Chinese English learners' second language writing development]. MA thesis, Guangdong Foreign Studies University.

12
MY FOOTPRINTS OF LANGUAGE LEARNING

Lijuan Li (李丽娟)

In this chapter, I first explain the importance of language that it is as a communicator of the message. And then I introduce my four different stages of language learning. Every stage includes the learning process and my feelings on the languages. Last, I made some summaries to my process of language learning.

Language learning is critical. "I like to say that we should study languages because languages are the only thing worth knowing even poorly" (Lomb, 2008). Needless to say, the process of language learning is tough but colorful. Language is close to our life. We communicate with each other by language. Language is more than verbal communication. It also involves many aspects: writing, reading, even academic monograph. Language has many uses, and the use depends on where we use it. When it comes to language, I have learned three languages, even four. As a medium of the message, the role of language is very dominant as a key to the success of the message delivered properly.

Learning the Naxi Language

My first language development was profoundly influenced by the traditional culture of ethnic minorities. Minority language is my first language. I'm a minority—Naxi. Of course, the Naxi language became my first language. We (Naxi)have our culture which only belongs to us. We also have our own script or characters. To my regret, I can hardly write in Naxi. Strictly speaking, there was no distinct process of Naxi language learning. We speak Naxi just like the Chinese eat with chopsticks. My parents communicated with me in Naxi when I was a baby (even though I couldn't speak yet). This is why I spoke Naxi from the day I could speak. Before I went to primary school, I always spoke Naxi. What's worse, I can hardly speak Mandarin. Nobody taught me Mandarin. My parents haven't got a good education, and they have no ability to teach me.

DOI: 10.4324/9781003288756-15

I remembered a terrible thing that made me ashamed for a long time when I was a little child. Every year during the Spring Festival, my aunt, who is my mother's youngest sister, comes back. She has a son who is one year older than me. I called him cousin. The biggest distinction between me and him is that our living environments are different. He was brought up in the city, but I was born in a village. His first language is not Naxi. My brother speaks a kind of Lijiang dialect which is similar to Mandarin. Lijiang dialect and Mandarin are only slightly different in tone. On that day, my mother let me play with my brother, and we were outside. My neighbor had a persimmon tree. My brother came from the city, and he was curious about that tree. He asked me, "What's this?" I completely drew a blank. There was no word in Mandarin or dialect that matched persimmon in my mind. For all this, I still didn't want to admit my ignorance. So I blurted out: "taozhi" (taozhi is the Naxi word for persimmon). My brother was confused. He understood it as peach because its pronunciation sounded like peach in Mandarin. I realized he misunderstood me, but I didn't want to explain anymore. I had no better explanation for it at that time. I just wanted to finish this topic quickly. Now I look back on it feeling ashamed. We couldn't understand each other at that time. The Naxi language has had a great influence on me. Because of my Naxi upbringing, I learned Chinese or Mandarin later than my peers, like my cousin.

Learning Chinese Mandarin

This means that I needed to speak Mandarin when I went to primary school. There are many signs on the walls of the school which said "please speak Mandarin." All teachers used Mandarin in teaching classes, and students also needed to use Mandarin to talk with teachers. Actually, all of my classmates, even all of my schoolmates, are minorities. We have our own minority language. At that time, we were good at our own minority languages over Chinese or Mandarin. We still used our own languages after class. Maybe we have been accustomed to using the minority language.

Our Chinese teacher was a very serious person who would detain us after school because we hadn't finished our homework or had made mistakes. She had an rigorous attitude towards her teaching. We needed to keep a daily diary. I learned a lot from her. I would finish my homework carefully every time because of her strictness. During primary school, I did a lot of writing (even though it was just superficial writing). I also learned "pinyin" which is difficult for me. "*pinyin*" is using Romanized spellings to transliterate Chinese. However, "pinyin" involves many elements, such as initials, finals, tone ... I always couldn't distinguish them clearly, especially the alveolar nasal and velar nasal. I still cannot distinguish them now. Our Chinese teacher asked us to buy a book that contained many excellent compositions. She thought we needed to improve our writing level.

Chinese and Mandarin are the same in a sense. If we have to figure out the difference between them, I think it should their range. Chinese include many dialects which belong to China. (All of dialects are inseparable from Chinese even though we may not understand because of our different living region). I think Mandarin is the basic of Chinese learning. In my hometown, there are many other minorities (such as Yi people, Lisu people) who live in the mountain. Many of them have no awareness of education. Some children stay their educational level in fifth or sixth grade. They have no motivation to get more knowledge. Most of them got married at a very young age. Some children even cannot speak Mandarin, let alone learn Chinese. Maybe one's educational level can change one's concept.

Learning English

I received my English textbook when I was grade three of primary school. However, if we discuss the stage of English learning, it should speak from my first grade of middle school. Our primary school have no professional English teacher, so the English textbook just a superficial book for us. We know about nothing about English. Even more ridiculous, we must take an English exam in such a situation that we never have English class. Fortunately, all types of questions of test paper are multiple choice and judgment questions. We lived without English for three years.

English appeared in my life when I went to the middle school. The period of middle school was a turning point on my road of English learning. It was also at that time that I made an indissoluble bond with English. I met my best English teacher whose name is Dorothy. Her charm attracted me. She is a quite patient person believing that there are no bad students in her eyes. She didn't regard score as the norm of balancing bad or good students. On the contrary, she believed every student can learn English well unless he is a lazy man. Those students who get poor English scores will become her "key protected object." She constantly encouraged them to learn English and never give them up. Many students began to learn English with her encouragement except those people who gave up his own. I love her teaching method. Her class was always full of vitality. She not only encouraged me but also indicated my deficiencies. She told me that I should pay attention to my English calligraphy, and she suggested me to buy some exercise book which can improve my calligraphy. She also has a good pronunciation of English. But we didn't pay much attention to oral English at that time. (It also caused my poor Oral English now.) She also helped us subscribe to the English newspaper every month. We can practice our listening, writing and reading. At that time, all of the subjects, English was my best subject.

When I went to high school, English become more important. We needed to take the college entrance examination. I didn't expect that I chose the English as my major during my college life. We made contact with English every day. Our teacher requested us to read some English masterwork. We also need to finish thesis in English. That thesis is the longest writing I have written so far. I also didn't expect that I chose English translation as my major during my postgraduate life. Maybe English has an indissoluble bond with me. At present, I have more chance to know about English writing. We have specialized writing class.

Learning Japanese

I only had one year experience of Japanese learning. I learned Japanese as my second foreign language when I was junior student of university. I think learning a language requires much time and effort. One year is too short to learn a language. So my Japanese is not very good. I feel not very interested in Japanese. We just learned the vocabulary, grammar and simple dialogue of Japanese.

Conclusion

Having said all of the above, is there any important element in language learning? Of course, I believe interest is the best teacher. I have my personal experience. I connected with Japanese when I was junior student of university. Before I learn it, it was full of excitements in my mind. However, good times don't last long; I lost my interest in Japanese soon. And it led to a terrible outcome that my Japanese become worse and worse. Interest is the basic of learning.

I can speak Naxi language because of my identity as a minority. Language is a valuable element in our life. "There may no other word that has as many connotations as this noun does with its few letters" (Lomb, 2008). Our background of family and learning will influence our language learning. When it comes to language, we should not only focus on speaking but also develop our reading and writing skills. Those famous writers whose works are popular in the academic community are involved in reading and writing. Reading and writing are very necessary for us in language learning.

References

LOMB K, 2008. Polyglot: How I learn languages[M]. Berkley, CA: TESL-EJ.

13

A WAY TO MEMORIZE

Reading and Writing

Yufeng Zhang (张玉凤)

Not being smart and having a poor ability to express myself, I've suffered various embarrassments uncountable times in front of the class or in public such as being too nervous to speak in a normal way. No one could expect that I would succeed in literacy, particularly in reading and writing in English. But I really made it, and here is the way I have progressed over the years with literacy, both Chinese and English, mainly in reading and writing.

Early Exposure to Reading

I was born into an ordinary family in Shandong province after my brother, who was two years older than me. There's no communication gap between us. Both my father and brother greatly affected me in my early exposure to reading for my mother was busy caring for us.

Learning Chinese Characters While Playing with My Brother

My brother brought me much happiness through his interest in reading and playing. My first reading must have come from 斗兽棋 which translates as Jungle or Dou Shou Qi ("Game of Fighting Animals"). It's a traditional Chinese board game played on a 7×9 board, also known as Jungle Chess, Animals Chess, or Children's Chess. With a piece of paper with 16 panes, each pane had a small picture of an animal (such as elephant, lion, tiger, leopard, wolf, dog, cat, or mouse. Each animal has two panes for the two-player game) with Chinese characters of animals' names like "象, 狮, 虎." All the panes can be cut individually from the whole paper. My brother and I played with those cards frequently.

I started learning the real Chinese characters when I was four years old. I was so interested in that game and curious about it that I wanted to play it every day.

DOI: 10.4324/9781003288756-16

According to Berlyne (1960)[22], "Curiosity is a way of managing arousal." Indeed, gradually, I understood the pithy formula "1 象 2 狮 3 虎 4 豹 5 狼 6 狗 7 猫 8 鼠" just by playing which helped me to win the game or avoid being beaten by my brother. But now, when I look back on those days, I am surprised to find that it's a good way to learn and to read during playing, especially for a small child, and it can greatly arouse interest in reading. At that time, with one set of Jungle Chess sold out, the markets began to introduce new samples. All the Chinese characters and pictures were still the same as the former ones except the color of the pictures was changed. However, I still liked to play the new Jungle Chess; anything new was always interesting to me. Though I couldn't write those Chinese characters at that time, I have learned how they were read and what they look like. Thanks to the Jungle Chess and my brother, they lead me in the way of early reading and learning Chinese characters. Concurrently, the Juggle Chess taught me the culture of the food chain and competition among animals. At that time, I just learned the weaker are eaten by the stronger. As I grew up, I realized that it is similar with humans. Although the competition is keen and tough, it is everywhere around us. What we can do is improve ourselves and make ourselves stronger.

Not long after that, my brother went to kindergarten while I was left at home as I was not old enough. Longing for his return to play with me, one day he showed me a magic paper secretly when he got home. Oh! It's money! Printed on the paper neatly in lines with different colors, they are so small and cute! While I was dreaming of buying new Juggle Chess in those days, I asked him hopefully: "We can use it to buy more new Jungle Chess, right?" Then, I was answered negatively, "No, we can't. It was just toy money or some pictures of money which cannot be used to buy anything. It's illegal." However, it didn't sweep away my interest in the magic toy; I was still crazy about it because I had never owned such a magic toy before. Cutting out the "money" from the paper, he began to teach me how much it all was and we played together to imitate buying something from him and then he made an exchange with me. However, I was too small and couldn't calculate much. But it was my early exposure to math reading with little Chinese characters and a new exploration for me. In addition, I had to bear in mind that it's illegal to use counterfeit money in society, more especially, in the world.

It reminded me of my uncle. He was once cheated by a customer who asked to pay in cash during a trade with over 20,000 yuan. My uncle fully trusted him because they were not strangers to each other and he didn't use the currency detector to determine whether the money was genuine. However, one day when my uncle used some of the money to pay for something, he was told that the money was counterfeit. It was not expected! A sense of being cheated came into his mind! After checking the remaining money, four hundred yuan was also counterfeit! It's unbelievable! My uncle felt very sad and burned the counterfeit on the fire to avoid someone else being cheated. That scene had a deep impact on me. It made me realize some twisted culture in our society in which someone pursued profit no matter what methods they used or how dangerous it was. In addition, I learnt that being kind as much as you can, no matter what happens, such as my uncle who chose to destroy the counterfeit instead of cheating someone else. Being a man with a heart of gold no matter where we are, who we become, or what we experience, that's also the essence of Chinese culture.

Listening to the Songs with Father's Tape Player

When I was a small kid, my father was fond of listening to music on his tape player. He would play it when he was free. Meanwhile, I was exposed to some songs he listened to and learned some lyrics such as "这里的山路十八弯" (The roads here of the mountains were crooked), "雾里看花，水中望月" (Watch the flowers through the fog while observing the shadow of the moon in the water) "父亲就像拉车的牛" (Fathers are like the horse pulling the truck), and "常回家看看" (Back home to visit your parents as often as possible). Though it's old-fashioned now, it stands for that era. According to Hermann Ebbinghaus (2013) who puts forth the Ebbinghaus Forgetting Curve and suggested that it is critical to review regularly to retain what has been learned Without understanding the meaning behind those lyrics at that time, I just memorized them for my father always played them.

It was not until I grew up that I really understood the meaning of those lyrics. In particular, reading, listening to, and memorizing those lyrics, on the one hand, greatly added to my happiness, and, on the other, drove me to understand my parents early on. Some lyrics such as "父亲就像拉车的牛" and "常回家看看" stand for part of Chinese traditional culture, especially filial piety. Chinese parents work exceptionally hard to support their family and raise their offspring without any expectation of being paid back. What they want is to look forward to their children becoming better and better in good health as well realizing their dreams and they expect nothing in return, even though they live a poor life. As they age, they just expect their children to come back to reunite as much as possible; even if it's just for a short time, that's enough for them. However, each time they see each other, the less time there will be. As I grew up, I began to comprehend the true meaning behind those lyrics and understand my parents more deeply. Indeed, the culture of lyrics greatly affected me. To some extent, that's also some essence of Chinese writing. According to You (2010)[142], "Observe both the natural world and human society and to capture their essence." To me, the essence of human society is the culture that binds its members together and shapes their ways of thinking and behaving.

Having My Own Story Books

Having admired my brother for having his own story books which were different to those books at home, I eventually got one when I was admitted into kindergarten. I began to read it again and again, especially those stories I preferred. What impressed me most deeply was a story telling me about keeping quiet when someone is sleeping. One day Miaoli's friend came to her home and her mother was sleeping. She spoke loudly: "我妈妈正在睡觉呢，你小点声。" (My mother is sleeping now, please keep in a low voice). Maybe she just wanted to warn others to keep quiet. However, she wasn't aware that she spoke more loudly than others. The story was ridiculous but educational. It has deeply affected me for many years. It has taught me to mind my words, attitude and manners no matter where I am, which situation I was in and what role I play. What's more, it has taught me to doit myself before asking others to do it. The lesson is similar to the Chinese teaching "吾日三省吾身" (I examine myself three times daily). Stories and words like these have shaped my character and taught me to make time for self-reflection every day to find where I'm weak, where I can improve, as well as consider the situation from another person's side as much as possible.

Calligraphy

In traditional Chinese culture, if someone can write Chinese characters squarely, he will be knowledgeable, educated, and well-cultivated. Similarly, if one student writes squarely and neatly in their daily life or during an exam, he will be praised by the teachers and achieve high sores on his paper. Therefore, almost all the teachers and the majority of parents pay great attention to calligraphy. According to the Chinese saying, "字如其人" (The characters you write is the same as your personal character).

Being Punished for not Writing Chinese Characters Squarely

I was punished during a dictation in grade four by my Chinese teacher who found one of my Chinese characters was not square and upright enough while other words were square and correct. The Chinese character "平" which I wrote on the first line was not straight enough, even a little crooked. Although it's not wrong, I was punished and had to write this Chinese character 50 times. Fortunately, it's only one simple Chinese character. Since then, I became more careful in her class, especially during the dictation about my calligraphy. It was my first time being punished and it taught me a great lesson in my calligraphy: write as squarely as possible. In addition, my mother was strict with my handwriting. She always looked over my homework and pointed out which Chinese character was not square. Luckily, there was no punishment from her, however, I had to correct them again. In Chinese culture, the attitude is more important in many aspects such as if I can't write squarely, then my attitude may be not right. If my attitude is right, then I will get better. They pay more attention to this.

Escaping from Practice Calligraphy

On entering middle school, which is a boarding school although not far from home, I couldn't go back until the weekend. On the other hand, I felt lucky to escape of mother checking my calligraphy. However, not long after that, we were asked to practice calligraphy every day, at least one piece of paper, according to the assignment from my Chinese teacher who wrote very square and upright. I practiced by tracing a model which is the "文言文" (Classical Chinese) in our textbooks. I reviewed what I learned while practicing calligraphy. At the very beginning, I did it very carefully because practicing calligraphy calmed me down and made me concentrate as well as creating the desire to write as square, upright, and neat as my Chinese teacher. As the saying goes, what you put in is what you gain. It works indeed. My calligraphy improved a lot after the first semester. However, with so much homework to do in the third semester, I stopped practicing calligraphy every day. Instead, I would trace the model with several pieces of paper in one day if I had time so that I could hand them in the following days without practicing every day. While I was feeling lucky to escape from practicing calligraphy, I was caught by our Chinese teacher. "Please show me your prepared calligraphy. You have traced for several pages." Having nothing to say, I had to hand in my "prepared calligraphy." Consequently, my handwriting deteriorated a lot. Luckily, I learned a lot of classic sentences according to the model such as "冰冻三尺非一日之寒" (Rome was not built in one day) which accounted for my calligraphy. Growing up, I began to feel more and more pitiful that I didn't persist in practicing calligraphy at that age for good handwriting really plays an important role in some areas. After having worked as a teacher, I always told my students to practice calligraphy as much as they can to avoid being like me. As mentioned at the start, in Chinese culture, all the teachers pay great attention to the calligraphy. I become one of them.

Writing Compositions/"Poems"

Resulting from my limited reading and poor ability of expressing myself, I was afraid of writing composition in primary school. Once my Chinese teacher asked us to write a composition about a person. I chose the title "我的爷爷" (My grandfather) and covered two pages and handed it in. The next day, my Chinese teacher praised me in front of the class and asked me to read it to our classmates. Then she asked me to copy it on the blackboard while my classmates wrote it down in their notebooks as a model passage. It was my first time being praised for composition which encouraged me a lot. Since then, my worry about being afraid of writing compositions seemed to reduce a lot. However, my composition was not good enough now that I read much. As we all know, reading has a direct correlation with writing. According to Ye (2017)[491], "Reading is the base of writing."

Another important event is that I used to write short "poems" or short passages on the QQ board during my university life. One of them got the second prize in a competition of compositions which motivated me a lot. As I look back on those "poems," I found them ridiculous and not even fluent. However, the process of writing or creating them still kept me calm at that time. See, for example, the following two poems:

冬日有感	Winter Thoughts
狂风肆虐枯蓬舞,	High wind howls and blows weeds away,
乱玉碎琼信满途。	With aspiration I stand in the snowy day.
寒梅傲枝影半墙,	Plum blossom with her tenacious branch casts shadow on the wall,
飞鸿踏雪胜三秋。	Swans clawing on the snow ground surpass the most beautiful fall.
陌	In a Trance
春风不喜参尤半,	The spring breeze comes with my mixed feelings,
浅禾摇曳雨中漫。	Seedlings flicker and diffuse in the rain drizzling.
残梦楼空三更钟,	Odd dream with empty building, it was already midnight,
惊起恍之前如颤。	I woke up, stunned, trembling before the dim light.

I don't clearly remember the backgrounds of why I wrote these "poems" at that time. Nonetheless, writing in Chinese remains an effective way for me to remember my past.

The Most Striking Memories of Writing in English

Memory is a storehouse filled with various experiences of our past life covering all aspects, including reading and writing. Reminiscing about the past, the most striking memory of my earliest writing in English dates back to my university life when I was a senior during the last winter holiday.

Having been looking forward to the winter holidays coming, I was suddenly told that something unfortunate happened to my family. With little money, I decided to take a part-time job and made an difficult decision that I would live in the classroom secretly. Then I moved ten desks to set up a "bed" to sleep on as well as a "desk" for reading and writing. With no hot water, heating, or lights, the first night I couldn't sleep at all with tears escaping continuously in the cold classroom. I began to comfort myself: "You are a tough girl with a strong mind. Everything will be better soon when you wake up." However, I didn't dare to turn on the lights for fear of being caught by security because it was forbidden to live in the classroom especially during the winter holiday. Instead, I just prepared for my lessons under the dim light of my computer screen; I was then teaching an English reading and writing course. Although it's very tough for me, I persisted because it's my duty to make a good lesson for all my students. Gardner (1979)[45] defines motivation in his social-psychological models as the "combination of efforts plus desire to achieve the goal of learning the language plus favor attitudes towards learning the language." My motivation came from my desire to do a good job as well as pressure from my job. It's my first time to work as a real English teacher. Wanting to make it as perfect as possible, I did a lot of reading and writing. What's more, surprisingly, I found that

I was more efficient and creative in that tough condition by myself. Meanwhile, I would mark the inspiration coming from a particular matter or objects around. This work experience improved my English writing to some extent. Gradually, I got used to this "secret" life although it was a little tough.

However, something unexpected happened. One day when I got off work to go to my "secret home," I was astonished to find that all of my bedding had disappeared! How could I do the English reading and writing for tomorrow's teaching? How would I live in the classroom tonight? Feeling anxious and scared, I tried to calm myself down and went to ask security who might have taken my bedding. "Why are you living here?" they asked. "A serious car accident happened to my father recently. The money has run out. I had found a part-time job already and promised not to cancel, also, I have little money to rent a house." Luckily, they returned the bedding to me, and I went back to my "secret room" happily. What impressed me most deeply was that two security men knocked on the door, one of them carrying a thermos and the other with an electric heater in his hand which he gave to me instead of using it himself. They moved me to tears, these warm-hearted people in front of me. What's more, another security man the same age as my grandfather bought me another new heater and blanket. I must be the luckiest and happiest girl in the world. There were no words to express my appreciation to them except to work hard and do more careful writing for my teaching. Those men with a heart of gold greatly affected me a lot, especially when I met someone who was in trouble. Maybe that's some essence of Chinese culture: help each other and pass it on.

With time passing by, I spent the whole winter holiday between the classroom and my workplace. Although many years have passed, that lucky warmth flashes occasionally in my memory. It encourages me to go forward, especially when I want to give up, and especially when I feel stressed with some difficult English writing. I always tell myself that "The most difficult time has gone; everything will be easier compared with before. There's no way to give up." As the Chinese saying goes, "吃得苦中苦, 方为人上人" (No pain, no gain). In Chinese culture, no matter how hard something was, it will be better one day. Also, I strongly believe that all that you have gone through will pay you back one day in another way, which will help you grow up well. As the saying goes, only those who endure the most, become the highest. Every time when I encounter difficult times, I will turn to writing to grab my attention and calm me down. It really motivates me a lot.

Reflections on My English Writing as a Postgraduate

Before becoming a postgraduate, I hadn't tried to keep weekly journals until my English writing teacher Mr Yang asked us to do so. At first, I had no idea how to organize the language natively and how to express what I thought clearly. Luckily, with Mr. Yang's help, I have improved a lot, although I am not the best. What we look forward to is seeing the comments he gives us on our English writing. It's a way to check and reflect. No mistakes, no progress. Over time, I have become less tired of writing weekly journals as I know it contributes to practicing and expressing myself better. What's more, I have learned to use writing to remember my daily life.

Furthermore, I have learned much from writing my literacy autobiography, as recounted in this chapter. My literacy autobiography helped me to understand my writer identity as rooted in my past life and literacy experiences (Ivanić, 1998). Without the autobiography, I would never reflect the past, the way of my literacy. It reminds me of the past and gives a lot of useful help in my following studying. Although the process is difficult, it's a way of growing up.

Conclusion

For me, literacy, in both Chinese and English, has been difficult because I was not smart and had a poor ability to express myself. The way covering past has benefited me a lot in shaping my personality and thought as well as some cultural views which will contribute to my future literacy level. My literacy autobiography, as informed by autoethnographic research (Chang, 2008), also demonstrates my literacy achievement to some extent.

References

CHANG H, 2008. Autoethnography as method[M]. Walnut Creek, CA: Left Coast Press.
(德) 艾宾浩斯著 [EBBINGHAUS H], 2013. 记忆的奥秘[M] [The secret of memory] (D WANG, Trans.). 北京: 北京理工大学出版社 [Beijing Polytech University Press].
GARDNER R, 1979. Social psychological aspects of second language acquisition: The role of attitude and motivation[M]. London: Oxford University Press.
IVANIĆ R, 1998. Writing and identity: the discoursal construction of identity in academic writing[M]. Amsterdam: John Benjamins.
叶圣陶 [YE SHENTAO], 2017. 好读书而求甚解[M] [Read well by not reading too well]. 北京: 开明出版社 [Kaiming Press].
You X, 2010. Writing in the devil's tongue: A history of English composition in China[M]. Carbondale, IL: Southern Illinois University Press.

14
MY ROAD ON ACQUISITION OF READING AND WRITING

Wanjun Shi (时皖君)

This is a chapter related to literacy autobiographical writing, a record of my process of reading and writing acquisition. I divide the chapter into three parts as important nodes to present what I have experienced regarding my early reading, my passion for writing, as well as my future expectation, analyzing the reasons for different behaviors in each stage and how such experience has sculpted me step by step. Based on my personal experience and relative theories, I concluded that the growth environment, educational background, culture, and the special people we meet "help [us] to construct a more complex identity" (Tso, 2020)[175] and have a profound impact on an individual's reading and writing development.

Back to My Early Reading

I was born and raised in an ordinary working-class family in the east of China, growing up in an environment where Jiangsu dialect was spoken. Like most other children whose parents were busy at work, I spent my childhood in the countryside with grandparents before kindergarten. Influenced by my grandpa, an art lover who operated a troupe after retirement, I was exposed to music, instruments, and opera since a little girl. It was my initial language acquisition way in which Mandarin, Cantonese, and Hokkien were all involved in different kinds of music. Though not learned systematically, such cultural edification in the early years stimulated my sensitivity to language to some extent. Also, with open-minded parents who were always willing to buy books and generous in my education, I was fortunate enough to do some reading in my pre-school age. Nowadays, with classics like 《唐诗三百首》 (*Three hundred Poems of the Tang Dynasty*) still lying on my bookshelf, although most of which were obscure for me to understand, I accumulated some literary literacy by rote.

DOI: 10.4324/9781003288756-17

However, such experience didn't make me stand out in writing during primary school, especially when I took my first composition class in the third grade. For me, that was a lesson in which everything was easy to understand but hard to finish, and I guess, what made it was my age, an age with little desire to express myself. After all, living in the deepest part of the alley with few buddies to communicate made me an introverted girl who was scared of speaking, let alone writing at length. Meanwhile, as most of the teachers in China only focused on imparting writing skills but ignored the development of our writing interest and ability, seldom did my writing teacher guide us on how to write essays step by step. He just provided us with writing templates (some sentences or paragraphs that can provide a frame suitable for all topics) to fight against exams, which was a test-taking strategy helping us improve scores quickly, but impeding our cognitive development (Ferris & Hedgcock, 2004).

A Passion for Writing Inspired

I can't remember when everything changed. Maybe it was in my junior high school period, what was also called adolescence. In my eyes, the richest time in a person's life is when he or she is a teenager, always with a wide imagination. Therefore, with an expression desire breaking through the restricting 'fence' of formal education, my writing door was suddenly opened by reading interesting literary works. It just so happened that the novels written by Guo Jingming were particularly popular at that time. His works such as *Most Novel* and *Tiny Times* were highly sought after by middle school students. So, as per most teenagers, I spent all of my pocket money buying his books, trying to imitate his vivid, descriptive, and graceful words. In fact, I still have no idea about the reason for my crazily addicted to his words today. But in this way, I did make great progress in writing, and to be exact, it was the start to feeling the magical power of words and literature. After that, I began to read diverse books, from masterpieces on paper to mixed literature online; I took part in writing contests, was active in the school newspaper and radio station. Gradually, with the assistance of my Chinese teacher Mrs Zhou who collected all my school writing, I published a composition collection named "且听君吟."

Of course, the surge of expression is the hallmark of adolescence, and I believe, I was absolutely not that special one. Moreover, I fell in love with a boy at that time, which I think was one of the motivations for my thinking and writing. So, whenever I recall that unforgettable time, I always sigh and remember that it was a rare thing that my desire to express myself, including delicate emotion, melodramatic words, and the mood that now seems childish, without being laughed at, instead, was carefully protected and encouraged by some special people including the teachers and classmates I met.

Writing, Never Far Away from Me

In 2014, I entered a college close to my hometown, studying a major chosen by my parents. In fact, it was such a boring major to me that, in addition to English class,

I had no interest in other professional courses at all. I don't know why but maybe it was still language that attracted me a lot. Here, I use "still" to emphasize the place of language in my heart. As a language learner from primary school, I have both experienced the achievement and challenge that writing brought to me. Four years' undergraduate study as a non-linguistic major student made me feel that writing has been moving away from me. However, an accidental chance broadened my reading and writing path. In my sophomore year, I joined the school English Literature Club together with my best friend Alice, one of my college classmates who had a great passion for writing. Surrounded by various foreign language books and lively discussion with international students, we shared stories and articles with each other, which brought me into a real literature paradise and simultaneously aroused my enthusiasm for becoming a translator. Being a translator, which was a new identity I constructed in my mind from that moment, has opened another door for my second language acquisition (SLA), and with unremitting effort I became an MTI student in the last year.

Nowadays, I write a lot in both Chinese and English, from simple film reviews to easy essays, literacy poems to an academic thesis, in which I explored my moods, thoughts, and imaginations and saw a different world, including a different me. I asked myself all the time, is writing far away from me? Absolutely not. Although not being a professional writer, writing, as a silent voice, has never left me. Instead, it lights me up whenever there is frustration, misery, confusion, or happiness. That's the power of writing, or more precisely, the power of language.

Conclusion

Looking back at the journey I've taken, my past experience has shaped me into what I am now. Our "personal growth has not been bounded and stable, but rather bounded by ideals and experiences that surround a dynamic learning process" (Chang, 2008)[201]. At first, I just loved reading, which filled me with fantasy. Later, I yearned to describe and record everything I had learned, seen, and thought of. The acquisition of reading and writing, in my eyes, is not a process achieved overnight; instead, it's formed in the drops of our growth. The growth environment, our education background, as well as the special people we meet become important factors that influence how we perform today.

References

CHANG H, 2008. Autoethnography as method[M]. Walnut Creek, CA: Left Coast.
FERRIS D R, HEDGCOCK J S, 2004. Teaching ESL composition: Purpose, process, and practice. New York: Routledge.
TSO B, 2020. Rediscovering heritage identity through literacy[M]//CANAGARAJAH S. Transnational literacy autobiographies as translingual writing. New York: Routledge. 175–180.

15

MY CONQUEST OF LANGUAGE

Zihan Zhao (赵子涵)

As a language learner, my L1 is my home language, L2 is Mandarin, and L3 is English. This article is the description of the whole process of my language acquisition, using the method of autoethnography. During my writing, I find it is difficult to recall the old memories about my language learning, hence I ask my relatives the detailed information of it, and they show me some photos which really help me to remind of the old things. This article consists of four parts. The first part is a preface introducing my talents in language when I was a little girl. The second part is the attitude to English and the home language. The third part is my introspection at every stage of English writing in my life. The last part is my feelings about Chinese and English writing.

Preface

I have to say when I was a little girl about one or two years old I started to show talent in language. I began to speak earlier to my peers. I also liked singing, especially Yu Opera and pop music. On my way to the kindergarten, my grandfather would carry me on his shoulders and teach me to sing the opera word by word, and surprisingly I learned very fast and finally could sing a lot of opera (although I almost forget now). Honestly, I was too young to understand the meaning of them at that moment, I just really enjoyed myself singing and performing, and also the praise of adults. However, as I grew up a little, almost three or four years, I began to understand the actual meaning of them, and what the lyrics of the song were about. I still remember when my father sang a song named *Mother* (《母亲》) performed by Yan Weiwen (阎维文), I cried long and bitterly and was afraid of telling him the reason why I was crying is my mother never wiped tears for me (there is a lyric of this song "your mother will wipe your wronged tears forever"). My father was shocked that such a little girl could understand the deep meaning of it. I have to say that I was born to know and understand it.

What a lively girl! Well, people change; I am not sure what I have gone through over these years and my friends now regard me as a sober person who is not so expressive and confident sometimes. Maybe I have grown up to be an adult, not the same as the bold girl who never felt shy or shame any longer. It is hard to say if it is good for me.

Attitude to English and Home Language

As a Henan native, I love my hometown and never give a hoot about some people's prejudice. I know it still has a long way to go to improve itself, but your hometown is the place only you can complain about, not other people.

Henan dialect is relatively similar to Mandarin so I change myself easily and do not have any difficulty communicating with other people in Mandarin. I never intended to learn it even in any detailed pronunciation as people in other places mispronounce the "看看" (*kan kan*) and "康康" (*kang kang*) just because they cannot distinguish the front and back nasals.

When I was in Henan Normal University, my undergraduate college, I was a resident with all Henan natives who come from Nanyang, Xinyang, and Zhoukou, Shangqiu. We all have no trouble talking with each other in Mandarin except the girl from Xinyang, because her dialect is so different from ours. Even when she speaks Mandarin, she cannot differentiate between "l" and "n". We have something in common: while each one of us is unique, gradually we learned from each other's dialect and finally we can communicate with each other fluently in our own dialect.

As for English, my L3 (L1 is my home language, L2 is Mandarin), I had neither passion nor hate for it at the beginning, because I just learned something I should learn arranged by the school. However, as an English major student, I gradually figured out something interesting in English, such as the different English accents, the cross-cultural communication, the beauty as well as imperfections of translation (E-C/C-E) and so on. Until now I still keep finding many other fancy and magic tales in the English-related world. I also keep discovering new insights by interacting with the English language…

Every Stage of English Writing in My Life

To be honest, my early memory of English writing is vague. I even cannot remember when I started to write in English, maybe in primary school or junior high school. To graduate from both schools successfully, I had to pass some big examinations, which included some English exams.

My misty recollections of English writing are that I imitated the sentences in the textbook to write some sentences by myself in trying to introduce myself. In some simple sentence structures like "My name is Zhao Zihan, I am a girl, and I like listening to music …" I still made a lot of mistakes. I feel frustrated; writing must be the most difficult thing in the world. However, when I see other students' papers, they are worse. I could be the greatest in this subject, so I did not feel that awful.

I have to say before college, I always tried to find some good sentence structures in other people's writing and then imitate in my writing. It worked in the examination, honestly. My grammatical mistakes have decreased greatly, and my sentences can be absolutely right. However, I ignored that the content or the idea is the most important thing in your writing. Writing means expressing yourself. It is useless to say a lot of beautiful words if nobody can tell the main idea of it. From my point of view, writing is a very persuasive action. You can tell the reader a truth and persuade them to believe that is true without a doubt. That is to say, if you have a lot of ideas to share with people, you definitely have no worry about the prescribed word limit, both in Chinese writing and English writing.

I fell in love with English writing when I was a college student. There was no need to worry about the score of my paper, so I felt better and truly loved it. I recorded my feelings and reflected in English on some big things that happened in my daily life. I was just like the little girl named Anne: I find a new best friend, and I can tell everything to her in English. I felt amazing and excited when I was writing. It helped me to know myself better and improve my English writing skills.

In my spare time at college, I took some part-time jobs such as English teacher, tutor, and foreign trade salesman and so on. When I apply for a job, it is critical for me to prepare my resume. However, what should I do to express myself appropriately? Regarding this question, I learned a lot from a blogger. He said the right way to write a resume is never to use beautiful words to describe yourself, give them the evidence. For example, never say you are an excellent English learner; tell them what certificates or prizes you have received in this field. This is like Lai Jingjing's (2020) point that in English writing, a direct and deductive reasoning is often preferred.

I was shocked when I was a teacher trainee in an English training school; I discovered a new learning method to improve my English spelling and writing. I never thought there would be an amazing way to help students easily grasp the key points of English spelling. When I was learning English, even my teacher had not heard this new way to learn English. If English learning were like a meal to me, my teacher's way of teaching did not really satisfy me. But now, by using this new teaching method, I can help my young students to enjoy learning English spellings like a full meal. How time flies! Recently I found out about Phonics in academic circles which is a method of teaching people to read and to recognize the sounds that letters represent. After learning the pronunciation of 26 letters and the letter combinations in the word, students can recognize the pronunciation patterns of letters and letter combinations, and then they can "pronounce the words as soon as see them, write down the words as soon as listen to them" (Qian Shuihua, 2019).

Now I have learned a lot about English translation, I understand a good translator is equal to a good writer. When you translate some literary works, you may not need to focus on the grammar, but concentrate on the beauty in sound, sense, and style. In translation, maybe you are supposed to enjoy the playfulness of English language.

At each stage in my growth, I had a different feeling about English writing. I hope that I will be surprised by my feelings of English in the next stage of my life.

My Feelings about Chinese and English Writing

First, I want to share my feelings about Chinese writing. I will never forget when I first learned how to write by myself, and my father shared with me some knowledge about handwriting. Since then I have realized the beauty of Chinese characters. When I was in grade three I started to learn how to write a whole passage, but I couldn't finish it by myself. My mother, who had been a teacher in my hometown before I was born, taught me how to organize the whole passage. She said some words and I would write them down and we would continue until we finished the whole sentence. After I went to school, I was praised by my Chinese teacher for good writing. Although I clearly know that this is not my work, I was still happy and had fallen in love with Chinese writing.

In contrast, I feel much less positive about English writing. Compared with Suresh Canagarajah (2001), whose family offered a rich Tamil and English bilingual environment for him, I lacked the occasions to listen and write down anything in English at home. Before grade 3, I hardly learned any English. Because of the lack of a telephone, Suresh Canagarajah and his family have to write letters to get in touch with the outside world, and this greatly influences his writing (Canagarajah, 2001). My case is different. As an L2 learner, I have always preferred spoken English to written English. I think the reason is that I am still not proficient in English writing due to my lack of using it in my daily life.

From my point of view, whatever language you learn, English or Chinese, you need to be curious about the new language, first, and create a lot occasions to practice. I still remember Suresh Canagarajah describing the situation when his dad suddenly whispered something in English to his mother and they both sneaked into the room to do something, making him wonder what his dad had said (Canagarajah, 2001). In his mind, English is secret and mysterious. This curiosity about English motivated him to learn the language. The strategies that helped Suresh acquire proficiency in the language inspired me a lot. Following his steps, I also want to develop "A curiosity towards the language, the ability to intuit linguistic rules from observation of actual usage, a metalinguistic awareness of the system behind languages, and the ability to creatively negotiate meaning in context" (Canagarajah, 2001)[24].

Conclusion

In my multiliterate life, I realize that each language represents a unique culture and contains traces of human development. Each language also reflects peoples' emotions about life. At the beginning of learning the certain language, we are usually innocent and ignore the whole process of learning. Then we gradually become an advanced learner and develop many language skills. We find more interesting things about language such as the differences and similarities between the two languages. Chronically, we know the cultural difference is the most important. The best way to learn a new language is to deeply understand and be friendly toward the new culture.

References

CANAGARAJAH S, 2001. The fortunate traveler: Shuttling between communities and literacies by economy class[M]//BELCHER D., CONNOR U. Reflections on multiliterate lives. Buffalo: Multilingual Matters. 23–37.
LAI J, 2020. Negotiating contrasting languages and rhetorics[M]//CANAGARAJAH S. Transnational literacy autobiographies as translingual writing. New York: Routledge. 218–227.
钱水华 [QIAN SHUIHUA], 2019. 牵手 Phonics 助力 Sound Time—phonics 融入译林版小学英语 Sound Time 的教学实践[J] [Use phonics to enhance Sound time: A teaching report of integrating phonics in Sound Time in elementary school English]. 小学教学研究 [Research on elementary school teaching], 27: 78–80.

16

MY JOURNEY TO LITERACY

Xi Wang (王茜)

I was born in a village in Hebei province and I grew up with my grandparents. My early access to reading began with my grandparents' stories. There was a power failure from time to time, and my grandparents were not busy when there was no electricity at night. Those were my most enjoyable moments, listening to their stories. All of the stories were told in their dialect. Instead of Mandarin, our daily language was a dialect which influenced me a lot. Heritage language scholar He (2004)[199] stated that "identity construction is intricately linked with heritage language learning."

After I entered primary school, my family attached great importance to my study and always bought books for me. From that time, the door of developing Chinese literacy was opened. Another obstacle in my language acquisition is that I didn't learn English in primary school which led to my failure in following the English class at the beginning of my junior high school. Encouragement from my teacher and parents saved me when I was in trouble. Since then, my way of developing both Chinese and English literacy was smoother. Now when I look back at the history of my literacy development, I find that different self-evaluations in which I think about myself influenced me a lot in constructing my identity. Both self-confidence and self-inferiority have complemented each other in the development of my identity.

Self-inferiority

Like every left-behind child I lacked security and confidence without my parents by my side, although my grandparents love me very much. The neighbors always made fun of me, saying "your parents don't love you." They were just joking, while for me, as a kid at that time, their words deepened my sense of inferiority. I did feel that my parents abandoned me. As for my future, I thought I might be a farmer like my aunt, so I didn't have any expectations in my study. However, deep in my heart, I was not defeated. I knew my parents were struggling for a better life. I could understand them although I was sad, and I believed that they loved me.

I moved to the city to live with my parents after entering junior high school. According to Hull and Schultz (2002), most people tend to believe that literacy development ties in to schooling. I began to learn English from Grade 7, much later than most students. I was poor in English because most of my classmates had already learned English in their primary schools, and they had learned English for many years. They had a moreorless foundational knowledge of vocabulary and grammar. However, I didn't even know ABC. It was difficult for me to read English words, let alone write them. I was depressed and such kinds of feeling pushed me to find a way out. My fellow classmate helped me in L1 and L2 literacy. Mendonça and Johnson (1994)[746] believed that students can "reconceptualize their ideas in light of their peer's reactions."

Self-confidence

My grandfather is the eldest child in the family. Under the pressure of life, he had to drop out of school to help his family. His two brothers, who got a college education, left the countryside and lived a better life. My grandfather has a deep understanding and agreement with "knowledge is power." He hoped that I could be well-educated and I was the best in my grandparents' minds. My families always encouraged me and praised me whenever I progressed in my study. Well, gradually I became more confident and thought maybe I could go to the university. That was the beginning of my dream.

However, I could not follow the English class at the beginning of my junior high school life. Luckily, I had very kind teacher and parents. Under their encouragement and my hard working, I became gradually more confident in English. My first writing in English was a self-introduction. It was a kind of "big thing" for me because it was the first time I wrote in English. I sat down, straightened my body, held the pen, got ready to write. But what I should begin with? I quickly recalled all the words I have learned and the way of composing the teacher taught. Oh! I can begin with my name. Ok, "My name is Wang Xi, and my English name is Cassie." I finished the first sentence, and it was a good beginning. Then I wrote step by step, about my hobby, my family members. After accomplishing it, I counted and wanted to know how many words I wrote: 52 words! It was an amazing number for me because I couldn't believe that I could write so many words all by myself. I read it again and again. Although it was a very simple self-introduction, it had a significant meaning in my English writing experience. From then on, I became more confident and interested in English. Gradually, I found I could follow the lesson and even did better than some other students. Thanks to my teacher and my parents, I did well in English in the following years. That's one of the reasons why I chose English as my major.

Conclusion

My journey in literacy is influenced by my self-evaluation. As I look back at my experience, guided by autoethnographic research (Chang, 2008), I found that self-inferiority has played a role as importantly as self-confidence. For me, my own literacy development is a miracle. Through it, I know more about myself and I feel I have become a better version of myself. Most importantly, it has lead me into a big world and new opportunities.

References

CHANG H, 2008. Autoethnography as method. Walnut Creek, CA: Left Coast Press.

HE A, 2004. Identity construction in Chinese heritage language classes[J]. Pragmatics, 14(2 & 3): 199–216. https://doi.org/10.1075/prag.14.2-3.06he

HULL G, SCHULTZ K, 2002. Connecting schools with out-of-school worlds[M]//HULL G., SCHULTZ K. Schultz, school's out! : Bridging out-of school literacies with classroom practice. Teachers College Press. 32–57. https://repository.upenn.edu/gse_pubs/171

MENDONÇA C O, JOHNSON K E, 1994. Peer review negotiations: Revision activities in ESL writing instruction. TESOL quarterly, 28(4): 745–769. https://doi.org/10.2307/3587558

17
AFTERWORD

Shizhou Yang

蝉颂 A Eulogy to Cicadas
入光之蝉鸣夏暖，回首往事知愚贤。
读写自传书世界，超语为窗心灵显。
亦读亦写求知铜，天雨流芳蝶破茧。
多稿写作终成文，众生亦将读写谈。

I summarize my book with *A Eulogy to Cicadas*, a traditional Chinese seven-character-per-line poem shown above. I will use each line to summarize each of the preceding chapters, thus continuing the poetic inquiry started in Chapter 1. In this book that features my own and my Chinese students' LAs, I began Chapter 1 with a poem in which I reflected on my struggles for voice in my earlier years and a liberating encounter with LA writing. I was like "入光之蝉鸣夏暖"—one of the North American cicadas that escaped the "dark damp dungeon underground" and could not help singing despite the scorching summer. Short as it may be, life in the light makes it worth living and singing. My quest for a meaningful life has thus been intertwined with my language learning and literacy journey. Using a poetic autoethnography, I reflected on a similar epistemological spirit of gazing outward, inside, back, and forward in Chinese literary traditions. Caught between the native and the foreign, I expressed a strong desire to write with my distinct voice and escape the long, deadly silence under the master narratives of material prosperity, Marxist principles, and modernization. I did so by embracing LA writing, poetic inquiry, and autoethnography as epistemological tools of the marginalized.

Chapter 2 featured my own LA, the writing of which was my process of "回首往事知愚贤" (looking back to know foolishness and gain wisdom). Through my LA, I narrated my humble roots, lofty aspirations, and extensive investment in English language and literacy following my Chinese learning experience. In particular,

I reflected on my journey of becoming an L2 writing teacher in the EFL context. It was influenced by my multiple identities, evolving language ideologies, and diverse literacy experiences, both at home and school, and within both national and transnational contexts. They all contributed to my upward social mobility. I used "愚贤" (*yu xian*), two contrasting Chinese cultural concepts that mean foolishness and wisdom, respectively, to suggest LA as a genre that enables the marginalized to express their own accents or differences.

Chapter 3 offered a reconceptualization of LA writing, "读写自传书世界" (composing LAs to write about the world). I argued that in the EFL context, LA writing (读写自传) constitutes critical pedagogy because it essentially repositions all participants in a classroom writing ecology. By "书世界" (meaning simultaneously the world of books and writing about the world), I considered LA as a multi-voicing genre that evokes the three realities outlined by Pavlenko (2007) about autobiographical data. Specifically, LAs voice (1) the *life* realities of LA writers, that is, their life and literacy experiences; (2) the *subject* realities of LA writers, or their evolving understandings about languages, literacies, and identities; and (3) the *text* realities of LA writers, that is, their synergic translingual orientation and manifestations. Adding to these broad claims, I argued that LA writing is an epistemological process of exploring, knowing, and authoring to address the world through wrestling with and critiquing master narratives about languages, literacies, and identities in the TESOL profession.

Chapter 4 zeroed in on translanguaging as an integral part of the classroom writing ecology. Translanguaging mediated understandings about LA writing, autoethnographic research, academic writing conventions, and revisions, ultimately contributing to a deepened understanding of the writer's literate identities. Translanguaging also constitutes an important step toward decolonization (García & Li, 2022), particularly in terms of how it challenges dominant monolingual views of languages. Hence, one can refer to "超语为窗心灵显" (translanguaging as a window to reveal the soul). It's a narrative rendering of my own and my students' moments of English language use, often in synergy with Mandarin Chinese and multiple modalities. It offers an autoethnographic account of pedagogical translanguaging and its impact on academic writing in a Global South context.

Chapter 5 traced the emergence of Chen's translingualism, as manifested through her words in her LA, "like special oriental spices added to Western food." It depicted Chen's LA writing as shaped by her family upbringing, the classroom writing ecology, and the transnational experience she gained through reading foreign literature, listening to "pop music in English and western rock," and ongoing exposure to translocal resources through English language and literacy experience. Translingualism or productive bilingualism seems achievable, especially for writers with privileged access, support, and resources. I use "亦读亦写求知铜" (read and write to know) to summarize Chen's literacy ideology: she reads to enlarge her vision, and she writes to leave an indelible mark on the world. Her case highlights both reading and writing as integral to a productive epistemological process.

Chapter 6 examined translingualism by scrutinizing a collection of 11 LAs and related data from my writing class in a Global South context. Using a creative autoethnography, which combined academic writing with diaries and poems, I proposed an expanded notion of translingualism. By doing so, I sought to validate local genres, non-Latin scripts, and non-literate experiences—in short, any epistemologically suppressed experience or knowledge that deprives the powerless of their voice. I suggested further that we should go beyond politicalized translingualism to consider internal and external translanguaging conditions in order to achieve any profound transformation of our learners. Hence the line, "天雨流芳蝶破茧" (as heavenly rain falls, butterflies emerge from their cocoons).

I borrowed "天雨流芳" (see Figure 17.1) from a double-voiced Naxi saying (TEL EEQ LU FAN or, in Dongba, pictorial script), and a Chinese expression (see Figure 17.2). First written in Chinese by the local Naxi chieftain Mu Gao on a huge memorial archway in Lijiang (my mother's hometown), "天雨流芳" indicated to the Ming Emperor that the Naxi people willingly submitted to the rule of the Han Chinese central government. To the Chinese readers, it praised the favor that the emperor bestowed on the Naxi people, comparing it to rain from heaven. To Naxi speakers and readers, however, a homophone to its Chinese text, literally means "use your eyes

FIGURE 17.1 The "天雨流芳" Memorial in Lijiang

Note: Photo by He Liming, used with permission

FIGURE 17.2 A Translingual Representation of "天雨流芳"

Note: Photo by He Liming, used with permission. The male statues dressed in Han Chinese style outfit and wearing a plait, the second boy in the standing boy on the right reciting a text, possibly the Chinese classic 三字经 or three-character classic, as written on the left side of the wall—all suggest that the literacy practice was steeped in the Han Chinese culture.

to read and your heart to comprehend books now," or, more concisely, "去读书吧!" (Let's read books!). "天雨流芳" thus embodies a Han cultural value for literacy and learning as adopted by the Naxi people.

I venture to suggest another possible reading in pursuit of justice in literacy education. True translingualism or translanguaging should go beyond mere mixing of horizontal cultures, discourses, languages, modalities, and even genres. True justice requires us to see human traditions and practices as inherently limited in that they tend to serve only the interests of the powerful while legitimizing the silencing of the powerless. For instance, in the collection of LAs, the practice of a teacher selecting one student's writing to read to the class as a model essay was repeatedly mentioned. The impact of this practice on the fortunate writers is great. However, is such a practice also fair to the class members whose writing was not chosen? Like the "天雨" (heavenly rain), true translingualism motivated by justice should entail perspectives, words, and practices that challenge epistemologies that oppress others or seek to justify oppression. To decolonize, then, requires us to exorcise any oppressing spirit within us or in our classrooms, whatever their recognizable origins in the Global North, South, East, or West. Through my autoethnography and my students' LAs informed by autoethnographic research, we have begun the quest, hoping that what we have produced so far is more than the noisy calls of North American cicadas and presents a consistent challenge to formal education that denies or restricts mobility and identity options of the historically marginalized.

Chapters 7–16 contained ten students' LAs, as completed at the end of the semester: "多稿写作终成文，众生亦将读写谈" (with multiple revisions comes the final version—student authors voicing their own visions of literacy). The first line reminds readers that the students' LAs were shaped by the classroom writing ecology, which entails multiple revisions. The second line highlights the student authors' own visions of literacy, as textually explored and displayed by their personal journeys with multiple languages (and dialects), literacy practices, and native genres. With regard to citations and references, the Chinese style GB-2015, which was also the style the MTI students had to use in their thesis writing, hence slight difference from the rest of the book.

These students' chapters, ranging from 1,000 to 4,000 words, have not been altered much from their final drafts. Only minor changes such as obvious grammar mistakes and spelling errors were corrected during the publication process to improve readability and clarity of ideas. These chapters attest to the importance of education in Chinese culture and to literacy as a socially situated practice. They further attest to the possibility of EFL student writers becoming creators and communicators of new knowledge from their own autoethnographic vantage points.

Knowledge production is never neutral. From a Global South epistemological perspective (Santos, 2014, 2020; Zavala, 2013), producing new knowledge involves contesting widely accepted assumptions, beliefs, and practices that have been normalized by power-holding institutions. The global spread of neoliberalism in language and literacy education makes generating new knowledge an even more challenging task (Surma, 2018; Yazan et al., 2021). For those who are historically marginalized, such as members of indigenous communities (Hokowhitu et al., 2021), knowledge production may involve liberating their mind from rampant but restricting ideologies, especially deficiency-entrenched ways of thinking about socially devalued languages, literacies, and cultures that have bonded them. By writing about and reflecting on their own lives, these marginalized and often voiceless subjects can begin to externalize, evaluate, and expel such ideologies, no longer internalizing them as absolute truths (Belcher & Connor, 2001; Canagarajah, 2020; Yazan et al., 2021). Ultimately, as the indigenous scholar Somerville (2021) wrote so thoughtfully about her "ricochet"-like journey of finding her place, this reflective writing becomes a matter of legitimizing, negotiating, and creating a textual home for one's previously suppressed personal experience, knowledge, and cultural perspectives. Teaching MTI students LA writing showed me that such a decolonization process seems to entail three major epistemological steps. The first step is to free the marginalized from restrictive ideologies, such as my early belief that reading non-textbooks was a waste of time and my students' belief that writing entails simply following a given template to pass an exam. The marginalized can gain this freedom by externalizing the abstract, internalized, and thus absolute-truth-claiming ideologies with images, labels, storytelling, and writing, as we did in the academic writing course for the MTI students. To facilitate this process, the marginalized can also be involved in reading, discussing, and reflecting on other multilingual speakers' ways of using languages and literacies. The contact zone (Pratt, 1991) featuring such interactions cannot be understated. As Gui reflected in a writing sample:

> After reading "Fortunate Traveler" by Canagarajah, a successful bilingual academic writer, I am finding it necessary to review my long-standing belief that Chinese writing is similar to English writing. In the light of his statement, writing, especially academic writing, is very much affected by ideology and cultural differences, and therefore readers/audience has to be taken into account.
>
> Canagarajah's essay was rejected by a journal as a consequence of his "direct" criticism of Western values, but was published by another, whose editor, sharing the same opinion with the author, is from Ireland. In addition, whether [a] piece of writing is a good one or not depends on a variety of factors, such as what kind of culture you are in, what situations you are in, who you are writing to.
>
> So, I am feeling a mixture of a little frustration—because English writing is not as easy as I thought, and encouragement—because of Canagarajah's saying that the conflict of be[ing] bilingual and bicultural is not always a "problem."

The minds of students such as Gui were freed because, through reading different stories, they were exposed to and had to wrestle with alien ways of viewing their own backgrounds and considered other tropes of becoming (Canagarajah, 2015; Pavlenko, 2003).

The second step is to display, recognize, and celebrate students' individualized pathways to literacy and diverse literacies in local cultural forms, such as native genres, languages (dialects), and games. This book contains numerous such examples: poems, songs, opera, games, and calligraphy, to name a few. Native languages and literacies often go hand in hand. Moreover, they progress as individuals participate more fully in their native cultural communities. This expansion of the translanguaging lens may further unleash its potential to decolonize a singular, that is, Western-centered, way of understanding literacy. That is, by breaking the artificial boundaries between named languages such as Chinese and English, a translanguaging perspective encourages us to see multilinguals' languages as an integral part of their unified repertoire. Nonetheless, without seeing native genres intertwined with native languages, and in some cases dialects as well, we may recognize and activate only part of multilinguals' translanguaging repertoires for written communication. Unfortunately, this may mean that the students' legitimate use of much of their dormant resources will rest on whether the Global North allows it, thus continuing the same process of suffocating other ways of knowing in the Global South (Santos, 2014), particularly in terms of how knowledge can be shared.

The third step is to facilitate the imagination, creation, and dissemination of hybrid literary forms as "identity texts" (Cummins et al., 2015) that humanize both the self and the other. Pursuing such a vision, this book, which features LA writing by Chinese graduate students majoring in MTI, attempts "to see research participants as human beings who are capable of genuinely participating in the studies more than simply providing data" (Edigo & De Costa, 2022). The LAs provide narrative accounts of their individual commitments, struggles, and pathways to literacy, as sponsored, supported, and nurtured by diverse social others. As such, this book may supplement existing studies that feature "non-native speaker of English" perspectives on the teaching and learning of English (Nunan & Choi, 2010) and English literacy in a global context (Belcher & Connor, 2001; Canagarajah, 2020).

My background has had a profound impact on my theorization of translingualism, de-colonization, and heritage. By exploring and exposing these connections, I engage in a process of decolonizing both myself as a researcher and my research (Datta, 2017), which to me is like removing the log in my own eyes (English Standard Version Bible, Matthew 7:5, English Standard Version). To begin with, true as it may sound, I reject the assumption that translingual orientation occurs naturally in multilingual societies. Even though I grew up in a multilingual environment, I did not automatically develop a translingual disposition. Instead, soon after I went to school, I began to develop a monolingual tendency or, more accurately, a major-lingualism that magnified the importance of dominant languages on one hand and disregarded minority languages and dialects on the other. Through my LA, I exposed the social origins of my language ideology, such as the textbook model of Marx's forget-your-own-language approach to learning English (Dong & Liu, 1984). My evolving language ideology, as discussed in detail in Chapter 2, taught me the importance of understanding our own relationships with our language(s)—in this case, as mediated by LA writing. In other words, our backgrounds—such as geographical locations, professional identities, and ethnicity—offer no immunization to the dominant language ideologies of a given society. Through formal education in particular, we may have been indoctrinated into a certain way of assigning more value to one language, literacy practice, or way of using language than another. I believe that embracing Global South epistemologies requires us to identify, wrestle with, and externalize these internalized views of language and literacy. Accordingly, literacy educators must design their classroom writing ecologies deliberately to stimulate productive affordances and uptakes from their learners.

Furthermore, my background has shaped my translingual vision differently from scholars raised in former colonies of European powers. My generation in China has not experienced direct military occupation by any foreign power. Nonetheless, history lessons about the two Opium Wars in the mid-19th century and the Nanking Massacre by the Japanese in the 1930s did instill in us a strong nationalist sentiment against imperialism. Some of the patriotic songs we sang every year at school and the anti-Japanese TV shows we watched reinforced the same position. As Chinese, we were taught to hate the British, yet we had to learn English no later than middle school; we hated the Japanese, yet in college we had to learn Japanese as our second foreign language. Learning foreign languages thus always involved for us a love-and-hate relationship. On one hand, these foreign languages promised us new possibilities for upward social mobility. Especially for those of us from the rural and ethnic backgrounds such as myself, English, together with English literacy, was the game changer that enabled college entry and a promising career (Yang, 2021). At the national level, foreign languages, especially English, have been promoted for the last century or so, mainly as a tool to gain advanced science and technological knowledge from the West so as to modernize China (Hu, 2021; You, 2010). "Our colonial experience traps us in the project of modernity" (Smith, 1999, p. 34). I understand that *us* to mean not only people from former colonies such as India, but also people from former semi-colonies such as China. On the other hand, we had to alienate ourselves from the cultures associated with foreign languages, constantly monitoring our ways of thinking, acting, speaking, writing, and believing lest we deviate from the official lines prescribed by the unmistakable government authorities. To decolonize, for me, thus means externalizing the myths or misguided beliefs about foreigners, foreign languages, and foreign literacy practices that once ruled my mind. I also need to stop demonizing the foreign. Ironically, this seems to be a process of distancing myself from the patriotic nationalist education I received in school and developing a cosmopolitan outlook that honors trans-border connections and shared humanity (You, 2016, 2018).

Moreover, my background has shaped my view of heritage by referencing interactions and hybridity to help me imagine new identity options in relation to ethnicity and humanity. Although I was ethnically Naxi though my mother, I grew up in a Lisu autonomous county within a Tibetan autonomous prefecture in southwest China—not in Lijiang, the traditional heartland of the Naxi. Consequently, heritage meant not a singular, fixed, and pure cultural root but a plural yet selective mixture of languages, traditions, and practices. More specifically, in my county, the Lisu people were the majority group, and they have practiced Christianity for more than a century. Yet as a teenager who had received atheist education and patriotic indoctrination, I had disdain for the Lisu people's Christian faith, regarding it as mere Western superstition. I also looked down upon the Lisu people, viewing them as ignorant, addicted to tobacco, and prone to drinking. Nor did I show any respect toward or appreciation of a local literacy miracle, the Lisu Syllabary script, which was invented in the 1920s by an illiterate farmer, Ngua-ze-bo (Sun & Han, 2020). This distance from the Lisu people meant that in constructing my heritage repertoire, I have borrowed little from them.

In contrast, the Tibetan culture has influenced me to a much greater extent. The Tibetans were the majority group in my prefecture, which includes my hometown and two Tibetan counties. My childhood friends and I grew up drinking yak-butter tea daily for breakfast. To this day, I still make yak-butter tea for my transnational family. I also liked singing Tibetan-style songs in Chinese and enjoyed telling people that my hometown is close to *Shangri-La*, an idyllic plateau of cultural diversity and harmony described in the novel *The Lost Horizon* by James Hilton (1933).

Besides, I cherished the memory of how a Tibetan saved my elder brother's life like a good Samaritan. According to a family legend, my brother was very sick one day in his early years, and my father was carrying him on his back, feeling anxious, as they left a local clinic. A middle-aged Tibetan man approached my father and said in a jolly way—in dialect Chinese with a thick Tibetan accent—that my brother was dying. Then, to my father's surprise, he gave them a big chunk of yak butter and gave my brother a Tibetan name. They never saw the man again, but my brother soon recovered.

These and many other connections with the Tibetans formed in me a more favorable disposition toward the Tibetan culture than toward that of the Lisu. In fact, in my first spiritual exploration as a college student, I tried out Tibetan Buddhism by visiting local lama monasteries and studying the lives of famous lamas. However, despite this attraction to Tibetan culture, I did not subscribe to it completely. For instance, I rejected the Tibetan propensity for fighting and laughed inwardly when a Tibetan "老乡" (a fellow from the same prefecture), at a gathering at my undergraduate university, dared us newcomers to "守住他们打下的江山" (keep the territory that they have claimed through fierce gang fighting). I was also bothered by family stories about my mother and aunt running for their lives as young girls when the "古宗" (an old name for Tibetans) ransacked the township, raped women, and burned houses, including my grandfather's house with his precious collection of musical instruments. Thus, the relationship between the colonizer and the colonized, which a Global South epistemology re-examines, is naturally translated to that between majority and minority groups. It's not a relationship of absolute hostility, nor of harmony as some Western literature portrays it. Rather, as far as my family history and personal life experience are concerned, it's a relationship of cultural entanglement and individual alignment.

Different from the Lisu culture, of which I appreciated little, and different also from the Tibetan culture, from which I appropriated much, the third heritage I now claim as my own is that of Christianity. I used to believe all religions were the "opium of the people," as Marx (1843, paragraph 4) famously said. That included Tibetan Buddhism, the Naxis' Dongba religion, and the Christianity of the Lisu—all of them were nothing but a drug to numb humans as to their pains and sufferings. Growing up in Communist China, I was educated to believe in science and communism only. My strong teenage commitment to atheism and science was vividly displayed when, with a kitchen knife, I heroically chased away two Dongba priests, the shamans of the Naxi people, whom my mother had invited to my home to perform rituals in the hope of healing her paralysis. In college, I joined the Communist Party to "serve the people wholeheartedly," as the Party repeatedly called it. Yet at the same time, I began to question a lifestyle, prescribed by Marxism, that concerned solely material reality. Back then, I had an intense struggle with human hypocrisy, such as people doing kind acts for show or forcing a smile despite inner bitterness. I also experienced difficulty in relating to others, including my own family. Tibetan Buddhism, which struck me as a form of escapism, offered no solution to my strife.

Eventually, after encountering Western Christians and reading the Bible in English, I began to view my life, family, and traditions differently and to claim my right to speak from a Christian perspective. I began to narrate my life as a Kingdom child—as obtained through grace and faith rather than political background and patriotic performance. I exorcised the dominant discourses of atheism, folk traditions of "朝天子" that paid homage to the earthly "son of heaven" through music (Yang, 2013), and my long-held monolingualism (Wang & Yang, 2022). My conversion to Christianity thus informed my cosmopolitan and translingual vision. It has offered me a way to relate to different races and ethnicities through the lens of brotherhood, initiated and sustained through compassion, humility, and forgiveness. It has also instilled in me a biblical notion of social justice, which centers on powerless groups such as women, orphans, and foreigners. Instead of numbing my mind, Christianity has awakened me to the dire reality of human sin, oppression, and injustice.

This multidimensional and evolving relationship between my background and my research is an important part of the story. After all, as some scholars have pointed out (Pennycook & Makoni, 2020; Smith, 1999), decolonization cannot be achieved through creating an insulated knowledge system that excludes all knowledge systems of the Global North. To move forward, we need to reform our "epistemic cognition" or "understanding of the nature of knowledge and knowing" (Avramides & Luckin, 2007, as cited in Mannay, 2016, p. 102) by drawing on multiple epistemologies and disciplinary traditions. In other words, we need to practice humility by not only admitting but also proactively addressing our blind spots, which we may have inherited from our native cultures or received from formal education and training. As someone born into cultural practices of diverse ethnic groups, I need to recognize that following traditions is not the equivalent of doing justice. On the contrary, traditions, especially ones shielded by their romanticized glory, tend to legitimize unequal relationships, such as one group treating another as less valuable in some way—be they women, children, or people from a different background.

Knowledge making, especially for scholars like me from the periphery, should thus start with recognizing our own experiences as important, our own insights from those experiences as valid, and our own critique of naturalized discourses as critical. Yet at the same time, we should maintain a Confucian epistemological position of a humble explorer: "知之为知之，不知为不知，是知也" (Know what we know, know what we do not know, and that is knowledge). Furthermore, we should be open to admitting our blind spots and engaging in dialogue with other knowledge systems. The self is thus turned into an instrument of knowledge production concerning cultures, languages, and literacies, similar to the gazing spirit of autoethnographic research and poetic inquiry. Unless we—the marginalized, uncivilized, barbarians, ESL/EFL writers, or however we are named—take such a step, knowledge will continue to be written *about* us, rendering us invisible, voiceless, and faceless in a similar fashion to how the West has invented the Orient as an exotic *other* (Said, 1978). Forsaking our obligation to engage in global epistemological reformation, we will continue to be neglected (i.e., not mentioned) or negated (i.e., represented negatively) in books, articles, and reports written about us.

I still have reservations, though. At the practice level, at least, many questions remain unanswered in this LA-based study from a Global South perspective. According to Pennycook and Makoni (2020), a Global South project is a systematic decolonization project that strikes a balance between appropriating and distancing oneself from Western epistemological traditions. Does that mean that I should have included more epistemologies from my mixed Global South ethnic heritage? If so, which ethnic group should I side with: Tibetans, Lisu, Naxi, or Han Chinese? And why? By singling out one tradition or group over another, am I rejecting the premise—on which translingual and translanguaging scholarship stands—that there are no concrete and fixed boundaries between languages? Is my embrace of Christianity—undesirable from the Chinese government's perspective—a result of colonialism and neocolonialism and thus requiring further decolonization? Or does it qualify as a return to the faith of the Lisu people of my hometown and thus an example of rooted translingualism? What does decolonization look like in a context where the dominant official ideology consists of atheism and communism, both imported from the West? Furthermore, what should we do when the dominant epistemology in a Global South context is based on Marxist premises regarding humanity, human history, and sciences? Given that I have received much of my education in the West, am I an insider of both the indigenous community (such as the class of students I taught) and the global professional community, or am I an inside neither of the two communities and able to speak only from a liminal space through hybrid practices? Is not the indigenous community another imagined community? As I wrote, inspired by Somerville's (2021) story of seeking a home, with many unpleasant twists and turns, for her racial, gender, and professional identity:

> am I indigenous
> to the Global South
> or to the human world
> of transnational ties, tides, and tyrannies
>
> under the eternal curse of passports
> power, and privilege,
> or lack thereof?

What can we do with the unequal relationship already inherent in the structure of an EFL writing classroom? How can power be used in such a way as to disrupt the epistemological injustices that plague the globe? Questions like these require me to engage in an ongoing search for truth in the midst of competing worldviews concerning ontology and epistemology advocated by different power holders.

These questions cannot be answered by anyone other than myself, as I have to assume responsibility as a dialogic agent ("Bakhtin.", 1981). Arguably, other

TESOL scholars will have to wrestle with their own backgrounds in a similarly reflective fashion to unravel their own heritage. Along the way, they will form, reform, and articulate their own visions of transnational and ethical human relations as mediated by accented (written) Englishes (You, 2016, 2018).

In this book, I have argued mainly for three positions from a Global South perspective. First, LA writing can be reimagined as critical pedagogy to teach academic writing in the EFL context and to form more flexible ways of writing and more translingual or productive bilingual subjectivities than form-based instructions can generate. Second, a translanguaging or translingual perspective needs to be expanded. Insofar as LA writing is concerned, the notion of repertoire needs to go beyond linguistic features alone, to include considerations not only of modalities but also of native genres. It also needs to be open to the possibility, at least in this EFL context, that to translanguage is not to use *all* available features but to select and use only *some* features deliberately, pragmatically, and strategically. Last, rather than focusing on translanguaging itself as a pedagogical outcome, we should pay attention to translanguaging as part of the classroom writing ecology and to both the internal and external conditions for translanguaging. Therefore, even though I have studied LA writing by borrowing concepts such as transnationalism, translingualism/translanguaging, and investment and have demonstrated their relevance in the EFL context, I hope that I have contributed a dialogic rather than a monologic voice to the discussion.

One final reflection on transnational LAs as translingual writing. Whereas Canagarajah (2020) theorized LA writing as providing a textual home for the diaspora, who have left their home countries and their literacy practices behind, what I learned from my own and my Chinese students' LAs is transnational and translingual in a different way. That is, what our LA writing textually explored is not a home country left behind or the alienation of its literacies by an all-English monolingual environment. Instead, collectively, we have explored, represented, and, to a lesser extent, critiqued home and previous language(s) and literacy practices. As Zhang wrote in her LA, "Without the [literacy] autobiography, I would never reflect [on] the past, the way of my literacy." My opportunity for cross-border travel and my students' lack thereof have shaped but not fully determined our individual tropes of becoming. As Wang Y. wrote in her LA:

> With keen interest in English, I really enjoyed becoming a bilingual learner. Learning a new word is like twisting a kaleidoscope. Through this, I seemly expose [have seemingly exposed myself] to a foreign country, speaking in their way, feeling in their way and thinking in their way. In other words, it seems that I was traveling by taking the "English" Airline.

To a great extent, all my students are like Wang Y., who experienced the transnational aspects of life primarily through the very experience of language learning. Our unique transnational aspirations, connections, and encounters with transnational resources have shaped our unique visions of an interconnected world.

Therefore, EFL writers are transnational beings in their own right. They desire that both their textual and lived identities can go beyond any singular, simplistic, and possibly suffocating label. Translingual writing may offer a strategy for EFL writers to pursue such hybrid identity options. As TESOL classrooms are filled with transnational beings like the ones described in this book, we as TESOL professionals must be mindful of the classroom writing ecologies, contact zones, and larger social, cultural, and historical realities that shape our learners' transnational learning experiences, literacies, and literate identities. I believe that we will be successful if our students find our classrooms to be a safe haven to display, explore, and develop an enriched sense of self as literate beings, despite—and especially because of—all the differences they embody.

References

Bakhtin, M. M. (1981). *The dialogic imagination: Four essays* (M. Holquist, Trans.). University of Texas Press.

Belcher, D., & Connor, U. (Eds.). (2001). *Reflections on multiliterate lives*. Multilingual Matters.

Canagarajah, A. S. (2015). "Blessed in my own way": Pedagogical affordances for dialogical voice construction in multilingual *student writing. Journal of Second Language Writing, 27*, 122–139. https://doi.org/10.1016/j.jslw.2014.09.001

Canagarajah, A. S. (2020). *Transnational literacy autobiographies as translingual writing*. Routledge.

Cummins, J., Hu, S., Markus, P., & Montero, M. K. (2015). Identity texts and academic achievement: Connecting the dots in multilingual school contexts. *TESOL Quarterly, 49*(3), 555–581. https://doi.org/10.1002/tesq.241

Datta, R. (2017). Decolonizing both researcher and research and its effectiveness in indigenous research. *Research Ethics, 14*(2), 1–24. https://doi.org/10.1177/1747016117733296

de Sousa Santos, B. (2014). *Epistemologies of the South: Justice against epistemicide*. Routledge.

de Sousa Santos, B. (2020). Decolonizing the university. In B. de Sousa Santos, & M. P. Meneses (Eds.), *Knowledges born in the struggle: Constructing the epistemologies of the Global South* (pp. 219–239). Routledge.

Dong, W., & Liu, D. (1984). How Marx learned foreign languages. In W. Dong, & D. Liu (Eds.), *Gāo jí zhōng xué kè běn yīng yǔ dì yī cè bì xiū* [Senior high school textbook: English (required)] (Vol. 1). People's Education Press.

Edigo, A., & De Costa, P. (2022). Research methods in applied linguistics. *Research Methods in Applied Linguistics*. Advance online publication. https://doi.org/10.1016/j.rmal.2022.100016

English Standard Version Bible. (2001). ESV Online. https://www.esv.org/Matthew+7/

Hilton, J. (1933). *The lost horizon*. G. F. Best.

Hokowhitu, B., Moreton-Robinson, A., Tuhiwai-Smith, L., Andersen, C., & Larkin, S. (Eds.). (2021). *Routledge handbook of critical indigenous studies*. Routledge.

Hu, G. (2021). English language policy in Mainland China. In E. L. Low, & A. Pakir (Eds.), *English in East and South Asia* (pp. 19–32). Routledge. https://doi.org/10.4324/9780429433467-3

Li, W., & García, O. (2022). Not a first language but one repertoire: Translanguaging as a decolonizing project. *RELC Journal, 53*(2), 313–324. https://doi.org/10.1177/00336882221092841

Mannay, D. (2016). *Visual, narrative and creative research methods: Application, reflection and ethics*. Routledge.

Marx, K. (1843). *A contribution to the critique of Hegel's philosophy of right*. https://www.marxists.org/archive/marx/works/1843/critique-hpr/intro.htm

Nunan, D., & Choi, J. (Eds.). (2010). *Language and culture: Reflective narratives and the emergence of identity*. Routledge.

Pavlenko, A. (2003). "I never knew I was a bilingual": Reimagining teacher identities in TESOL. *Journal of Language, Identity & Education, 2*(4), 251–268. https://doi.org/10.1207/S15327701JLIE0204_2

Pavlenko, A. (2007). Autobiographic narratives as data in applied linguistics. *Applied Linguistics, 28*(2), 163–188. https://doi.org/10.1093/applin/amm008

Pennycook, A., & Makoni, S. (2020). *Innovations and challenges in applied linguistics from the Global South*. Routledge.

Pratt, M. L. (1991). Arts of the contact zone. *Profession*, 33–40.

Said, E. (1978). *Orientalism*. Random House.

Smith, L. T. (1999). *Decolonizing methodologies: Research and indigenous peoples*. Zed Books.

Somerville, A. T. P. (2021). Ricochet: It's not where you land; it's how far you fly. In B. Hokowhitu, A. Moreton-Robinson, L. Tuhiwai-Smith, C. Andersen, & S. Larkin (Eds.), *Routledge handbook of critical indigenous studies* (pp. 49–64). Routledge.

Sun, B., & Han, G. (2020). Lisu Syllabary: A folk creation in the Yunnan-Tibetan borderland. *Journal of Chinese Writing Systems, 4*(2), 87–104. https://doi.org/10.1177/2513850219888033

Surma, A. (2018). Writing is the question, not the answer: A critical cosmopolitan approach to writing in neoliberal times. In X. You (Ed.), *Transnational writing education: Theory and practice* (pp. 61–76). Routledge.

Wang, G., & Yang, S. (2022). Socializing strategies, family language policies and practices: An auto-ethnographic study of a transcultural family in southwest China. In J. Gube, F. Gao, & M. Bhowmik (Eds.), *Identities, practices and education of evolving multicultural families in [the] Asia-Pacific* (pp. 15–30). Routledge.

Yang, S. (2013). *Autobiographical writing and identity in EFL education*. Routledge.

Yang, S. (2021). From hoeing the cornfields to teaching English. *The Font—A Literary Journal for Language Teachers*, 1.

Yazan, B., Canagarajah, A. S., & Jain, R. (2021). *Autoethnographies in ELT: Transnational identities, pedagogies, and practices*. Routledge.

You, X. (2010). *Writing in the devil's tongue: A history of English composition in China*. Southern Illinois University Press.

You, X. (2016). *Cosmopolitan English and transliteracy*. Southern Illinois University Press.

You, X. (Ed.). (2018). *Transnational writing education: Theory, history, and practice*. Routledge.

Zavala, M. (2013). What do we mean by decolonizing research strategies? Lessons from decolonizing, indigenous research projects in New Zealand and Latin America. *Decolonization: Indigeneity, Education & Society, 5*(1), 55–71.

INDEX

50-word poem 72, 99, 102, 104, 106–107, 111

academic literacies 63, 87
agency 24–25, 29, 41, 44–46, 52, 83
Ahearn, L. M. 41, 45
authoritative discourse 48, 99
autoethnography 62, 84, 113–114, 144, 161, 169, 171; poetic autoethnography 3–14; creative autoethnography 97

Bakhtin, M. M. 48, 99, 103, 179–180
Belcher, D. 173
Bourdieu, P. 100, 107

calligraphy 21–22, 64–65, 120, 153–154
Canagarajah, S. 37–47, 51, 60, 81–84, 92, 106, 112, 164, 174–175
capital 23, 32, 92, 107–108
Chang, H. 61
Christianity 10, 26, 31–32, 98–99, 176–179
classroom writing ecology 45–49, 63, 85–88, 91–93; defining of 81
College Entrance Exam 19, 23–24, 29–30, 138
Communist 62, 99, 177, 179
Confucius 52, 143, 178
Connor, U. 43, 107
contact zone 41, 44, 50, 91, 101, 103, 174, 181
cosmopolitanism 176, 178
critical pedagogy 40–53, 170, 180
cultural confidence 99

Dai (people) 128–132
Darvin, R. 83, 92, 107–108, 110
de Sousa Santos, B. 8, 11, 114
De Costa, P. 175
decolonization 4–5, 113–114, 172–179; of academic writing 59, 105–106; and translanguaging 170
deficiency 101, 104, 111, 173
dialects 19, 31, 43–44, 64, 99–102, 104, 109–114, 119–121, 129–132, 136–137, 140, 147, 158, 162, 166, 173–177; Cantonese 102, 128, 158; Hokkien 121, 158
diaspora 46, 180
dominant narrative 43, 48, 94, 99, 176, 179
Dongba script 171
Dörnyei, Z. 23
Douglass, F. 43
Duckworth, V. 104

Elbow, P. 11, 50
Ellis, C. 58, 113
epistemological imbalance 4–5, 18, 40, 46–48, 61, 113, 173; Global South epistemologies 8–12, 32, 103–104, 170–181
epistemological disruption 46–53
epistemological gazes 12
ethnic languages 62, 65–66, 73, 101–102, 111–112; Lisu (people) 170, 177, 179; Naxi (people) 8, 19, 27–28, 99–101, 114, 176–179; Tibetan 19, 21, 62, 112, 176–179
externalization 173

Index

Freire, P. 48, 103, 52
Fujieda, Y. 39

Gao, Y. 82, 90–94
García, O. 59–60, 73–74, 107, 170
global souls 113
Global South 59, 62, 97, 103, 106, 110, 113–114, 170–180
Grant, A. N. 8
Guo Chen 123–127
Guo Jingming 131, 160

Hanauer, D. 27, 41, 52
Harklau, L. 99, 113
Hassall, P. 106
He Zhizhang 14
heritage culture 112–113, 172
Horner, B. 48, 52, 106
Hu, G. 4, 176
hybridity 45, 59–60, 73, 81, 91, 109–111, 175–176, 181
Hyland, K. 103

identity 83, 90–93, 101–104, 107–108, 130–132, 157–158, 160, 166, 176; nature of 29
identity texts 175
ideology 23, 28, 39, 73, 75, 83, 92–93, 99, 107, 110–111, 170; defining of 83
Iida, A. 10, 12, 39, 44
imagined identities 23–24, 29, 32, 51–52, 83, 92, 107–108
inequalities 5, 74
investment 83, 108
Ivanič, R. 45, 51

Jian Wu 136–139
Jinling Li 140–145

Kaplan, A. 141–142
Kramsch, C. 48–49

LA *see* literacy autobiography
language ideology 30–32, 84, 92, 174–175; Major-lingualism 111–113; monolingualism 30, 39, 43, 46, 59, 61, 73, 75, 84, 91, 93, 109, 113, 170, 175–180
Lee, I. 18
Li Gui 133–135
Li, W. 46, 59, 75, 105
Lijiang 147, 171
Lijuan Li 146–149
Lisu script 176

literacy autobiography: as a "foreign" genre 11–15; critique of existing studies 37–46, 81–84; as critical pedagogy 40–53; defining of 37; evaluation criteria 71, 76; in EFL context 12, 39–40; in ESL context 37–39; of the teacher 18–34

Makoni, S. 18, 178–179
Mandarin 19–20, 23, 30–31, 64, 73, 91, 101–104, 111, 128–131, 133–134, 146–148, 161–162
marginalized writers 18, 28–30, 43, 45, 51–53, 101, 103, 170
Marx, K. 30, 177
Marxism 177
Master of Translation and Interpreting (MTI) 5, 63, 69, 73–74, 84, 87, 110, 112, 173–175
Matsuda, P. K. 7–8, 21, 29, 44, 50–51
Menard-Warwick, J. 52
metaphor 8, 14, 65, 90, 114, 141–142
minzu 15
mobility 29, 83, 101–102
moment analysis 64, 73

native genres 174; couplets 9; Da You Shi 44; games 106–107, 109, 120, 137, 150–151, 174; Haiku 44; martial arts novels 134; nursery rhymes 72, 136–137; opera 104, 109, 121, 158, 161, 174; songs 21, 101, 152, 161, 175; *sanwen* 97; Sijo 44; Tang poems 22, 104, 158; *zui* novels 66; three-character classic 172
native speakerism 73, 92, 175
neoliberalism 4, 11, 173
Norton, B. 23, 51, 83, 92, 103, 107–108, 123, 133
Nunan, D. 175

Opium Wars 175

Park, G. 13
Pavlenko, A. 99, 103, 170
pedagogical design 63–64, 75, 84, 93, 129, 185; dialogical pedagogy 63, 84, 88, 92; multi-draft writing 61, 70–71, 85, 86–94, 105; students' autoethnographic process 63, 64, 67, 85, 104, 114, 157
pedagogical translanguaging 58–62, 64–76, 170; and modalities 59–61, 66, 72, 75, 109–111; defining of 60; redefining 110; translanguaging conditions 61, 73, 75, 114, 171

Pennycook, A. 178–179
poetic autoethnography 5–15
poetic inquiry 13
Poetic Inquiry 13
Poma, G. 12
Postmodernism 11–13
Pratt, M. L. 12, 41, 50, 91, 101, 103, 174
productive bilingualism 83

Qian, Y. 39

Rao, R. 90, 126
Richardson, L. 10–11
rooted translingualism 82, 89–94

Scientificism 112
self-authoring 105
Shen, F. 92
Silva, T. 44
Southern Barbarians 98–99, 103
Street, B. 28
Surma, A. 173
symbolic violence 100

The Bible 25–26, 175, 178
Tibetan Buddhism 177
TOEFL 25, 29, 67
translanguaging: defining of 58, 59, 60, 109; space 66, 73, 109

translingualism *see* translanguaging; defining of 109
translingual practice *see* translanguaging
transnationalism 81, 83, 88–89, 91–94, 112, 179–181
transnational space 83, 91, 179
trope of becoming 81, 112, 174, 180
Turnbull, B. 60–61

voice 3–4, 7–14, 30, 50; Dialogical voice 50–52, 88, 99, 103–105
Vygotsky, L. 27

Wanjun Shi 158–160
Weixi 9, 10, 19
White, M. 45, 104
Wiebe, S. 13, 106
writing templates 66, 100, 102, 131, 143, 159, 173

Xi Wang 166–168

Yazan, B. 91
You, X. 4, 24, 43, 81–82, 91, 97, 106, 176, 180
Yuejia Wang 128–132
Yufeng Zhang 150–157

Zapf, H. 49–50
Zihan Zhao 161–165

For Product Safety Concerns and Information please contact our EU
representative GPSR@taylorandfrancis.com
Taylor & Francis Verlag GmbH, Kaufingerstraße 24, 80331 München, Germany

www.ingramcontent.com/pod-product-compliance
Lightning Source LLC
Chambersburg PA
CBHW051358290426
44108CB00015B/2071